# Dickens's Clowns

Edinburgh Critical Studies in Victorian Culture
Series Editor: Julian Wolfreys

**Recent books in the series:**

*Rudyard Kipling's Fiction: Mapping Psychic Spaces*
Lizzy Welby

*The Decadent Image: The Poetry of Wilde, Symons and Dowson*
Kostas Boyiopoulos

*British India and Victorian Literary Culture*
Máire ní Fhlathúin

*Anthony Trollope's Late Style: Victorian Liberalism and Literary Form*
Frederik Van Dam

*Dark Paradise: Pacific Islands in the Nineteenth-Century British Imagination*
Jenn Fuller

*Twentieth-Century Victorian: Arthur Conan Doyle and the* Strand Magazine, *1891–1930*
Jonathan Cranfield

*The Lyric Poem and Aestheticism: Forms of Modernity*
Marion Thain

*Gender, Technology and the New Woman*
Lena Wånggren

*Self-Harm in New Woman Writing*
Alexandra Gray

*Suffragist Artists in Partnership: Gender, Word and Image*
Lucy Ella Rose

*Victorian Liberalism and Material Culture: Synergies of Thought and Place*
Kevin A. Morrison

*The Victorian Male Body*
Joanne-Ella Parsons and Ruth Heholt

*Nineteenth-Century Settler Emigration in British Literature and Art*
Fariha Shaikh

*The Pre-Raphaelites and Orientalism*
Eleonora Sasso

*The Late-Victorian Little Magazine*
Koenraad Claes

*Coastal Cultures of the Long Nineteenth Century*
Matthew Ingleby and Matt P. M. Kerr

*Dickens and Demolition: Literary Afterlives and Mid-Nineteenth-Century Urban Development*
Joanna Hofer-Robinson

*Artful Experiments: Ways of Knowing in Victorian Literature and Science*
Philipp Erchinger

*Victorian Poetry and the Poetics of the Literary Periodical*
Caley Ehnes

*The Victorian Actress in the Novel and on the Stage*
Renata Kobetts Miller

*Dickens's Clowns: Charles Dickens, Joseph Grimaldi and the Pantomime of Life*
Jonathan Buckmaster

**Forthcoming volumes:**

*Her Father's Name: Gender, Theatricality and Spiritualism in Florence Marryat's Fiction*
Tatiana Kontou

*The Sculptural Body in Victorian Literature: Encrypted Sexualities*
Patricia Pulham

*Olive Schreiner and the Politics of Print Culture, 1883–1920*
Clare Gill

*Victorian Auto/Biography: Problems in Genre and Subject*
Amber Regis

*Culture and Identity in Fin-de-Siècle Scotland: Romance, Decadence and the Celtic Revival*
Michael Shaw

*Gissing, Shakespeare and the Life of Writing*
Thomas Ue

*The Arabian Nights and Nineteenth Century British Culture*
Melissa Dickson

*The Aesthetics of Space in Nineteenth Century British Literature, 1851–1908*
Giles Whiteley

*Women's Mobility in Henry James*
Anna Despotopoulou

*The Persian Presence in Victorian Poetry*
Reza Taher-Kermani

For a complete list of titles published visit the Edinburgh Critical Studies in Victorian Culture web page at www.edinburghuniversitypress.com/series/ECVC

Also Available:

*Victoriographies – A Journal of Nineteenth-Century Writing, 1790–1914*, edited by Diane Piccitto and Patricia Pulham

ISSN: 2044–2416

www.eupjournals.com/vic

# Dickens's Clowns

## Charles Dickens, Joseph Grimaldi and the Pantomime of Life

Jonathan Buckmaster

EDINBURGH
University Press

Edinburgh University Press is one of the leading university presses in the UK. We publish academic books and journals in our selected subject areas across the humanities and social sciences, combining cutting-edge scholarship with high editorial and production values to produce academic works of lasting importance. For more information visit our website: edinburghuniversitypress.com



Edinburgh University Press Ltd
The Tun – Holyrood Road
12(2f) Jackson's Entry
Edinburgh EH8 8PJ

First published in hardback by Edinburgh University Press 2019

Typeset in 11/13 Adobe Sabon by
IDSUK (DataConnection) Ltd

A CIP record for this book is available from the British Library

ISBN 978 1 4744 0695 6 (hardback)
ISBN 978 1 4744 6392 8 (paperback)
ISBN 978 1 4744 0696 3 (webready PDF)
ISBN 978 1 4744 0697 0 (epub)

# *Contents*

# *Series Editor's Preface*

'Victorian' is a term, at once indicative of a strongly determined concept and an often notoriously vague notion, emptied of all meaningful content by the many journalistic misconceptions that persist about the inhabitants and cultures of the British Isles and Victoria's Empire in the nineteenth century. As such, it has become a by-word for the assumption of various, often contradictory habits of thought, belief, behaviour and perceptions. Victorian studies and studies in nineteenth-century literature and culture have, from their institutional inception, questioned narrowness of presumption, pushed at the limits of the nominal definition, and have sought to question the very grounds on which the unreflective perception of the so-called Victorian has been built; and so they continue to do. Victorian and nineteenth-century studies of literature and culture maintain a breadth and diversity of interest, of focus and inquiry, in an interrogative and intellectually open-minded and challenging manner, which are equal to the exploration and inquisitiveness of its subjects. Many of the questions asked by scholars and researchers of the innumerable productions of nineteenth-century society actively put into suspension the clichés and stereotypes of 'Victorianism', whether the approach has been sustained by historical, scientific, philosophical, empirical, ideological or theoretical concerns; indeed, it would be incorrect to assume that each of these approaches to the idea of the Victorian has been, or has remained, in the main exclusive, sealed off from the interests and engagements of other approaches. A vital interdisciplinarity has been pursued and embraced, for the most part, even as there has been contest and debate amongst Victorianists, pursued with as much fervour as the affirmative exploration between different disciplines and differing epistemologies put to work in the service of reading the nineteenth century.

Edinburgh Critical Studies in Victorian Culture aims to take up both the debates and the inventive approaches and departures from convention that studies in the nineteenth century have witnessed for the last half century at least. Aiming to maintain a 'Victorian' (in the most positive sense of that motif) spirit of inquiry, the series' purpose is to continue and augment the cross-fertilisation of interdisciplinary approaches, and to offer, in addition, a number of timely and untimely revisions of Victorian literature, culture, history and identity. At the same time, the series will ask questions concerning what has been missed or improperly received, misread, or not read at all, in order to present a multi-faceted and heterogeneous kaleidoscope of representations. Drawing on the most provocative, thoughtful and original research, the series will seek to prod at the notion of the 'Victorian', and in so doing, principally through theoretically and epistemologically sophisticated close readings of the historicity of literature and culture in the nineteenth century, to offer the reader provocative insights into a world that is at once overly familiar, and irreducibly different, other and strange. Working from original sources, primary documents and recent interdisciplinary theoretical models, Edinburgh Critical Studies in Victorian Culture seeks not simply to push at the boundaries of research in the nineteenth century, but also to inaugurate the persistent erasure and provisional, strategic redrawing of those borders.

Julian Wolfreys

# *Acknowledgements*

This study began life as a 2012 doctoral thesis, and like Grimaldi's *Memoirs* grew under my subsequent alterations 'much better than I supposed possible'. For their help on the first part of that journey, many thanks must go to my supervisors Sally Ledger, Anne Varty and Adam Roberts at Royal Holloway, University of London, as well as my examiners Paul Schlicke and Matt Rubery.

To nurture this fledgling work into the form you now find it, I owe much gratitude to my editor Julian Wolfreys for his initial interest in my proposal, and the reviewers at Edinburgh University Press for helping me get the overall shape of the book set from the start. After that, I am incredibly grateful to have been in the excellent hands of the EUP editorial team especially Nicola Wood, whose careful and patient reading of my work informed and enriched the final necessary polish. During the drafting stage, I had some wonderful support and encouragement from a group of academics who lent their valuable time and discerning eyes towards reading embryonic versions of the individual chapters. So many, many thanks to Emma Curry, J. Hillis Miller, Kate Newey, Bob Patten, Amber Regis and Matt Sangster.

Bliss was it to be alive as a PhD candidate during the years surrounding the 2012 Dickens bicentenary, and so thanks must also go to the wonderful community of Dickensians, Victorianists and Neo-Victorianists whom I heard, spoke to and always learnt from at the panoply of conferences celebrating the work of the Inimitable.

Final thanks are due to my family and support network at home: my partner Sarah, who now knows most of Grimaldi's anecdotes off by heart (for which I can only apologise), and our two wonderful boys Finn and Sam, the latter of whom is definitely more of a Weller than a Pickwick.

This book is dedicated to the memory of Sally Ledger, in whose company all of us spent too, too little time; as one of Sally's last

PhD students, I hope this work is in some small way a deserving tribute to her enthusiastic guidance and expert insight into all matters Dickensian.

Some material in Part 2 has appeared in other forms in two journal articles: '"We are all actors in the Pantomime of Life": Charles Dickens and the *Memoirs of Joseph Grimaldi*', *Victorian Network* 3.2: Theatricality and Performance in Victorian Literature and Culture (Winter 2011); and '"A man of great feeling and sensibility" – the *Memoirs of Joseph Grimaldi* and the Tears of a Clown', *19* 13 (May 2012).

Some material in Chapter 6 has appeared in another form in '"Ten Thousand Million Delights": Charles Dickens and the Childhood Wonder of the Pantomime Clown', in Peter Merchant and Catherine Waters' edited collection *Dickens and the Imagined Child* (Ashgate, 2015).

Some material in Chapter 7 will appear in another form in 'Brutal Buffoonery and Clown Atrocity: Dickens's Pantomime Violence', in Louise Lee's forthcoming edited collection *Victorian Comedy and Laughter: Conviviality, Jokes and Dissent* (Palgrave).

George Cruikshank's illustration 'Mr Grimaldi as Clown in *Harlequin and Friar Bacon*' is © Victoria and Albert Museum, London.

All other images are reproduced by courtesy of Charles Dickens Museum, London.

# *Abbreviations*

Throughout, I have cited the Norton and Penguin editions, due to their general availability and reliability as scholarly editions. However, if I have consulted other editions, I have included their bibliographical details below, and made this clear in the citations.

## Works by Dickens

*AN* — *American Notes*. Ed. and Int. Patricia Ingham. London: Penguin, 2000.

*AYR* — *All the Year Round*. Ed. Charles Dickens. 20 vols. London: Chapman and Hall, 1859–68.

*BoL* — *The Battle of Life*. In *The Christmas Books: Volume 2*. Ed. and Int. Michael Slater. London: Penguin, 1978.

*BH* — *Bleak House*. Ed. George Ford and Sylvère Monod. New York and London: W. W. Norton and Company, 1977.

*BR* — *Barnaby Rudge*. Ed. and Int. Gordon Spence. London: Penguin, 1986.

*Ch* — *The Chimes*. In *The Christmas Books: Volume 1*. Ed. and Int. Michael Slater. London: Penguin, 1985.

*CC* — *A Christmas Carol*. Ed. and Int. Michael Slater. London: Penguin, 2003.

*DC* — *David Copperfield*. Ed. and Int. Jeremy Tambling. London: Penguin, 2004.

*DS* — *Dombey and Son*. Ed. and Int. Andrew Sanders. London: Penguin, 2002.

*GE* — *Great Expectations*. Ed. Edgar Rosenberg. New York and London: W. W. Norton and Company, 1999.

*HT* — *Hard Times*. Ed. Fred Kaplan and Sylvère Monod. New York and London: W. W. Norton and Company, 2001.

*HW* — *Household Words*. Ed. Charles Dickens. 19 vols. London: Bradbury and Evans, 1850–9.

*LCD* — *The Letters of Charles Dickens*. Ed. Madeline House, Graham Storey, Kathleen Tillotson, Angus Easson and Nina Burgis. 12 vols. Oxford: Clarendon Press, 1965–2002.

*LD* — *Little Dorrit*. Ed. and Int. Stephen Wall and Helen Small. London: Penguin, 2003.

*MC* — *Martin Chuzzlewit*. Ed. and Int. Patricia Ingham. London: Penguin, 2004.

*MED* — *The Mystery of Edwin Drood*. Ed. and Int. David Paroissien. London: Penguin, 2002.

*MJG* — *Memoirs of Joseph Grimaldi*. Ed. Charles Whitehead. 2 vols. London: Bentley, 1846.

*NN* — *Nicholas Nickleby*. Ed. and Int. Mark Ford. London: Penguin, 2003.

*OCS* — *The Old Curiosity Shop*. Ed. and Int. Norman Page. London: Penguin, 2000.

*OMF* — *Our Mutual Friend*. Ed. and Int. Adrian Poole. London: Penguin, 1997.

*OT* — *Oliver Twist*. Ed. Fred Kaplan. London and New York: W. W. Norton and Company, 1993.

*PI* — *Pictures from Italy*. Ed. and Int. Kate Flint. London: Penguin, 1998.

*PoL* — 'The Pantomime of Life'. *Dickens's Journalism: Sketches by Boz and Other Early Papers 1833–1839*. Ed. Michael Slater. London: Phoenix, 1996. pp. 500–7.

*PP* — *The Pickwick Papers*. Ed. and Int. Mark Wormald. London: Penguin, 2003.

*SkB* — *Sketches by Boz*. Ed. and Int. Dennis Walder. London: Penguin, 1995.

## Works by Others

*SR* — Carlyle, Thomas. *Sartor Resartus*. Ed. Mark Engel and Rodger L. Tarr. Berkeley and Los Angeles: University of California Press, 2000.

*LTC* — Carlyle, Thomas and Jane Welsh Carlyle. *The Collected Letters of Thomas and Jane Welsh Carlyle*. Ed. Charles Richard Sanders et al. 32 vols. Durham, NC and London: Duke University Press, 1970–2005.

*MWS* — Scott, Sir Walter. *Memoirs of the Life of Sir Walter Scott, Bart*. Ed. John Gibson Lockhart. 7 vols. Edinburgh and London: Robert Cadell and John Murray, 1837.

Chapter 1

# Introduction

On the morning of 1 June 1837, the period's most celebrated clown Joseph Grimaldi was found dead by his housekeeper, after a night of convivial roistering with his friends. This may have marked the physical end of Grimaldi the man, but critics had been bemoaning the cultural death of the clown ever since he retired fourteen years earlier. In his 'Ode to Joseph Grimaldi' of 1825, Thomas Hood sums up the general mood when he despairs:

> For many a long, long year must go,
> Ere Fun can see thy like again –
> For Nature does not keep great stores
> Of perfect Clowns – that are not *Boors!* (1906: 19)

Just seven days earlier (25 May 1837) Charles Dickens had moved into 48 Doughty Street not far across town and may have read Grimaldi's obituary in *The Morning Post* or *London Standard*. Although May had been a month of creative paralysis, due to his mourning for his sister-in-law Mary Hogarth (who died on the 7th), Dickens still had two popular serials in progress – *The Pickwick Papers* and *Oliver Twist* – and was editor of *Bentley's Miscellany*. As Kathryn Chittick describes, this was the year in which Dickens 'entered upon the flood-tide of his early reputation' (1990: 114) and his move to Bloomsbury was a sign of his rising status, both literary and financial, as well as of his growing family – his first son, Charles Culliford Boz, had been born in January.

Dickens and Grimaldi never met each other, even though Dickens had lived in London since 1822, but they were connected by a shared acquaintance: George Cruikshank, Dickens's illustrator for *Sketches by Boz* and *Oliver Twist*, was a close friend of Grimaldi's, and as a member of his 'Crib' drinking club, may have been present at that final evening of drinking. This book tells the story of a work that links these three figures from across the artistic spectrum. The *Memoirs of Joseph Grimaldi* (published 1838) is generally regarded as an outlier in the Dickens canon – it was his only biography, it was a text which he 'edited' based on an original manuscript written by another hand, and perhaps most obviously it was one of his few commercial and artistic failures. However, in this book I will make a case for the redefinition of its status as, if not a major work, a work of significant impact on Dickens's subsequent writing, his attitude to life and on his sense of the comic.

At least one observer has linked Grimaldi and Dickens previously, based on their shared participation within an annual Christmas tradition and their embodiment of seasonal goodwill and conviviality: reviewing *The Cricket on the Hearth*, *The Mirror of Literature* piquantly observed that a Dickens Christmas story had become 'as regularly expected as pantomime' and 'hailed with as much delight as that of Grimaldi' ([Anon.] 1845: 402). I want to explore this interrelation more carefully to understand how the figure of Grimaldi's pantomime clown informs more of Dickens's other writing than has been hitherto discussed.

As I shall contend, Dickens had a unique imaginative engagement with Grimaldi which shapes his treatment of a number of topics, including the consumption of food and drink and his presentation of violence. To briefly introduce the ways in which Dickens's pantomimic sensibility is registered in both Dickens's works and by others making sense of those works, I want to look at three examples. They neatly convey how Dickens uses pantomime elements in his work and demonstrate the effect these elements have on his readers.

One technique of Dickens's characterisation, his creation of what John Carey calls 'violent effigies' from animated collections of inanimate objects, has antecedents in Grimaldi's act. In his renowned tricks of construction, Grimaldi composed vital, living figures from disparate objects, such as a boxer composed of Covent Garden vegetables or a horse made up from a workman's bench, broomsticks and an animal skull. In *Dombey and Son* the description of Captain Cuttle's friend Mr Bunsby is framed in a way that simultaneously composes and decomposes him, as Dickens collects a variety of seafaring objects to construct him as a living embodiment of all things nautical:

> Immediately there appeared, coming slowly up above the bulk-head of the cabin, another bulk-head – human, and very large – with one stationary eye in the mahogany face, and one revolving one, on the principle

> of some light-houses. This head was decorated with shaggy hair, like oakum [. . .] The head was followed by a perfect desert of chin, and by a shirt-collar and neckerchief, and by a dreadnought pilot coat, and by a pair of dreadnought pilot trousers, whereof the waistband was so very broad and high, that it became a succedaneum for a waistcoat: being ornamented near the wearer's breast-bone with some massive wooden buttons, like backgammon men. (*DS* 367)

Another example of Dickens's pantomimic sensibility is his manner of noting the absurd incongruities that life sometimes presents to us. In one of Jingle's rambling disquisitions on the general nature of existence, he makes the following observation:

> 'Rather short in the waist, an't it?' said the stranger, screwing himself round, to catch a glimpse in the glass of the waist buttons, which were half way up his back. 'Like a general postman's coat – queer coats those – made by contract – no measuring – mysterious dispensations of Providence – all the short men get long coats – all the long men short ones.' (*PP* 33)

In a much later novel, the narrator Pip makes the following rueful comment on life's ineffable way of throwing together comical mismatches in the most inappropriate of circumstances:

> The two convicts were handcuffed together, and had irons on their legs [. . .] One was a taller and stouter man than the other, and appeared as a matter of course, according to the mysterious ways of the world both convict and free, to have had allotted to him the smaller suit of clothes. (*GE* 175)

The tones of these two novels are polar opposites – the gentle high jinks and comfortable resolutions of *The Pickwick Papers* chafes against the more embittered and mature reflections of *Great Expectations* – yet both novels find a shared space to accommodate Dickens's vision of life's pantomimic nature.

Finally, this observation by G. K. Chesterton encapsulates how Dickens's pantomimic lens infiltrates his readers' apprehension of the characters he creates:

> The thing about any figure of Dickens [. . .] is that he cannot be exhausted. A Dickens character hits you first on the nose and then in the waistcoat, and then in the eye and then in the waistcoat again, with the blinding rapidity of some battering engine. (1911: 203)

Chesterton closes on a military metaphor, but in the evocative image of the vivid physicality of Dickens's characters assaulting the reader, he uses language that is closer to the slapstick violence of the irrepressible clown. There is comicality in the relentless by-play between the character and reader suggestive of the mechanical back-and-forth assault of the clown on Pantaloon.

My exploration focuses on the aesthetic effects of both artists across a wide range of scenarios like these examples, but I also want to consider why pantomime's political potentialities made it such an attractive form for Dickens to draw upon in his own writing. This continues important recent work on Dickens's radical antecedents such as Sally Ledger's *Dickens and the Popular Radical Imagination* (2007) as I explore how Dickens draws on Grimaldi's subversive side to celebrate the glorious grotesqueries of the human body, declare resistance towards rigid conformity and social convention, and direct a defiant blast of laughter towards the violence of everyday life. While these elements of Dickens's writing have been explored individually elsewhere, here I draw them together and situate the pantomime clown as a single unifying force at work within this process.

This book also participates in a conversation initiated by several key studies of Dickens's creative dialogue with popular forms of entertainment. Paul Schlicke's wide-ranging *Dickens and Popular Entertainment* (1985) charts Dickens's engagement with public spectacles such as the circus and the fair, but only briefly mentions pantomime, while Juliet John's *Dickens's Villains* (2001) takes another theatrical genre as its key focus, tracing Dickens's adaptation of the melodramatic villain within his work. My study takes further impetus from the only major work to address Dickens's use of the pantomime in a sustained manner, Edwin Eigner's *The Dickens Pantomime* (1989). Eigner's work is the most substantial consideration of Dickens's imaginative relationship with the pantomime to date, as it is only treated elsewhere as a small element within broader treatments of Dickens's humour. He argues that pantomime was the primary dramatic genre within Dickens's theatrical aesthetic, claiming that his 'fascination with pantomime was as great, perhaps, as his general interest in the theater and equally long-lasting' (1989: 4). He regards pantomime as the creative wellspring for much of Dickens's writing, in relation to which all the constituent parts of his works – 'the dramatis personae [. . .], the movements of his plots, and even the meaning of his vision' – can be read. For Eigner, pantomime's influence on Dickens spreads yet further, informing 'the essential pattern of Dickens' comedy, the basis for his psychological insights and his social vision, as well as the modus operandi of his aesthetics' (1989: 8).

Eigner persuasively traces the value of pantomime for Dickens, as its fluid, magical and anarchic free-form approach offered him an adaptable mechanism for 'changing genres and thus changing world-views' (1989: 40). However, Eigner's attention centres round the pantomime plot, as he shows how Dickens's characters fulfil the narrative functions of the major figures of pantomime – Harlequin, Columbine, Clown and so on. My study therefore breaks new ground by moving beyond Eigner's more abstract framework to examine how the specific mechanics of Grimaldi's pantomime performances find their way into Dickens's work, comparing what Grimaldi did onstage with what Dickens did on the page.

Part I, 'Dickens, Grimaldi and the Pantomime Clown', outlines the broader critical context for Dickens's interest in the pantomime and its principal protagonist. Chapter 2 describes the status of pantomime as popular entertainment from the Regency years up until the 1850s, a period which ran parallel to Dickens's childhood, adolescence and formative years as a writer. This chapter also considers the different functions that laughter at the pantomime performed and shows how this 'unlicensed' form of theatre was a politicised mode of entertainment. Grimaldi's clown can be situated as an important agent of this politicisation, functioning as an avatar for the vicarious release of subversive feeling and for the articulation of popular opinion on a number of social issues. The chapter closes by contextualising Grimaldi's clown in relation to the other model of clowning most available to Dickens, the Shakespearean clown. Although several critics have previously recognised Dickens's creative debt to the Bard, his friendship with William Charles Macready has channelled most of this critical attention towards Dickens's engagement with Shakespeare's epic and tragic characters. However, he was also thoroughly conversant with Shakespeare's comic tradition and two principal topics for Dickens's humour – his interest in the 'romantic side of familiar things' and the bathetic deflation of pretence and pompous conventionality – are as firmly grounded in the tradition of the Shakespearean clown as that of Grimaldi.

This broader framing of pantomime lays a foundation for Chapter 3, which uses a close reading of his journalism on the topic to examine how Dickens viewed and understood the pantomimic. This chapter outlines two main themes which shape my argument for the rest of the book: firstly, Dickens's perception of life as a pantomime, founded upon both his acute social observation of the play-acting within everyday life and his sense of everyday life's comic absurdity, and secondly, his identification of the pantomime as a source of fancy and wonder within the toughened and unsentimental modern world, with the pantomime's transformation scene serving as a rich metaphor for the aforementioned 'romantic side of familiar things'. From Dickens's general assertions about the cultural and political value of pantomime, the chapter shifts to Dickens's interest in Joseph Grimaldi and his clown. I primarily draw on Dickens's journalism again, but closely analyse the brief glimpses of Grimaldi as a named character in Dickens's novels expanding these references out from the mere footnotes they have been in most editions thus far.

In Part II, 'Dickens and the *Memoirs of Joseph Grimaldi*', I demonstrate the creative value that this biographical project had for its author, looking at both his own creative additions to the work and the elements from Grimaldi's life story that became persistent imaginative concerns in his other work. Critics often relegate Dickens's role in the *Memoirs* to that of a hack editor who rushed out the final product with little investment in its content. However, I extend recent reappraisals of the *Memoirs* by tracing how it became a key influence on Dickens's later work rather than an embarrassing anomaly within the canon. By drawing from both traditional and more recent theories of life writing, I prove how Dickens belies his status as 'editor' to produce an interpretative and creative work that develops the ideas around theatricality and identity that he was exploring in other contemporary work.

Chapter 4 shows how the *Memoirs* comprises three principal and overlapping discourses and epitomises the unstable and multivalent status of life writing at that time. Firstly, I argue that the *Memoirs* has affinities with contemporary biographies of the Romantic poets, which, rather than reflecting conventional Romantic ideals of the unitary 'genius' subject who exists apart from the world, domesticate and humanise their central artist-subjects. In its focus on Grimaldi 'offstage' life rather than his art, and most crucially its insistence on the interrelation between the two, I assert that the *Memoirs* embodies what Julian North calls a 'transgressive publication of domestic privacies' (2009: 23), and gestures towards the more popular, radical modes of the period that Sally Ledger has traced elsewhere in Dickens's work. My primary point of comparison will be Lockhart's *Life of Sir Walter Scott* (1837–8), which Dickens eagerly read in its serialised form. Lockhart constructs a Scott who engaged with his art and the wider world despite personal bereavement and ill health, and, as I shall show, Dickens constructs a similar Grimaldi in the *Memoirs*. However, by carefully synthesising Thomas Egerton Wilks's manuscript (which was itself an abridgement of Grimaldi's own written account), Dickens also eschews Lockhart's lengthy, ten-volume form and anticipates the later, more concise style of Victorian 'Lives and Letters'.

Secondly, I will show how the *Memoirs* also draws upon the eighteenth-century genre of the stage biography, a mode which underscores and highlights the links between theatrical art and life. This technique consciously uses the theatre as a means of evaluating the lives of its subjects, and by comparing the *Memoirs* to several significant examples of the form I will demonstrate how Dickens similarly foregrounds the themes of theatre and performance in his construction of Grimaldi's life.

Thirdly, I will explore how this dual strategy – domesticating Grimaldi's life while also presenting it as a public performance for an audience – reflects what recent biographical scholarship has defined as the 'relational life'. Rather than depicting its subject as an impermeable 'great' figure who stands apart from their social milieu, the 'relational life' is a wholly inter-subjective one, with those who surround and interact with the subject having a significant investment in their construction. In particular, I will argue that the *Memoirs* exemplifies all three of Paul John Eakin's categories of 'relationality': Grimaldi is involved in a number of interrelated social environments, most prominently the theatre and his home; his life is regularly held up for contrast and comparison with key individuals around him, particularly fellow performers; and the narrative also dramatises the relationships between Grimaldi's own multiple selves, most obviously between his 'onstage' persona and his 'offstage' one. In portraying this domestication of the artist-subject, I develop the work of critics such as Malcolm Andrews who have described this creation of a shared, intimate space for reader and artist to co-exist as a central and abiding objective of Dickens's art.

Chapter 5 explores the role of George Cruikshank in the reconstruction of Grimaldi's life. I regard Cruikshank's accompanying plates as equal in artistic status to Dickens's text, and reflect Cruikshank's longer creative and personal relationship with the subject since the early 1800s. Building on earlier research, I will analyse Cruikshank's pictures in dialogue with Dickens's text and explore how they operate as what Martin Meisel calls 'realisations' and 'illustrations', giving both a 'concrete perceptual form to [Dickens's] literary text' and an 'interpretive re-creation' (1983: 32) that further enriches and embellishes Grimaldi's life. Moreover, I will show how Cruikshank's style wholly supports Dickens's motif of theatricality in a manner representative of the symbiotic relationship between theatrical and pictorial traditions.

Although the *Memoirs* is often criticised for inadequately exploring Grimaldi's onstage life as a pantomime performer, Dickens's awareness of Grimaldi's life and performances provides an important imaginative impulse for his own fictional clowns. This is the subject of the third and final section of this book, 'The Clown at Large', which focuses on three key tropes of Grimaldi's pantomime routine – the excessive consumption of food and drink, the use of slapstick violence against vulnerable people and the transformative power of clothing – and analyses how some of Dickens's comic characters draw on these tropes in their own 'performances' within Dickens's texts. Like Grimaldi's own pantomime performances, these move beyond incidental amusements to become the vehicle for the exploration of more radical concerns around authority, identity, violence and the body. I primarily approach these topics through theories of laughter and comedy, positioning the treatment of these themes upon a spectrum that broadly stretches from 'Bakhtinian' inclusive, democratic comedy at one end and 'Bergsonian' normative, corrective laughter at the other. I will demonstrate how the clown figures of both Grimaldi and Dickens are contingent and protean figures that oscillate between these two poles, sometimes even within the same performance or work.

In Chapter 6, I explore one of the principal attractions of the pantomime clown for Dickens, namely his ability to transcend the ordinary, particularly as manifested through the clown's feats of eating and drinking. The comedic consumption of food and drink was a versatile tool for both Grimaldi and Dickens, as the laughter experienced by the viewer/reader pulls them in contradictory directions. Building on Michael Hollington's work on Dickens and the grotesque, I initially use Mikhail Bakhtin's theories of the grotesque body and the democratising form of the carnivalesque as a theoretical lens through which to view these spectacles of eating and drinking. I will show how through a celebration of the bodily grotesque the clown becomes a force for democratisation, who teaches us to acknowledge that as humans we share the same basic humanity including all its faults. However, informed by Henri Bergson's theory of corrective laughter I also analyse how Grimaldi and Dickens use this trope for more normative and satirical purposes, elevating the viewer/reader above the clown and inviting us to participate in a ritual of ridicule to correct these faults. In the final section of this chapter, I explore an example of how this ambivalence between celebration and derision presents itself, analysing Dickens's presentation of Christmas feasting, which represents a fault line between the attitudes of the Regency period and those of the Victorian period.

Chapter 7 continues to trace Dickens's attraction to the superhuman qualities of the clown through an exploration of the trope of slapstick violence, which Dickens regarded as one of the principal attractions of the pantomime. I discuss Dickens's two main uses of this trope, which were his presentation of action in carefully choreographed slapstick scenes and his use of language in a way that dematerialises and reconfigures the violent spectacle. I will focus on the three principal targets of violence in both Grimaldi's pantomime and Dickens's fiction, who arguably represent the most vulnerable members of any society – the elderly, women and children.

By relating these scenes back to the more general spectrum of comedy's 'movement', this chapter demonstrates how certain presentations of violence within Dickens's work operate as a 'diverting' force, simultaneously entertaining and disrupting – the democratic accommodation of violence as part of our human experience is offset against the more exclusive vicarious enjoyment of the misfortunes of others, which becomes particularly troubling when directed against a vulnerable target. As I will show, this tendency towards chaos and amusement in cruelty directly pulls against the gentler comedic impulse towards harmony, as well as Dickens's own impulse towards sentiment.

Chapter 8 shows how Grimaldi and Dickens use the clothing of their clownish characters (and its transformative power) as a versatile signifier for exploring ideas about the materiality of the world. The methodological underpinning of this chapter is provided by fashion theorists who recognise clothing as simultaneously both a private insulation for the ego and the public projection of it. I also develop Foucault's views on the manipulation of 'the docile body' through clothing and Barthes's distinction between 'costume' (the garments of conventional societal norms) and 'dress' (garments which project the individual ego) to show how clothing for Grimaldi and Dickens becomes a multivalent trope to both de-humanise and re-humanise the body. In their hands, garments become, on the one hand, a constituent of the pervasive and oppressive mechanisms of conservative society that is particularly ripe for satire and ridicule, but on the other, a symbol of individual liberty against that society.

My argument here also positions this cultural work by Grimaldi and Dickens within what was an already vibrant critical debate at the time. I recover the significance of Carlyle's *Sartor Resartus*, using Carlyle's theories of clothing as lenses through which to scrutinise the clothing of Grimaldi's clown and of Dickens's characters. Finally, this chapter analyses the clothing of two related cultural archetypes – the dandy and the swell – as case studies in the comical presentation of clothing by both Grimaldi and Dickens. There has been much important work on the dandy and constructions of nineteenth-century masculinity, but little of it adequately accounts for the cultural lampooning of the figure through pantomime and literature.

## A Brief Note on Methodology

Before continuing further, I must briefly acknowledge the difficulties faced by all theatre scholars (including those 'just visiting' like myself) in trying to recover a proper sense of a live performance in the eighteenth and nineteenth centuries. This is particularly problematic for an outsider and 'illegitimate' genre like pantomime, unsanctioned by the Licensing Act and so outside of the documentary mechanisms of state control. As the theatre historian Michael Booth notes, it is 'impossible to speak in any meaningful way of the relationship between performance and an established text in pantomime' (1981: 75), a predicament largely caused by a paucity of material available to modern scholars (although of course more material becomes available as time moves on).[1]

Many promptbooks, one of the actors' most immediate resources (and therefore one most revealing for the scholar), have been lost, while 'official' published 'books of words' were often only brief outlines with limited relation to what actually occurred on stage. Those copies submitted to the Examiner of Plays often present the barest of details, and deliberately omit vital (and potentially censorious) information on dances and ballets, processions, transformation scenes, speciality acts, acting of low comedians, and other visual and spectacular elements. Therefore, as Booth notes, if one is to somehow reconstitute even a partial sense of the felt experience of an actual performance, 'One has to fall back on press reviews', which he pragmatically notes 'can be most helpful but repetitive, and too often unspecific' (1981: 86).

Moreover, analysis of this material generates a further challenge, for such reviews are inevitably compromised by the bias of the reviewer and must be handled according to this partiality. Recent pantomime critics have taken up this challenge with fascinating results: Jill A. Sullivan's *The Politics of the Pantomime: Regional Identity in the Theatre 1860–1900* (2011) questions the critical hegemony of the dominant nineteenth-century essayists such as Dickens, Percy Fitzgerald and Andrew Halliday, who deliberately position Grimaldi as the zenith of a 'pure' pantomime, while simultaneously presenting contemporary pantomime as an inferior form degraded by variety and less 'intellectual' visual spectacle. Furthermore, Dickens's prejudices come under scrutiny from Jim Davis and Victor Emeljanow in their *Reflecting the Audience: London Theatregoing 1840–1880* (2001), in which they view the descriptions of particular London theatres embedded within Dickens's accounts of his theatregoing as 'carefully constructed to support his argument in favour of popular amusements' (2001: 40). They call Dickens's account of his visit to the Britannia Theatre 'a highly impressionist point of view' (2001: 78) and his descriptions of the audiences at the Victoria and Britannia Theatres as 'formulaic and contrived' (2001: 90) and operating as part of a wider polemical manifesto. Within such works, Davis and Emeljanow contend, Dickens aimed to demonstrate how theatres were orderly and self-regulating sites of moral education, largely thanks to their alleged 'reclamation' by theatre managers such as Samuel Phelps at Sadler's Wells. Davis and Emeljanow sum up the pervasive nature of such mythologising as follows:

> Such was the authority of the journalistic accounts which appeared in *Household Words* both of the exotically distinct colonies and the exotic reaches of London, that the consumer of his myths read them, to borrow Barthes's analysis, as a factual system, instead of recognising them as a semiological one signifying the efficacy of cultural intervention, and in the case of Phelps himself, embodying its very presence. (2001: 102–3)

Given my primary subjects for this study, my early chapters inevitably draw on these 'compromised' sources, as I try to piece together the general view of pantomime's popularity as a theatrical form, particularly as it was performed by Grimaldi and experienced by Dickens. This book is a literary study rather than a history of pantomime, primarily concerned with Dickens's views on pantomime, focusing less on the veracity of what he describes and more upon what these descriptions reveal about how pantomime affected him both in the immediate moment as a writer and in his wider work. However, I recognise the cultural damage that such value-laden interventions can cause and where appropriate I acknowledge where the accounts of Dickens and others are calculated attacks against anti-theatrical prejudice rather than as objective accounts.

Moreover, my study at least attempts to speak to the work of Sullivan, Davis and Emeljanow (*inter alia*) by presenting as broad a picture as possible of Dickens's experience of pantomime – from letters as well as journalism – and tracing a variety of reasons for

Dickens's privileging of Grimaldi's pantomime. I also offer some examples which describe Dickens's experiences of contemporary pantomime positively, and by showing some apparently contradictory pieces by the same authors side-by-side I hope to demonstrate that their response to pantomime was a complex, multi-faceted and contingent one. For example, while Dickens views popular entertainment as morally instructive on one platform in one moment, on another occasion he fends off one anxious moralist, Mary Taylor, when she asks him to write a new version of *Punch and Judy* in which 'the faces of Virtue and Innocence were presented oft to the popular eye [. . .] instead of the face of Vice'. He declines, dismissing popular entertainments such as *Punch and Judy* and pantomimes as 'extravagant reliefs from the realities of life which would lose [their] hold upon people if [they] were made moral and instructive'. He explains that such diversions are 'quite harmless' in their influence and consist of 'outrageous joke[s] which no-one [. . .] would think of regarding as an incentive to any course of action, or a model of any kind of conduct' (*LCD* 5: 640). As this study shall reveal, other examples from Dickens's own work belie such statements.

## Notes

1. In the past few years, the *Eighteenth-Century Theatre: Censorship, Society and the Stage* online project has provided access to an invaluable archive of rich and diverse material that comes together and builds more rounded picture.

# Part I: Dickens, Grimaldi and the Pantomime Clown

Chapter 2

# Pantomime and Pantomime Clowning

## Introduction

This chapter describes the conceptions of pantomime and clowning that inform the rest of this study, focusing on the forms that Dickens would have known, firstly a child and then later as an equally enthusiastic adult spectator. After sketching a brief history of pantomime up to the time of Dickens's death, I trace a similar chronological development of its principal protagonist, the clown, who for Dickens was the most interesting and important character. I will also briefly delineate the figure of the Shakespearean clown, who was another attractive figure for Dickens, being the most significant incarnation of the English stage fool prior to pantomime and a figure who bequeathed a measurable cultural legacy upon future theatrical clowning.

From its inception in the 1720s, English pantomime's cultural significance was debated by a variety of individuals, who all brought personal concerns and interests to their responses to watching pantomime. The final section of this chapter draws out the key debates that form the apparatus for understanding Dickens's own pantomimic sensibility, which both supported and challenged aspects of this framework in equal measure. I will particularly focus on those involved in the pantomime business, other writers who were either suspicious of or inspired by the pantomime, and professional reviewers who articulated an experience to readers who were also audience members themselves.

As I noted in my introduction, the historical and critical evaluation of pantomime carries a particular set of challenges to the researcher. Some of these are the more general challenges of theatrical scholarship: the evanescent and physical nature of performance-based art forms limit both the quantity and quality of available documentary evidence – as another of Grimaldi's biographers Richard Findlater admits, compared with the live experience of the clown's performance, the 'surviving patter, and [. . .] words of his comic songs, are meaningless dust and ashes' (1968: 14). Moreover, pantomime's status as a popular form of entertainment operating outside 'official' culture makes it critically problematic for anyone approaching the limited material that does exist. Responses are inspired both by desires to contain the form in the cultural hinterland as a demotic and coarse form and by desires to embrace it and acknowledge that it has a dignity and aesthetic value comparable with more established forms. Moreover, the responses of those working within pantomime are equally divided, between those who wish to innovate and push the form forward versus those who are suspicious of new developments and nostalgic for 'better' times: Jeffrey Richards cites declamations of pantomime not being 'what it was' across nearly seven decades (2015: 2). As I shall explore further in Chapter 3, Dickens's own responses to pantomime are equally variegated, ranging from (a somewhat calculated) enthusiasm for its ability to engage the working classes to discomfort with how that engagement affected theatrical experience.

As will become clear, then, accounts of pantomime become the debating ground for a variety of competing interest groups which necessarily determine the composition of the pantomimic discourse, including which pantomime performances are discussed and how they are discussed. However, armed with this awareness, such debates are of immense interest in themselves and tell a story of pantomime's evolution which complements any straightforward account of performance dates and box office receipts.

## A Brief History of English Pantomime

English pantomime began as John Thurmond's 'afterpiece' entertainment *Harlequin Dr Faustus* at Drury Lane on 26 November 1723, with John Rich's rival production at Lincoln's Inn following soon after. Such was their immediate popularity that Garrick's predecessor at Drury Lane, Charles Fleetwood, observed in 1744 if 'the Playhouse may be considered as the general mart of pleasure' then 'the receipts of the house are a sufficient evidence [. . .] how necessary the addition of [pantomime] is towards procuring the *best play* a *numerous audience*' (1744: 1) and James Lynch has calculated that Rich's pantomime could bring in £1,000 per week, twice as much as the serious dramas of Wilks or Cibber (1953: 232). Thus *The World* urged theatres to invest 'none but the principal performers' into producing pantomimes, since 'people of taste and fashion' now regard it as 'the highest entertainment the stage is capable of affording' (qtd in Chambers 1881 2: 765). Garrick's 1757 revival of *All's Well that Ends Well* only survived 'several nights' by including a pantomime afterpiece (Lynch 1953: 238) and even as late as 1838, Macready's *King Lear* took second billing to the 'TRAGICAL – COMICAL – HISTORICAL – PASTORAL GRAND CHRISTMAS PANTOMIME, called HARLEQUIN AND PEEPING TOM OF COVENTRY: or THE LADYE GODIVA AND THE WITCH OF WARWICK' (Poole 2004: 137).

The pantomimes of the early eighteenth century were mime- and dance-based, built around alternating 'serious' and 'comic' sections. The 'serious' parts told a familiar tale from classical mythology in the form of operatic songs and movement, while the 'comic', or 'grotesque', parts presented the *amours* of their principal character Harlequin. He battles against the patriarchal odds to secure Columbine's love, using a variety of tricks and pranks, such as pulling down buildings or disguising himself as animals to attack Pantaloon's clownish servant. The 'grotesque' sections also contained transformation scenes, in which men and women became wheelbarrows or stools and everyday objects became ostriches or serpents in a process of fantastical and imaginative escapism.

All of pantomime's elements – mythological narrative, continental *commedia*, operatic spectacle, physical farce, court masque and fairground tricks – were familiar theatrical staples, but pantomime's innovation was to combine them, in contradiction of neoclassicism's rigid demarcation of serious and comic drama. This blending of high and low art is registered in the very term 'pantomime', coined by dancer John Weaver to describe this new form of theatrical performance. In its deliberate evocation of the 'pantomimi' dances of ancient Rome, which enacted mythological scenes in dumb show, such a term was suggestive to the eighteenth-century playgoer of classical 'civilising' theatre although in fact those original spectacles had been wholly public and democratic.

Pantomime's permanent place in the annual theatrical repertoire was secured by David Garrick, who, after several failed literary attacks on the form, attempted to exert control by staging his own pantomimes, starting with *Queen Mab* in 1750. Moreover, by staging his *Harlequin's Invasion* on Boxing Day 1759, he tried to delimit and institutionalise pantomime as a strictly festive spectacle. In its closing scene he pointedly expressed his view of the real dramatic hierarchy by having a bust of Shakespeare chase Harlequin offstage in a symbolic victory of 'high' art over 'low', yet ironically the popularity of *Harlequin's Invasion* kept the form firmly in the public consciousness. It also established pantomime as a Christmas entertainment to the extent that one critic in 1822 could jokingly assert that 'This ancient usage [of producing pantomimes at Christmas] is now become law' (Creed 1822: 126).

The next significant change in pantomime was a structural one, inaugurated by Sheridan's 1781 *Robinson Crusoe; or, Harlequin Friday*. Instead of interleaving the serious and comic scenes, the comic section became sandwiched between the serious opening and conclusion. Gradually the comical 'harlequinade' became the longest and most intricate part of the show and the novelty upon which the appeal of pantomime rested, occupying an average of eighteen scenes. The romance plot of the opening became a flimsy pretext for the harlequinade's stunts, pratfalls and more topical or satirical references spanning a variety of locations: exotic or fantastical (China, Vulcan's Cave, The Tower of Forty Virgins); romantically sublime (St Michael's Mount); and specifically local (Bedford Nursery, Ouse Bridge in York, the Steyne at Brighton).

This account written by Percy Fitzgerald in 1864 describes the harlequinade of his adolescence in the early 1850s and encapsulates its keynotes of chaos, transformations, acts of theft and slapstick violence:

> Then set in the old confusion, convulsing all round – houses changed into kitchens, gardens into steam-boats, and vegetable shops into railway trains. The clown and his decrepit friend took lodgings together, and when they sat down found their seats lifting them to the ceiling. Articles of food were purloined from traders' shops, the shopman always coming out into the street to arrange his bargain, and thus leaving his wares an easy prey to the evil-disposed and designing. Customers' heads were cut off, and fastened on again by the adhesive agency of the first glue-pot that chanced to pass by. (1864: 40)

David Mayer claims that during this second phase 'the importance of the pantomime in English life was extensive' (1969: 9) and traces intellectual responses from the likes of Leigh Hunt, Hazlitt and Byron, as well as regal patronage. Most pantomimes could now fill the house for at least twenty consecutive nights (although Grimaldi's managed over thirty, with *Mother Goose* going past a hundred), which was particularly remarkable during a time when a greater alternation and variety in a theatre's repertory meant that a run of ten nights was regarded as a success. According to A. E. Wilson, *Mother Goose* earned the Covent Garden theatre 'more than £20,000' (1949: 30) and in a harmonious circle of capitalist growth, large attendances generated the budget for more innovative, exotic and opulent spectacles, which in turn attracted yet greater audiences.

During this period, the clown also became the key protagonist within the developing theme of transformation within the pantomime. Beyond the crude metamorphosis of the opening characters into their harlequinade roles (via the removal of giant *papier mâché* heads) came the clown's more complicated tricks of construction. Reflecting Renaissance concepts of Folly (defined by Peter Berger as 'an act of magic by which a counterworld [was] made to appear' [1997: 193]), Clown fashioned costumes, machines, vehicles, and even people out of ordinary items, improvised from whatever was available. Cheeses became cart wheels, coal-scuttles became helmets, and bunches of carrots became hands, revealing a fantasy world hidden just beneath the surface of the audience's everyday environment. This alternative perspective on the world also served pantomime's satirical intent, such as when in *Harlequin and the Swans, or the Bath of Beauty* (Covent Garden, 1813), a clown recruiting officer created an 'awkward' squad of troops from inn-yard odds and ends, in a critique of the poor state of England's conscripted army. This shift in agency from the external, invisible stage directors of early pantomime to the figure of the clown foregrounded his intelligence, resourcefulness or ingenuity.

However, after Grimaldi's retirement in 1823 pantomime began to gradually absorb the similar dramatic forms of the extravaganza and burlesque, which altered the transformation scene that bridged the opening and harlequinade into a transformation of scenery rather than characters. The clown (and his harlequinade) receded in impact and interest, and by 1853 Edmund Ollier noted that visual spectacle and technical innovations such as diorama and panorama dominated what he regarded as 'the more intellectual features' (1853: 397). The extravaganzas of William Beverley and James Robinson Planché were elaborate, lengthy and collaborative spectacles, marshalling machinery, lighting, scenery and multiple performers. By the time that the dramatic critic Dutton Cook came to write in 1881, this shift had gone so far that 'In modern pantomime it may be said that the opening is everything and that the harlequinade is deferred as long as possible' (1876 2: 285).

While Michael Booth views the 'degeneration of popular taste' and 'lack of strong actors' (1981: 29) as contributing factors to this shift to the spectacular, it was also a way for theatres to showcase their financial might and technical talents which made the most of the latest scientific developments. As he recognises, any aesthetic benefits were regarded as a happy by-product:

> [N]ew materials, new stage machinery, and new methods of lighting impelled [pantomimes] into a dramatic structure which in part existed to display the ingenuity of machinist, gasman, head carpenter, costume designer, and stage manager. (1981: 64)

One of Dickens's periodical contributors similarly observed this pre-eminence of the technical over the aesthetic: 'gas, it may truly be said, has been the father (and the electric light the mother) of gorgeous modern scenery' ([Anon.] 1867a: 190).

The transformation scene also began to reveal a different type of fantasy world from that of the classical world of myth and legend. Fairy stories were enjoying a revival across the arts, including literature, opera, painting and photography, and within pantomime the fairy extravaganza gradually superseded the classical burlesque. According to Ollier, the use of fairy tales rather than tales from Greek mythology with pantomime was part of a wider initiative to improve its 'grace, elegance, and fancy', which also moved away from Harlequin's 'absurdity and profanity' and replaced Clown's broader comedy with moral edification (1853: 398). This final development was aided immeasurably by the introduction of spoken word into pantomime after its parliamentary deregulation in 1843.

This reform of pantomime morals also aligned with a recalibration of the role of children as both performers and spectators – more children attended pantomime after it became a festive spectacle, which in turn bolstered the orientation of Christmas as a family festival. The new wholesomeness of pantomime was given a spiritual dimension when Percy Fitzgerald described a formative childhood experience of 'that place of Paradise, THE PANTOMIME!', in terms that suggest a religious conversion during which heathen fairies and sprites become Christian angels. Fitzgerald's narrator reads the 'heavenly' programme in the manner of a holy relic, calling it an 'enchanted document' with its own fragrance and 'a gentle cerulean light' around it. Part of its effect comes from its 'superlatives and rapturous expressions of personal self-laudation', which overwhelm the child: 'I was struck with awe at the enormous number of persons [. . .] who had contributed to the gigantic work', which the wiser adult notes 'might have been the intended effect of these announcements'. When inside, 'theatre' is 'far too earthy a word' for the experience as he describes the:

> Soft realms of celestial light, happiness, and joy! The light ambrosial – the gay colours of Paradise – and bright circles, not surely of men, women, little girls and little boys, but of men, women, and children glorified. (1864: 41–3)

Alongside such effects, the themes of pantomimes were also 'improved' appropriately. In *Lindley Murray's Grammar; or, Harlequin A.E.I.O.U. and Y* (Surrey Theatre, 1842), Murray the grammarian leads the Vowels, Aesop and the arithmetician Edward Cocker to victory against King Ignorance, Vice, Indolence, Envy and Folly – pantomime's festive roots were now so distant that rather than celebrating Folly in the Erasmian tradition, he was a villain to be defeated. The programme for *Harlequin and Old Cocker, or Arithmetic Hall and the Rule of Three* (Olympic Theatre, 1842) promised 'high morality and profound instruction', and this style of pantomime was lauded for its ability to 'show in an amusing form those principles of prudence and morality which are aimed at in the legitimate drama' (qtd in Wilson 1949: 58). Other observers noted this pedagogical imperative underlying the pantomime's 'entertainment': Halliday observed that 'It cannot be said that *Hercules and Omphale* is destitute of a high purpose, since we find the author combining amusement with instruction in an effort to teach the proper pronunciation of Greek' (1865: 233), and the 'River of Life' scene in Boucicault's 1872 *Babil and Bijou* drew praise from *The Morning Post* for having 'made one of the most popular forms of English entertainment, pantomime, subserve the needs of education' by producing a spectacle 'by which the eye is educated [in the theory of evolution] while it is pleased' ([Anon.] 1872b: 6).

This earnestly pedagogic direction left a dissenting reviewer at *The Times* lamenting in the early 1840s that 'Pantomimes are grave matters now-a-days! Very little roaring, or giggling, or grinning, or any frivolity of that sort, is to be got out of a modern harlequinade'. When one show converted Shakespeare's characters into figures from popular theatre (Oberon becomes Mr Punch, Titania Judy and Puck Toby the dog), the show was criticised for its over-intelligence: Mr Punch had 'lost that ready sense for the practically humorous and become a fanciful theorist', replacing 'the exaggerated *vis comica*, which appeals to the coarser sense, and unites old and young in roars of laughter' with the 'ingenious and whimsical' ([Anon.] 1842: 5). The pantomime that Dickens watched as an adult had materially changed from the form that he had watched as a child, and the same can be said for the figure of the clown.

## The Stage Clown from Shakespeare to Grimaldi

During the Regency period, the clown had usurped Harlequin's position as pantomime's main protagonist and was the most prominent figure in the pantomimes of Dickens's childhood. *The Monthly Mirror* observed in 1807 that 'The Clown of Mr. Grimaldi' was 'the principal cause of crowded lobbies and scarcely standing room', as interest focused on the anti-hero's comedy rather than hero's acrobatics ([Anon.] 1807: 437). Attention also shifted from the romance plot to the comic anti-plot, which left pantomime precariously balanced between a classical, conservative concept of comedy, which progressed towards harmony and resolution, and a modern, democratic concept of comedy that was distinctly more inharmonious and discordant. Looking back even further, the pantomime clown has a complex and culturally rich genealogy, which includes folk festival figures (the French *sottie* and Gros-Guillaume) and *commedia dell'arte* characters (such as Pulcinella and Arlecchino). He also inherited traits from the Vice figure of English mystery and miracle plays, court jesters, rustic Clodpates, Clodpolls, 'cuddies' or 'cullies', Jack Pudding and the stage clowns of Elizabethan theatre, including Shakespeare's clowns, with whom Dickens was particularly familiar.

Shakespeare was the first English writer to fully grasp the imaginative possibilities of the clown, and Bente Videbaek's taxonomy of Shakespeare's clowns demonstrates just how prolific he is, spanning a spectrum of significances and becoming 'more function than character' (1996: 3). Shakespeare crafted his clown roles in collaboration with his actors, carefully balancing participation and distance, and verbal and physical contribution, but always positioning them as mediators between character and audience or 'high' and 'low' cultures. They were flexible figures, adaptable to both the playwright's purposes and the actor's particular style, whether it be Will Kemp's boisterous physicality or Robert Armin's more thoughtful verbal wit.

Shakespeare's clowns not only offer comic relief to audiences, but function as their guides and interpreters of the themes of the play, and have come to be viewed as complex and important figures. David Wiles situates the clown 'at the heart of the Elizabethan debate'

(1987: x) about acting and the nature of audience participation and Shakespeare's approach underpinned a more concerted attempt to give fools a significant point of view on stage. The performances of Dick Tarleton and Kemp were memorialised in eyewitness accounts, while Armin raised the fool's profile with his own fool literature, and Wiles sees such clowns as a 'response to post-medieval social conditions', whereby they 'helped to foster in Londoners a new sense of community, shared values, and active participation in the making of a culture' (1987: 23).

Tarleton and Kemp's 'Clown' was initially a stock role within the acting company, who combined communal (social) and normative (moral) functions. He amalgamated the itinerant, extemporising minstrels and amateur lords of misrule (roles that operated amongst the people) with the stage Vice, who instructed through the demonstration of aberration rather than a shared humanity (a role that operated apart from the people). In his new habitat of the playhouse, the once independent performer now faced the competing 'author-ity' of the playwright and Shakespeare initially inscribed this 'Clown' as a largely superfluous figure, confined within standalone set-pieces of acrobatic fooling. This suited Kemp, whose fooling was extemporised, participatory and less narrative-driven; he continued fooling after the 'official' performance, further cultivating his close relationship to the audience outside the bounds of the play, which began prior to the show with his mustering of the crowd and collection of tickets.

Even these brief cameos offer an alternative perspective on the play's events, placing other characters' actions into relief and broadening our range of experience. Clown appears in just two short scenes in *Titus Andronicus*, but still manages to serve as a practical foil to both Titus's absurdist madness and Saturninus's cruel hyperbole. Similarly, the exchanges between Cleopatra and a clown as she contemplates suicide draw out her real feelings for Anthony and fear of death. In the festive comedies, the clowns are often 'natural' fools who participate in a traditional inversion-restoration narrative. They serve as household drudges (Grumio), employees of authority (the watchman Dogberry), or royal subjects (Bottom), and this proximity to socially higher figures enables them to closely analyse the follies of their 'betters', and imitate them to the point of absurdity. Grumio unconsciously parodies his master Petruchio's violence, and Dogberry is a weak incompetent hiding behind the trappings and (misappropriated) language of his office in a way that mocks official rhetoric.

In the next stage of the clown's development, Armin integrated the clown's fooling into more rounded characters, who became foils to the original servant-type clowns. He also gave clowning a more intellectual basis in texts such as *Fool upon Fool* and *A Nest of Ninnies* (1608), which proposed a multivalent role for the clown – 'the fool as sinner, the fool as privileged critic of society, and the fool as merry-maker' (Bell 2011: 21) – and was a development of the Erasmian concept of folly.

During the Middle Ages, the fool had been an ambiguous figure. From the observer's supposedly superior viewpoint, he was an object of pity or ridicule: 'folly' derives from the Latin 'follibus', meaning 'bellows', reflecting the empty-headedness of the original character. However, this unworldliness made him the privileged 'Fool in Christ' and conduit for God's word – Jesus had embraced the simple in heart, and St Paul preached that wisdom was best discovered by first becoming less wise. These scriptural precedents licensed the fool to speak as he wished without recrimination, and these 'natural' fools were retained by the nobility to remind them of their own imperfections.

However, they were increasingly joined at court by 'artificial', professional clowns who exploited the natural fool's licence to actively point out the follies of others. During the Renaissance, this mandate adopted a more intellectual and pedagogic impetus, when Erasmus's *Moriae encomimum* (1511) further established the fool as a figure who could teach humanity to improve itself. Erasmus suggested that to live with 'nothing else than to be govern'd by reason' is only a partial existence compared to living with folly and being 'given up to the will of our Passions' (2003: 14). This sophistication of the clown's role gave folly a much broader cultural remit: as Robert Hornback asserts, the 'religious, political, and ideological elements were indeed often an, if not *the*, animating spark in the comic repertoire of much Renaissance clowning' (2009: 5). Rather than being mere comic relief within a wider scheme of authorised subversion, clowning began to consider deeper questions about humanity and knowledge.

Folly's recognition that all men were potentially fools regardless of social standing undermined established hierarchical roles, and so Shakespeare and Armin's 'artificial' clowns – such as Feste, Touchstone and Lavatch – operated in between the play-world and the audience's world. These clowns participate within the play-world enough to elicit sympathy with key characters and bridge the separate 'high' and 'low' social groups, but also keep sufficient distance to guide the audience through the play and prevent them from becoming entrenched within any set position. Such a clown remains a perpetual outsider in a position described by Leszek Kolakowski as simultaneously 'outside good society [. . .] observ[ing] it from the sidelines in order to unveil the nonobvious behind the obvious, the nonfinal behind the final' but also a frequenter of that society 'so as to know what it holds sacred and to have the opportunity to address it impertinently' (1968: 34).

When such clowns close the play, they leave the final impression on the audience back in their own world: when Puck calls the foregoing performance as a 'weak and idle theme, / No more yielding but a dream', he is neither an actor stepping out of character nor a character displaying self-awareness. Instead he is a figure who offers a final blurring of the boundaries between the 'real' world and the playworld, complicating the ostensibly conservative nature of the playworld endings so we are left pondering whether the *status quo* has been entirely re-established after all (Shakespeare 2008a: V, ii, 60–1). In later plays such as *King Lear* or *Troilus and Cressida*, this artificial fool becomes the 'bitter fool' whose laughter at society's follies carries either painful disappointment or caustic contempt.

Shakespeare's most integrated clown is Falstaff, who again redefined the playwright's creative relationship to clowning. Although Falstaff was an actor-centric role, who Robert Bell calls 'Kemp's apex and the zenith of clowning', Shakespeare invested equally as much, for 'Everything [he] knew, loved, and distrusted about clowns goes into Falstaff' (2011: 19). For Samuel Johnson, Falstaff encapsulates the paradox of the fool as a 'compound of sense and vice; of sense which may be admired but not esteemed, of vice which may be despised but hardly detested' (1968: 523), and Falstaff's repertoire transcends merely exposing the folly of the court's theatricality. His large girth, excessive appetites for food, drink and sex, and presentation of bodily excrescences (sweat, grease, laughter) align him with Bakhtin's grotesque body, and its attendant carnivalesque festivities, to the extent that Neil Rhodes calls him 'the supreme dramatic embodiment of the Elizabethan grotesque' (1980: 104).

Falstaff's juxtaposition with more sober figures generates diverting confusion and laughter, but also interrogates the constructed nature of identity. As Hal's tempter he acts as a Vice figure, but he also acts as Hal's teacher (presenting alternative world views and instructing his pupil through his own folly) and his scapegoat when the prince wishes to reject his past indiscretions. This uneasy relationship (coupled with Falstaff's association with food and drink) echoes the folk battle between (fat) Carnival and (lean) Lent, which continues in Falstaff's challenges to Justice Shallow (Falstaff's 'lawless law of nature' (Kayser 1964: 235) *versus* artificial, man-made law) and Hotspur (Falstaff's grounded and realistic perspective *versus* an 'official', glory-laden version of history).

However, through Falstaff, Shakespeare moves from celebrating universal folly to moralising through sermon – jester turns priest. In *Henry IV 1* he enjoys the bodily excesses in the Saturnalian tradition, but his subsequent appearances are admonitory lessons on the consequences of those excesses – disease, physical incapacitation and death. Hale and hearty England becomes overfed, sick England, and Falstaff becomes a scapegoat for the removal of its ills. At his nadir in *The Merry Wives of Windsor*, he is not a distanced and witty jester but the butt of the play's physical comedy, who indirectly teaches us through his sorry example. His obesity is no longer a source of celebration, but an impediment to his functioning within 'normal' society – as Rhodes has it, it is now 'the fat body mercilessly baited by tricksters' (1980: 122).

Echoing Falstaff's decline, Clown's cultural importance gradually diminished: Charles I was the last monarch to employ a court fool, and William Rowley (who died in 1626) was one of the last notable stage clowns before Grimaldi. Shakespeare had sophisticated the clown's role to the point at which the lettered elites believed that he had over-reached his original servile status, and even presumed to play the king. In a Hal-like rejection, Clown had to become a comic simpleton again, and as Willson Disher describes, the Restoration's fool was 'a whipping-stock for the gallants' (1925: 72). Clown was 'othered' as the countryside 'Clodpoll', whereas Harlequin reflected the nobility's self-image as fashionable men about town. If Clown presumed beyond his bounds and came to town, he was deservedly gulled and punished by its smarter inhabitants.

However as Regency pantomime become what Jane Moody calls 'a theatrical form which dramatised the pleasures, fears and absurdities of urban life' (2000: 209) Clown became its 'urban anarchist', balancing gullibility with tricksterism of his own and deriving comedy from his exploitation *of* the city, not just his exploitation *by* the city (2000: 211). In 1853, Ollier described the cultural capital that Clown had earned (or more fittingly, stolen) for himself, calling him the 'matchless rogue of modern times' and 'the veritable propagator of that embodiment of London impudence, knowing and sly [. . .] whom we cannot help in some sort admiring for the geniality of his humour and the southern existence of his spirits' (1853: 398).

This highlights Clown's modern, metropolitan nature, and indicates an acceptance of his vices because his humour is inclusive rather than cruel. If Dickens is felt to embody and possess London through his writing, Grimaldi's clown does the same; *The Times* noted that 'Grimaldi belongs to Covent-Garden theatre as completely as St. Paul's belongs to Ludgate-hill', and Grimaldi was a London monument in himself, born in London and performing in her theatres for his entire career ([Anon.] 1823: 3).

Contemporary commentators drew parallels between Grimaldi's pantomime and 'higher' theatrical modes, suggesting that Garrick's battle between the forms remained unresolved. H. D. Miles's pantheon of comical ghosts traces a line of descent from Shakespeare to Grimaldi, including 'Falstaff, Autolycus, and the two Dromios [. . .] Grimaldi and [. . .] Punch', who protect spectators from being 'lectured, educated, institutionalised and feelosofised into one eternal dead-level of knowledge!' (1838: 8). Recalling his constructions in *Harlequin and Asmodeus* (Covent Garden, 1810), in which he created a man from fruit and vegetables, *The Times* described Grimaldi as 'a sort of Shakespeare in his way – he exhausted natural monsters, and then "imagined new". Frankenstein was nothing to him. Place him in any warehouse, and he soon produced a creation that you would have sworn was indigenous to the soil' ([Anon.] 1828b: 3). During this period, then, Clown kept esteemed company – England's most revered playwright and the latest literary scientist. Such comparisons are also indicative of the relative struggles of Shakespeare's plays on the late eighteenth-century stage: while, as James Lynch notes, 'no dramatist came along who found the means to translate the melancholy Dane or the fat knight of the Boar's Head Tavern into the universal man who might walk the streets of Georgian London', Grimaldi's pantomime clown clearly could (1953: 301–2).

Accounts of Grimaldi's popularity highlighted his innate abilities rather than any learned trickery. Grimaldi was not a 'natural' fool in the medieval sense, but Halliday suggests that Grimaldi's humour *appeared* natural, and therefore superior to the 'artificial' stunts of other clowns. *The Times* astutely identified the craft required to convincingly perform guileless stupidity, calling Grimaldi the 'most assiduous of all imaginable buffoons' ([Anon.] 1813: 3), and Charles Dibdin felt that his studious professionalism emulated pantomime's greatest theatrical enemy: 'there was so much mind in everything he did. It was said of Garrick that, when he played a Drunken Man, he was "all over drunk" – Grimaldi was "all over Clown"' (1956: 41).

The versatility of Grimaldi's Clown is indicated by Horatio Smith, who recognises the comedy in all his undertakings:

> whether he have to rob a pieman or open an oyster, imitate a chimney-sweep or a dandy, grasp a red-hot poker or devour a pudding, take snuff, sneeze, make love, mimic a tragedian, cheat his master, pick a pocket, beat a watchman, or nurse a child. ([Smith] 1822: 59)

In these activities, Grimaldi negotiated between the naïve natural and scheming trickster, and between the Romantic man-child who merely follows his instincts and the worldly adult who fashions art from his buffoonery. *Oxberry's Dramatic Biography* described him as 'always appear[ing] to us to represent a grown child, waking to perception, but wondering at every object he beholds' ([Anon.] 1825a: 119–20) and even descriptions of his voice recognise this duality of juvenile innocence and adult knowingness; it was at once 'richly thick and chuckling, like the utterance of a boy laughing, talking and eating custard, all at once' (Hood 1868: 115) *and* 'a gin voice, heaved from the very bottom of the chest' (Robson 1846: 236). Clown (and his supporters) used this 'naturalness' to excuse his crimes, for although 'robbery became a science in [Clown's] hands', it was also 'a portion of his nature [. . .] for which he was neither blameable nor accountable' ([Anon.] 1825a: 119). One *Times* reviewer admits even that if Clown 'took a red-hot poker to anybody, we never could interfere, though it had been to save our own father – and when he stole apples, we really doubted whether common honesty was not a kind of prejudice' ([Anon.] 1823: 3).

As these complex responses attest, the precise nature of the laughter Clown generated was determined by an unstable compound of his own intended function and the audience's reception, ranging on a broad scale between 'democratic' and 'normative'. Bakhtin describes democratic laughter as a communal reaction shared *with* the clown at the relatable experience that he enacts, which affirms our common humanity for all its faults. All classes can participate in democratic laughter, despite any subversive context: 'The people's ambivalent laughter [. . .] expresses the point of view of the whole world; he who is laughing also belongs to it' (1968: 12). Thus by laughing with the court fool, the monarch was reminded that he was still subject to the foibles of his humanity regardless of any divinely-ordained status.

This aligns with Erasmian folly, which, according to Horatio Smith, continued to inform perceptions of comedy into the nineteenth century:

> 'All wisdom is folly,' says the philosopher; but we often incline to think the converse of the proposition correct, when we see thee put thy antic disposition on, and set the audience in a roar by the magic of thy powers. ([Smith] 1822: 58)

By echoing Hamlet's deliberate deployment of folly to uncover fundamental truths, this description refutes the 'naturalness' of the clown's fooling but acknowledges its social utility, also recognised by Leigh Hunt when he urged all adults who disliked pantomime to 'grow young again and get wiser' (qtd in Wilson 1949: 12).

However, Bakhtin describes how during the sixteenth to the eighteenth centuries the universal humour of this 'carnival satire' was forced to compete with a more exclusive 'modern satire' which rejected rather than embraced a shared humanity. The modern satirist was one 'whose laughter is negative and places himself above the object of his mockery' (1968: 12). Private entertainments replaced communal celebrations as the cultural elite uncoupled themselves from popular culture, and the newly 'mannered' audiences who looked into theatre's mirror no longer wanted to see Clown's face staring back. Philip Sidney's *Defense of Poesy* rebuked dramatists who 'thrust in the clown by the head and shoulders to play a part in majestical matters, with neither decency nor discretion', and his designation of such plays as 'mongrel' is loaded with a rhetoric of breeding, purity and class (1890: 50).

According to this more normative view, given full expression by Thomas Hobbes and later developed by Bergson and Freud, laughter is a tribal mechanism for crudely asserting superiority. The clown becomes a scapegoat for society's abnormalities and subversive feelings – who is now laughed *at* rather than *with* – in order to 'improve' society. Halliday also sees these normative values at work in the pantomime, as Clown punishes vices such as vanity:

> The clown cuts off the head of a dandy who is proud of his whiskers, and the children clap their hands with delight. There is a moral, d'ye see? He was inordinately vain of that figure-head of his, and he was punished. Serve him right. (1863a: 5–6)

A number of caustic reviews from *The Times* also describe Clown performing this normative function: as one observed, 'it is in the nature of man to enjoy the ridicule (though it recoil upon himself) which is flung first upon his fellow' (1824: 3), while another commented that 'Hobbes must have been deep in the philosophy of pantomimes', because 'It does one good to see how heartily the clowns and pantaloons [. . .] cuff and bang each other.' This is because as self-appointed 'moralists' we can identify with 'those idiosyncrasies of disposition which make the annoyance of a fellow-creature the only business and comfort of existence' (1832: 3).

Moreover, when Clown 'robs unwary tradespeople right and left, and their discomfiture is the greatest fun in the world' (Halliday 1863a: 6), this symbolic punishment of gullibility produces what Findlater has called laughter with 'gratitude and contempt', a shared response of public distancing which masks a shameful personal recognition (1978: 159). Halliday indicates that this laughter creates an uncomfortable relationship between the observed onstage performance and the lived offstage existence. After asking 'Where is the witticism that can compete with sitting on a baby, and flattening it to the shape of a pancake?' or the 'ludicrous object [of] a policeman with his hat knocked over his eyes?', he recognises that this laughter is not universal when these activities occur offstage – the mother does not find the idea of her own baby being flattened amusing, and the policeman could not keep order if he were a comic butt offstage (1863a: 5). According to this view, Clown is no longer an empathetic figure, since in Bergson's terms 'laughter is incompatible with emotion' (1956: 150), and the source of this humour is 'a growing callousness to social life' (1956: 147).

Pantomime comedy also enacted social control in other ways; by stereotyping popular figures, identity becomes bounded and the apparent freedom offered by a comic mask becomes an imposition of fixed attitudes. In this sense, comic theatre could be said to subvert authority only to finally reaffirm it, either by providing an ending sympathetic to authority (when Clown is ultimately punished for his transgressions) or simply through the material conditions of its performance (which occurs within an officially sanctioned site, financially undergirt by the authorities). Lent follows Carnival, not vice versa, and often concludes with a trial for the Carnival figure or even the emphatic closure of a ritual execution and burial. Thus pantomime sometimes appears more conservative than carnival; Jill A. Sullivan regards the latter as a more participatory spectacle in 'the public spaces beyond the theatre' (2011: 130).

However, rather than fulfilling a single comic function, Grimaldi's performance constantly changed position through the course of a pantomime to satisfy both polarities of 'democracy' and 'authority'. Pantomime appealed across all classes, from those in the pits to the royalty in the boxes, and the clown's complication of the boundaries between the theatre (staged performance) and the world beyond it (lived reality), makes it a more pervasive form that is closer to Peter Burke's description of carnival as:

> a huge play in which the main streets and squares became stages, the city became a theatre without walls and the inhabitants, the actors and spectators, observing the scene from their balconies. In fact there was no sharp distinction between actors and spectators, since the ladies on their balconies might throw eggs at the crowd below, and the maskers were often licensed to burst into private houses. (1994: 182)

The harlequinade further encouraged this elision of boundaries through its use of real locations and shop-fronts advertising real commercial interests. Conversely events such as the Old Price Riots (1809–10) reveal theatregoers to be active participants in a symbiotic actor–audience dynamic, in which, as Marc Baer has it, a 'place in the audience was also a voice' (1992: 177).

Pantomime's cross-class appeal to a wide range of social groups is therefore not incompatible with the carnivalesque, which Bakhtin felt was set up in opposition to the *official* culture rather than any particular class. Pantomime is what Burke describes as a 'polysemous' event, 'meaning different things to different people', which should be 'read as a palimpsest' of different value systems, rather than one system triumphing over another (1994: 191). Members of the nobility and clergy could enthusiastically participate within the carnival without hypocrisy, and a variety of events (the Martin Marprelate controversies, early evangelical ceremonies and festivals of misrule) indicate how orthodox religion opportunistically embraced the tactics of the carnivalesque in their own battles against opposing religions.

Normative laughter directed at a scapegoat thus becomes ambivalent, when those traits decreed as 'officially' undesirable are not universally abhorred. Distancing laughter can become accommodating laughter, and villain can become hero, especially when presented as an embodied reality. Kristen Poole describes the failure of attempts to ridicule Martin Marprelate in the form of a stage grotesque; the audience varied from a 'jeering mob seeking retribution for Marprelate's affront to ecclesiastical authority' to 'a crowd of carnival celebrants enjoying the antics of a lord of misrule' (2004: 28).

## Pantomime's Attraction – and its Threat

Pantomime's early success meant that it became what John O'Brien calls a 'ubiquitous [object of discourse] from the 1720s until at least mid-century'; as he puts it, 'once you go looking for Harlequin, he shows up in every imaginable context' (2004: xx). A contemporary observer noted that 'Harlequin was to frisk, and frolick, and leap over the heads of the best writers of the age' and so unsurprisingly the views of 'serious' dramatists like Garrick and novelists like Henry Fielding (a creator of afterpieces himself) differed from those of theatre-goers or profit-hungry theatre-owners (qtd in Murphy 1801: 242). Colly Cibber only reluctantly allowed pantomime on his stage, claiming that 'they were obliged at Drury Lane either to comply with the public taste or starve' (qtd in Wilson 1949: 53). Shakespeare may have nourished the soul, but not the proprietor's stomach it seems, and Cibber plaintively observed that 'the severer might cry out against these mummeries', yet

> as the managers laying out some hundreds on a piece of this description would bring them in many thousands, who can be surprised they continued them while they turned out so much to their account? (qtd in Wilson 1934: 52–3)

In 1860, the Christmas pantomime was still being called 'the sheet anchor of the drama' ([Anon.] 1860b: 5) for theatre managers, upon which was predicated the survival of more 'literary' and intellectual drama the rest of the year: 'If it were not for that raddled face and those spangled pantaloons, what would become of Shakespeare and Sheridan. The former bring grist to the mill, the great immortals gobble it up.' Even then, the playwright James Robinson Planché recognised the very different priorities at work:

> a thousand pounds were frequently lavished on a Christmas pantomime [. . .] while the plays of Shakespeare were put on the stage with makeshift scenery, and, at the best, a new dress or two for the principal actors. (1872 1: 52)

Such complaints became a *leitmotif* of pantomime's early history, as this *arriviste* form asserted its cultural position to equal measures of critical distaste and popular commercial appeal. Thus *The Drama* laments pantomime's prominence at the patent theatres, as 'the leading houses descend to the embodying [of] such grotesque fancies, as are displayed in these ridiculous violations of nature'. It dismisses any comparison between contemporary pantomime and its classical predecessor, feeling that pantomimes, in their 'Grotesque dresses, barbarous action, and the invocation of "poetry run mad"', 'differ but little from the whimsicalities of a country fair' ([Creed] 1822: 126–7).

A neat parody of anti-pantomime sentiment is offered in Halliday's 'My Pantomime' (1863), which humorously depicts a frustrated tragedian forced through straitened circumstances to write pantomimes, regarded as the lowest form in the theatrical hierarchy. Popularity and profit supersede artistic expression and originality as the theatre manager Moberly explains that 'the scene-painter [is] the horse, and the author [is] the cart'. Thus the narrator must 'manage [his] story to fit' the scenes that have already been painted, so 'lower[s]' and 'unscrew[s]' his script 'down to the proper pitch' by filling it with slang and punning. Artistic licence is also curtailed by audience taste and financial speculation, for as Moberley again explains, 'everything's been done so, and new things are hazardous'.

During rehearsals, the narrator's romantic conceptions are further disabused as he finds himself not in the 'pillared and curtained apartment' of 'lofty-mannered tragedians assembled in solemn conclave' but 'in a little dark mouldy room, in the midst of a throng of low comedians, and singing chambermaids, and acrobats, and ballet-dancers, who paid me no respect whatever, but regarded me with marked suspicion and distrust' (Halliday 1863c: 273–4). Fitzgerald's 'Harlequin Fairy Morgana!' also adopts a pattern of reversed transformation and disappointing reality, as the naïve boy-narrator discovers that the 'surpassing lovely Queen Morgana' was not perpetually 'Glorified, and in her habitual medium of ambrosial pink light' (1864: 44) but became by day a 'sickly unwholesome' creature, 'as yellow as a guinea' who 'looked as if she had lately been ill' (1864: 48).

But despite aesthetic qualms, pantomime was ever-popular: *The Times* wryly noted that 'Everybody pooh-pooh's the pantomime; but everybody goes to see it. It is voted "sad nonsense" and played every night for two months.' This same review captured pantomime's cross-class appeal in a tangible demonstration of its popularity, likening the frenzied conduct of spectators to a street riot, in which the 'dreadful' 'squeeze' at the entrance was followed by alarming 'attempts [. . .] to force open the doors of boxes', by a group of 'assailants'. It further notes how 'the whole neighbourhood was in a state of active commotion' as the playhouse's mood spreads to the environs. In a replication of pantomime's mixing of class and gender, 'Bow-street officers, – ladies who thought themselves ill-treated, – and dandies, whose pockets were rendered just as light as their heads were shaken together in a most delectable confusion' ([Anon.] 1823: 3). *The Era* in 1867 strengthens this sense of pantomime's populism by likening it to other triumphs of popular agitation: 'Time in his course has built up the Pantomime into an institution, as venerable as Magna Charta, as sacred as the "Bill of Rights", as dearly cherished as Habeas Corpus' ([Anon.]1867b: 10).

A number of Dickens's periodical writers went beyond box-office economics to promote pantomime as an earnest dramatic profession. Halliday's later 'Poetry and Pantomime' (1865) counterweighs the caricature of 'My Pantomime' by highlighting its literary merit. He contrasts the 'well-skilled lively young men [. . .] condemned to write our burlesques and pantomimes' with 'the unskilled dull dogs [who] are nearly always selected to write our comedies and dramas' and places the pantomime writer in the company of literary greats (1865: 233). Towers's *Goody Two-Shoes* is compared with 'the writings of the immortal Shakespeare' in its 'bold defiance of rhythm [. . .] rugged force of expression, and [. . .] great earnestness of purpose', and further parallels are drawn between Homer, who 'glorified the heroes who fought under the walls of Troy' and 'the pantomime poet of the East [who] glorifies the British heroes who have fought and bled for the honour of their country in the prize ring' (1865: 230–1).

During an age which lauded hard work in quasi-religious terms, a potentially more persuasive argument was one which acknowledged the significant physical endeavours involved in pantomime's production. G. A. Sala's piece 'Getting Up a Pantomime' (1851) is a clever inversion of one of *Household Words*' 'process' articles, which were usually accounts of prosaic industrial processes (for example, manufacturing paper or making glass) written in a way that, as Harry Stone puts it, simultaneously transformed 'those processes (and by extension the entire workaday world) into something rich and fanciful, a transformation that could help people survive in an iron age' (Dickens 1969 1: 137).

Sala reverses the usual pattern and reimagines the 'rich and fanciful' world of the pantomime as a series of more 'workaday' activities, and in the process refutes common misconceptions about the pantomime (for example, the insubstantiality of stage carpentry). He asserts a parity between stage technicians and non-theatrical tradesmen, and demonstrates how the pantomime world of impermanent pain that the audience enjoy can only be constructed through backstage suffering and anguish. In doing so, Sala breaks the illusion of pantomime and exposes the poverty of the reality behind the pleasure of the spectacle. This poverty and pleasure are delicately balanced in such images as the 'noble knights and ladies' who 'feast richly off wooden fowls and brown-paper pies, quaffing meanwhile, deep potations of toast-and-water sherry, or, haply, golden goblets full of nothing at all'. Sala exclaims how 'Dreadfully deceptive are these stage banquets and stage purses' and notes the pangs of the actors involved in the empty nourishment of the spectacle: 'the haughty Hospodar of Hungary' toasts with a 'liquorless cup', while the actor is 'vainly thirsting meanwhile, for a pint of mild porter from the adjacent hostelry' (1851: 293).

The piece builds to a crescendo of industriousness as the Boxing Day opening approaches. The word 'work' is repeated in a rhythmic pattern that echoes the steady efforts of the pantomimists, 'Work, work, work, everywhere'; 'Work, work, work, and Christmas-eve is here', 'Work on the stage [. . .] Work in the flies, and work underneath the stage' (1851: 295). Nor is it just the technicians, as the performers rehearse 'until their bones ache, and the perspiration streams from their limbs'. Christmas Day brings no respite from the labour, just the 'Incessant fiddling from the repetiteur. "Trip", "rally", and "jump", for the pantomimists'.

Sala closes rhetorically, returning to the 'ants behind the baize' who have 'laboured so hard at' the pantomime, that they become begrimed by their toils like other manual labourers. He requests the reader to 'Consider how hard they work, how precarious is their employment, how honestly they endeavour to earn their living, and to do their duty in their stage of life' (1851: 296). The laziness, itinerancy and indolence that anti-theatrical prejudice commonly associated with stage people are replaced by a redoubtable work ethic, as 'the ants behind the baize' cry 'Give us more nails, hands, Venetian red, velvet, and glue, and we'll not fail' (1851: 295).

Augustus Harris's account of his management of *Mother Goose* supports Sala's view, and is summarised as 'ten weeks, without one moment's peace, without time for eating, drinking, or even sleeping'. Harris employs military metaphors in describing the discipline required: 'everything has to be ordered, everyone to be drilled' and he is 'Constantly besieged from morning till night'. His working days are narrated as a hyperbolic whirl of time, space and activity: he has a 'hundred daily interviews' with a long catalogue of people, 'more people than [he] can remember', and 'at least twenty people always waiting to see [him]'. The frantic back-and-forth activity of the harlequinade is echoed in his 'Rushing, for forty-eight hours at a time, to Newcastle, Birmingham, and Paris', 'returning to the hotel only to find a score of telegrams calling for my immediate return to London'. Others who observed Harris at work corroborate his reports of incessant toil; for example, when rehearsing *Aladdin* in 1885, he has 'the semblance of a pantomime demon' darting 'from one end of the stage to the other like a globule of quicksilver'. The observer employs anaphoric uses of 'Now' and 'Anon' to pile activity upon activity, and Harris is no longer a struggling human labourer, but a multi-tasking magical superman (qtd in Booth 1981: 76–7). The accounts of Sala and Harris thus represent carefully crafted defences of pantomime as a theatrical form, which use a dual strategy to both elevate pantomime through comparisons with other enterprises and engage with pantomime's methods to transform and enrich everyday experience.

Pantomime's popularity, then, was indisputable: the financial facts forced even its most conservative critics to acknowledge its success and importance to the survival of other dramatic forms. Its success was partially based on its appeal to both the mind, through its radical politics, and the body, through its delight in the corporeal. I will briefly introduce these themes here in anticipation of further analysis to come in subsequent chapters.

Pantomime's alluring radicalism stemmed from it being outside the purview of the 1737 Licensing Act, which Lynch describes as 'the formal and parliamentary recognition of the theater as a powerful social instrument'. This only permitted spoken drama at three theatres and sought to punish unlicensed 'minor' theatres which performed any 'Interlude, Tragedy, Comedy, Opera, Play, farce or any other entertainment of the Stage' 'for hire, gain or reward' (1953: 2–3). Even after the 1843 Theatre Regulation Act, the non-verbal harlequinade lay outside of the control of the Lord Chamberlain's office, which only oversaw the written parts of the pantomime, and only received summaries of the comic business from around 1850.[1] However, pantomime was relatively well-protected compared with popular entertainments such as the circus, which was literally an outsider form; circuses were rarely granted licences during the Christmas period and risked fines or closure without one.

Pantomime utilised this liminal legal status to present material which subversively ridiculed authority figures and deflated the pretence of social and official rituals. Bergson has recognised the latent comicality of officialdom, whereby 'Any image [. . .] suggestive of the notion of a society disguising itself [is] laughable' since its participants give 'the impression of puppets in motion' (1956: 89–90). Pantomime exposed this risible charade by critiquing the instruments through which power is asserted and performed – the ceremonies of government, law courts and the military. This drew the praise of radicals like Leigh Hunt, who identified pantomime's 'animal spirit' in its unsettledness, violence and possibility of transformation. For Hunt, pantomime could also fulfil the wishes of spectators discontented with their own lot and struck out against an array of targets that included 'the hypocritical, the selfish, the self-sufficient, the gossiping, [. . .] the ostentatious, the canting, the oppressing, [. . .] the money-scraping, [and] the over-squeezing' ([Hunt] 1817: 9).

This satirical direction also aligned pantomime with the vibrant visuals of such artists as Gillray and the Cruikshanks, a link cemented when Grimaldi 'introduced a series of Caricature Scenes somewhat similar to the Print Shop Caricatures, and, like them, allusive to the reigning follies of the day' (Dibdin 1956: 102). While pantomime may have been gentler in its approach, its embodied nature increased its piquancy: Clown's flesh-and-blood realisation of the wittiest visual observations of the day prompted the *New Monthly Magazine* to describe him as a 'Hogarth in action' ([Anon.] 1837: 384).

Pantomime carried significant political import, rather than being a simple diversion: Halliday might well expect that 'Some [. . .] members of parliament [. . .] will one of these days fill a column with the statement which the pantomime poet has expressed in two lines' (1865: 232). This was no abstract anti-authoritarianism, and was, as *The Times* put it, an annual 'running commentary [. . .] upon the whims and speculations of the year' ([Anon.] 1824: 3). This currency was supported by pantomime's movement from a timeless rustic countryside to a specific contemporary and urban setting; as *The Times* observed 'If comedy holds the mirror up to nature, it is pantomime, with her concave glass, that should, peculiarly, caricature the deformities of the town' ([Anon.] 1825b: 3). Such 'deformities' were uncovered through themes as various as the Napoleonic wars, the British Empire, the Regency crisis, sartorial fads, the rise of consumerism, the social costs of the Industrial Revolution, new modes of travelling and other contemporary inventions.

The clown was praised by Horatio Smith as 'the finest practical satyrist [*sic*]', who entertains through his 'acute observation upon the foibles and absurdities of society, and his happy talent of holding them up to ridicule' ([Smith] 1822: 57). Grimaldi's more mischievous Clown became the principal agent for the subversive fantasies of his audience, committing crimes against authority and property with impunity. As Findlater suggests, the outrageous nature of these crimes was proportional to the harshness of the penal code: 'If any Clodpoll in real life had been caught in one of these man-traps, set for those criminals who trespassed on private property, he might have been transported for life to Australia' (1978: 118). While several commentators attempted to disavow the corrupting potential of such criminal displays – Charles Dibdin claimed that 'every immorality' committed by Clown 'was almost invariably followed by some appropriate punishment, through the agency of Harlequin' (1956: 89) – audience testimonies of Grimaldi's performances relish and even excuse his crimes while simultaneously glossing over their moralising conclusions.

Such antics were attuned to the darker tone of Regency humour: for example, Grimaldi's gluttony reflected what Bryant calls 'the national vice of stuffing' (1950: 151) which produced gigantic meals of many courses, as the clown became 'a parody of Georgian greed' (Findlater 1978: 158). Similarly, his impersonation of a drunken watchman drew on the same tradition of malicious tricks depicted by Pierce Egan and Douglas Jerrold. This seam of black comedy is described by historians in varying shades of savagery: Gerald Frow feels that Clown reflects the sensibilities of a time when 'lords thought it a fine thing to hob-nob with pugilists, marquises grew famous for practical joking, and gentlemen on a night out as a matter of course beat the watch' (1985: 73), while Arthur Bryant suggests that Regency humour is 'to throw a drunk in a dunghill, drop a live coal on sleeper's head, rob a blind man of his dog and swear in the presence of ladies and clergymen' (1950: 326). Pantomime competed with such violent spectacles as cock-fighting, bear-baiting and bare-knuckle fighting, and the tourist Robert Paulet lamented the effect of the proximity of these different 'diversions': 'men can see a monkey dangling from a wire, or a fellow creature expiring at the gallows, with equal unconcern' (qtd in Cradock 1828: 35). As Moody describes, Grimaldi's act carried 'a malicious, sinister undertow' along with it and this could abruptly transform 'from pleasure to menace, approbation to abhorrence', thus evoking not only wholesome John Bull but 'those dastardly *sans culottes* and demonic villains of patriotic serio-pantomime' (2000: 213).

This thread of subversive politics was allied with pantomime's bodily aesthetic, which looked predominantly to the spectator's body for its response. The recourse to the corporeal was partly due to the original prohibition of dialogue as well as the large and noisy performing spaces, but as O'Brien (2004) explains, it became a tool deliberately deployed against the authoritarian verbal poetics. Leigh Hunt remarked that 'It is better to act folly than to talk it', and because the true 'essence of pantomime is practical absurdity keeping the wits in constant chase' (1820: 573), pantomime was felt to achieve its best effects at a more bodily, sensational level. One *Times* review attributes the popularity of the pantomime to the audience's unconscious acknowledgement that 'it is pleasant to laugh without an effort, and to hear such jokes as do not require the fatigue of comprehension', and asserts the superior appeal of the bodily and communal spectacle over the verbal and private experience of reading a novel: 'A pun tells only once – but it is not so with a poke in the eye [. . .] Thousands of us notoriously lay down even the Waverley novel for a fire – or a dog-fight – or a hackney-coach overturned' (1823: 3).

Grimaldi's Clown articulated this bodily vocabulary so expertly that commentators assigned it an equivalence to the literary as a means of expression: *The Times* called him 'a living epigram, so terse and pointed, as to set translation entirely at defiance' ([Anon.] 1828b: 3), while the *New Monthly Magazine* similarly felt that he transcended verbal communication's power as a semiotic code: 'Speech would have been thrown away in his performance of Clown', for 'Every limb of him had a language' ([Anon.] 1837: 383). His corporeal performances were anatomised in forensic detail; his face became 'a living jest-book, in which may be read all the whimsical notions which owe their birth to his prolific fancy', which in turn prompted a concomitant *bodily* response by the audience:

> all parties seem convulsed with laughter, and their arms, shoulders, features, and whole body, are at once set bustling with delight. In the pit, there immediately appears a sea of pleasure; and the people roll backwards and forwards like waves. ([Anon.] 1815b: 421)

## Conclusion

This chapter has not only marked out the principal waypoints in the history of the pantomime form, but also tried to trace the broader cultural currents along which it moved through the theatre world. Moreover, in outlining a sense of what Dickens would have understood as 'pantomime', I have hopefully also drawn out its attractions and imaginative possibilities for this most imaginatively voracious of writers.

Pantomime's principal protagonist the clown was a peripheral figure who could not only provide a humorous and oblique running commentary on more 'serious' and substantial themes. He also reflected Dickens's own values of conviviality, the ameliorative powers of laughter, and the recognition of a common humanity amidst what would become, in Dickens's eyes at least, an increasingly inhuman society. The clown also processed and mediated the urban experience and carefully constructed anarchy.

The clown carried a cross-class appeal, and could amuse and entertain across social boundaries, nimbly slipping between the radical and the conservative. Dickens also engaged with pantomime in this open-ended way – neither entirely democratic and populist nor entirely superior or critical of aberrant behaviour.

Dickens's stated intentions within *Household Words* and *Bleak House* were to 'show to all, that in all familiar things, even in those which are repellent on the surface, there is Romance enough, if we will find it out' (*HW* 1.1: 1) and dwell upon 'the romantic side of familiar things' (*BH* 4). In the pantomime clown, a figure capable of transforming himself and the world around him through tricks of construction, Dickens found an ideal conduit for identifying the fantastical latent within the everyday, in order to reimagine and reinvigorate *quotidian* experience.

The pantomime clown's ability to generate laughter and thus forge a direct bodily response and link with his audience also spoke to Dickens's desire to 'sit down upon the very hobs' of his readers 'and take a personal and confidential position with them' (*LCD* 4: 327–8) and his sense of the 'peculiar relation (personally affectionate, and like no other man's) which subsists between me and the public' (*LCD* 8: 539–40). However, Dickens also learnt from the experience of the clown that this relation was a precarious one, as the audience could provide a sense of validation and communality with the individual but just as quickly transform into the mob, threatening to overwhelm and engulf his individuality.

## Notes

1. Thanks to Professor Kate Newey, who is tracing the Lord Chamberlain's requests for copies of the comic business alongside the scripts of pantomime openings.

Chapter 3

# Dickens at the Pantomime

## Introduction

In *David Copperfield*, Dickens's favourite and most personal novel, a young David takes in 'Julius Caesar and the new Pantomime' at Covent Garden. David is overwhelmed by the experience:

> the mingled reality and mystery of the whole show, the influence upon me of the poetry, the lights, the music, the company, the smooth stupendous changes of glittering and brilliant scenery, were so dazzling, and opened up such illimitable regions of delight, that when I came out into the rainy street, at twelve o'clock at night, I felt as if I had come from the clouds, where I had been leading a romantic life for ages, to a bawling, splashing, link-lighted, umbrella-struggling, hackney-coach-jostling, patten-clinking, muddy, miserable world. (*DC* 295–6)

In its recognition of pantomime's ability to combine the familiar with the magical, its potential to open new topographies of experience, its breathless accumulation of the sensory excess of the pantomime, and finally its contrast with the damper ordinary world, this description neatly captures much of Dickens's thinking about the nature and role of pantomime.

Dickens's interest in pantomime was manifested in many ways. He attended pantomimes throughout his life, both inside and outside the theatre. Letters spanning thirty Christmases until 1868 detail his spectatorship in various capacities: on family trips, both as a child and with his own children; with male friends within an evening's revels; and professionally as a reviewer. He alleges to have seen Grimaldi perform on two occasions during his childhood, firstly when he was 'brought up from remote country parts [. . .] to behold the splendour of Christmas Pantomimes and the humour of Joe' aged about eight (before he 'aspired to the dignity of a tail coat'), and again in 1823 when he applauded 'with great precocity' (*LCD* 1: 382). However, these claims appear in an unpublished letter to the 'Sub-Editor' of *Bentley's Miscellany* – a non-existent role, effectively making it a letter to himself – in which he defended the *Memoirs* against *The Athenaeum*'s claim that he lacked 'that great and utter Clown-love, which maddens those who have laughed with and at Joe' ([Anon.] 1838d: 165). He admits his 'recollections of [Grimaldi's] acting are [. . .] but shadowy and imperfect' (*LCD* 1: 382) because of his youth, and while his claim could be another autobiographical fiction perpetuated by Dickens, it is consistent with the wider narrative of childhood pantomime experience within his writing.

Later, as an adult, he searched for new pantomime theatres on his travels, proudly telling one correspondent that 'In Paris last February, I found a new little Theatre open for Pantomime and comic singing and dancing' (*LCD* 7: 690–1), and returned to old haunts such as 'my old blackguard theatre, the Funambules' (*LCD* 6: 120). He sought out the latest and best shows, asking Collins 'Are you keeping your eye on the Marylebone Theatre?' (*LCD* 7: 506) or telling Clarkson Stanfield that 'I have heard that the Princess's [pantomime] is best' (*LCD* 10: 15), and recommended promising talent, telling manager John Willmott that 'It is really worth your while to see the Columbine at the Pavilion', for she 'would do you good service, I think, at the Lyceum' (*LCD* 4: 460). He was well acquainted with those in the profession: Stanfield ('Stanny'), a scene-painter whom he first met at a Covent Garden rehearsal in December 1837 was a particularly close friend. He also knew the pantomime writer and actor J. B. Buckstone, and the work of the harlequin George Weiland, referring in one letter to 'a jolly mask – such as Weiland would have if he were a grinning spirit' (*LCD* 4: 14).

Even when not attending, Dickens keenly followed a pantomime's progress; he asked Mark Lemon 'how "Jack and the Beanstalk" goes', after having read 'a favourable notice [. . .] in the *Galignani*' (*LCD* 8: 11). Such knowledge formed part of his comprehensive view of London's theatre scene, which enabled him to confidently delineate 'the state of the Theatres' in his correspondence, such as when he asserts that 'Drury Lane opens at Christmas for Pantomime, and any cheap thing that can be crammed into the same bill' (*LCD* 8: 689).

Dickens also acted in and directed his own pantomimes in his private theatricals, including an adaptation of Planché's *Fortunio and his Seven Gifted Servants* in 1855. He offered the part of Gobbler to Wilkie Collins, promising him 'great Pantomime opportunities [. . .] to devour Property Loaves'. Collins accepted, and apparently performed with great relish: Henry Dickens described how he 'gulped down a quantity of enormous loaves in *papier mache*, which he brought in on a large barrow' (*LCD* 7: 488).

Dickens's rich experience of pantomime prompts his correspondingly complex responses to it. He sometimes viewed it as a childish treat, playfully asking Lemon 'Are you for a pankelmime on Thursday?' (*LCD* 5: 680), or telling Macready before an opening night that 'I am so excited about tonight, that I can do nothing' (*LCD* 2: 453). He also viewed it as a diversion from the sober duties of an author and parent, proudly telling Forster that 'I have determined to resist the Pantomime and to come straight home like a good boy' (*LCD* 2: 1).

But Dickens's spectatorship could also exercise his aesthetic and technical scrutiny. In a blend of the childish and discerning, he once instructed Stanfield not to go to the pantomime without him, so that 'We can go so snugly from the office, and fix our critical eye on [set designer William] Beverley' (*LCD* 9: 537). On another occasion, Stanfield is the keenest to attend, 'having been maddened by accounts [. . .] of mechanical wonders at the Britannia' (*LCD* 7: 510). Their trips became like military operations, as Dickens instructs Stanfield to get himself 'into working Pantomime order!' (*LCD* 10: 170) months before they will attend, and even family trips feel like formal observances: he informed his Swiss friend W. W. F. De Cerjat that Christmas 'is the time of year when Theatres do best, there being still numbers of people who make it a sort of religion to see Christmas pantomimes' (*LCD* 11: 293).

Through this multi-faceted engagement Dickens makes pantomime a flexible and polysemic vehicle for his own ideas, which he articulated in his writing and cultivated in the writing of others within his circle. This chapter will trace two particularly informative theoretical strands in his thinking about pantomime: firstly the way in which real life events have specifically pantomimic qualities, which are revealed through the agency of the clown; and secondly, how pantomime serves an important cultural and social function as a source of fancy and wonder within a toughened and unsentimental modern world, whereby the transformation scene becomes a rich metaphor for uncovering 'the romantic side of familiar things'.

## The Pantomime of Life

One of Dickens's earliest explorations of pantomime, 'The Pantomime of Life', first appeared in March 1837. It was included in *Bentley's Miscellany* as a 'stray chapter' (*PoL* 500), to fill the gap left by a short instalment of *Oliver Twist*. Although Dickens had told Bentley that he was 'compelled – *really* compelled [. . .] to defer [the missing pages] to some future opportunity' (*LCD* 1: 227), he finally produced a piece that has been acknowledged as a 'fluently-written' 'artistic manifesto' (Slater 2009: 95–6) that insists on an 'association [. . .] between pantomime and our everyday lives [that is] essential in terms of the carnivalesque in his work' (Eigner 1989: 14).

For the epitome of Dickens's personal experience of 'the pantomime of life', one might move forward twenty-three years to 1860, when he attended a 'dull' Boxing night performance of J. V. Bridgeman's *Blue Beard*. The show proceeded as expected when 'suddenly and without a moment's warning, every scene on that immense stage fell over on its face and disclosed Chaos by Gaslight, behind!'. The comic business continues:

> In the uproar, some moon-calf rescued a porter-pot, six feet high (out of which the clown had been drinking when the accident happened), and stood it on the cushion of the lowest Proscenium Box P.S. beside a lady and a gentleman who were dreadfully ashamed of it. The moment the House knew that nobody was injured, they directed their whole attention to this gigantic porter pot in its genteel position (the lady and gentleman trying to hide behind it), and roared with laughter. When a modest footman came from behind the Curtain to clear it, and take it up in his arms, like a Brobdingnagian Baby, we all laughed more than we had ever laughed in our lives. I don't know why. (*LCD* 9: 354)

The unscripted irruption of the pantomime beer mug into the real world, and the way in which its incongruous size jars against both the gentility of the couple and the modesty of the footman is more entertaining for Dickens and his fellow spectators than the official show.

To underscore how far the performance has escaped from its regulated margins, Dickens then relates a similar episode on the street outside:

> We have had a fire here, but our people put it out before the Parish Engine arrived, like a drivelling Perambulator – with the Beadle in it – like an Imbecile Baby. Popular opinion, disappointed in the fire having been put out, Snowballed the Beadle. God bless it! (*LCD* 9: 354)

The initial tone of peril is averted by the image of the beadle in the pram, echoing the 'Brobdingnagian baby' from within the theatre. The slapstick violence enacted against authority at the conclusion also links this real event directly to the pantomime.

In this account and 'The Pantomime of Life', Dickens persuasively reassigns 'serious' theatre's ability 'to hold [. . .] the mirror up to Nature' (Shakespeare 2008b: III, ii, 21–2) to a less earnest form by interweaving pantomime scenes and characters with those from real life. In 'Paradise Revisited', for example, co-written with Henry Spicer, the narrator's experience has taught him that 'Pantomime is truth – truth coloured, condensed, elaborated – but truth itself'. This is seen in the way that the *dramatis personae* exhibit the traits of universal mankind – 'Clowns, boisterous, mischievous, unscrupulous; harlequins, gay, plausible, vindictive, mysterious; columbines, fair and fickle; pantaloons, with every attribute of age, except its reverence' – and in pantomime's capacity to reveal humanity's histrionic capacity, and punctures pomposity in all its forms (*AYR* 15.352: 31). After attending the 'amazingly good' *Harlequin Guy Fawkes* at the Olympic, Dickens declared that it was 'a comfortable thing to see all conventional dignity so outrageously set at naught' (*LCD* 7: 585), and the comfort that Dickens takes from the 'outrageous' levelling of form and decorum was a persistent motif in his treatment of the pantomime. In 'The Pantomime of Life', a session in the House of Commons is transformed from an earnest political discussion into a comically mechanical and physical spectacle: every night, the MPs 'twist and tumble about, till, two, three, and four o'clock in the morning; playing the strangest antics, and giving each other the funniest slaps on the face that can possibly be imagined, without evincing the smallest tokens of fatigue'. Empty rhetoric and affected moral conviction are comically exposed by Harlequin's magic wand, which strikes members dumb or makes them 'all life and animation [. . .] pouring forth a torrent of words without sense or meaning'. It can also instantly change one's opinions or allegiance, echoing the contest between the 'Buffs' and 'Blues' in *Pickwick*: 'one gentle tap on the back will alter the colour of a man's coat completely' (*PoL* 506).

Other more threatening forms of officiousness are also neutralised through transforming them into pantomime form. When the tyrannical Mr French borrows a gun to kill stray cats at Dickens's Boulogne residence, he 'discharges it twice in vain and throws himself over with the recoil, exactly like a clown' (*LCD* 8: 153). Dickens similarly deflates the pretensions of high art when describes how the operatic actress 'Miss Romer walked upon her knees to an extent which we never saw equalled, saving by the clown at Astley's' (1843: 660). In this perfectly weighted comic line, the superlative description of the first clause raises the sentence to the highest pitch, before crashing down in the bathetic sub-clause.

Yet while this diminution of authority in all its forms (political, domestic, cultural) might align with the carnivalesque democratic humour I described in Chapter 2, Dickens could also employ pantomimic images for the purposes of normative self-regulation. In 'The Pantomime of Life', the Pantaloon's function reveals a darker and more Hobbesian strain of humorous violence. Dickens initially describes an 'elderly gentleman' who is 'comfortable in circumstances, and well-to-do in the world', but 'suddenly loses his footing and stumbles'. He is in fact an onstage Pantaloon, set upon by a 'noisy and officious crowd' and left 'despoiled of hat, wig, and clothing, [. . .] battered to pieces and his watch and money gone'.

The audience, who are 'convulsed with merriment' and 'exhausted with laughter', initially laugh democratically at the levelling of power when we are told the higher the 'real life' Pantaloon's status, the more gleeful the reaction to his subsequent fall: 'the more suddenly, and nearer the zenith of his pride and riches, the better'. But this becomes more troubling when the 'real world' audience abandon their passive spectatorship and become a harrying mob, 'whoop[ing] and yell[ing] as [he] lies humbled beneath them'. Dickens is keen to point out 'how eagerly they set upon him when he is down; and how they mock and deride him as he slinks away'.

In fact, Dickens's sympathy seems to have evaporated as attempts to exculpate Pantaloon's rough treatment, characterising such figures as those who perform in real-life society 'with as much liquorish energy, and as total an absence of reserve, as if they were on the very stage itself'. He is a 'most worthless and debauched' Pantaloon who disrupts conventions of age and acts in a way 'highly unbecoming his gravity and time of life'. Acting as a greedy opportunist, he is further guilty of 'enticing his younger companion, the clown, into acts of fraud or petty larceny', as well as 'improper' 'amorous propensities' towards young ladies. This serves to justify the mob's violence, as the old man becomes a scapegoat both onstage and offstage, and the villainous clown is absolved as a gullible dupe led astray by the cowardly Pantaloon (*PoL* 501–2).

Dickens's pantomime of life motif also attempts to reconcile the magic and excitement of the onstage performance with the everyday reality lived offstage, and in 'Paradise Revisited' he and co-author Henry Spicer demonstrate how that reality is regularly disguised by illusion. He describes the mundane reality obscured behind the glittering artifice, as we revere the pantomime's 'gorgeous temples', not the 'men behind, in corduroys and dirty shirt-sleeves, pushing them on', and operators of the enchanted waves who are 'punching each other's ribs, in a cloud of slate-coloured dust'. Dickens reminds us that this is replicated in life outside the playhouse and that we encounter all of these things 'only in a far less honest form [. . .] beyond the wall of the theatre' – but 'if it soothe me to sit and witness their reproduction, under circumstances which can no longer betray, who shall censure?' (*AYR* 15.352: 31).

For Dickens, even entire towns can exhibit such histrionic tendencies. The simple and lightweight nature of pantomime scenery (required to facilitate smooth and rapid transformations), made it an apt metaphor for what Dickens viewed as the superficiality experienced in ordinary life, not least of all that which he encountered in America. He told Macready that he went to America expecting to find its people 'applying themselves in a new world to correct some of the falsehoods and vices of the old' but was soon disappointed (*LCD* 3: 176). When describing a trip to Boston, the pantomime's garish and flimsy scenery seems to suit his satirical purpose perfectly:

> the air was so clear, the houses were so bright and gay: the signboards were painted in such gaudy colours; the gilded letters were so very golden; the bricks were so very red, the stone was so very white, the blinds and area railings were so very green, the knobs and plates upon the street doors so marvellously bright and twinkling; and all so slight and unsubstantial in appearance – that every thoroughfare in the city looked exactly like a scene in a pantomime. (*AN* 75)

This description encompasses colours, gaudiness and brightness, carrying a combination of vividness and insubstantiality, and the revelation of the artifice beneath the illusion. It soon moves past admiration towards an accumulation of hyperbole that stretches, and finally breaks, credulity.

American businesses are regarded as similarly ephemeral, as their air of impermanence reminds Dickens of a transformation scene:

> As I walked along, I kept glancing up at [the shop] boards, confidently expecting to see a few of them change into something; and I never turned a corner suddenly without looking out for the clown and pantaloon, who, I had no doubt, were hiding in a doorway or behind some pillar close at hand. (*AN* 75)

Such enterprises lack 'proper' distinction, establishment or tradition, and this motif of insubstantial newness returns in his later descriptions of Lowell. There it seemed 'every "Bakery", "Grocery", and "Bookbindery", and other kinds of store, took its shutters down for the first time, and started in business yesterday', and in New England more generally – 'All the buildings looked as if they had been built and painted that morning, and could be taken down on Monday with very little trouble' (*AN* 75).

The acting profession seems particularly susceptible to this transfer of values from one type of stage to another. In his sketch 'Astley's', immediately after the clown has escaped his master in a seeming victory for fancy over reality, Dickens switches tone, asking 'Did any of our readers ever notice the class of people, who hang about the stage-doors of our minor theatres in the daytime?' (*SkB* 132). The 'lower class of actors' (*SkB* 135) switches from one type of performance to another, carrying 'an indescribable public-house-parlour swagger' and a 'conscious air' (*SkB* 133), as performance becomes a means of survival, both financially and socially. As Dickens observes, 'They always seem to think they are exhibiting' and 'the lamps are ever before them', yet the contrast between their lives onstage and offstage could not be starker: one actor has to 'boast night after night of his splendid fortune, with the painful consciousness of a pound a-week and his boots to find' (*SkB* 133–4). Elsewhere, he notes that the grinding actor 'lives, at best, in a little world of mockeries', in which he has to 'paint sorrow over, with burnt cork and rouge' and 'give away a great estate six nights a week, and want a shilling; to preside at imaginary banquets, hungry for a mutton chop' (*HW* 1.1: 13).

Dickens's most substantial embodiment of the individual social play-actor is the pantomime clown, who is portrayed as an audacious shape-shifting con-man attempting to selfishly improve his lot by any means necessary. In 'The Pantomime of Life' Dickens initially suggests through a neat inversion that the clown's performance is mimetic rather than hyperbolic: 'the close resemblance which the clowns of the stage bear to those of everyday life is perfectly extraordinary'. Clown appears 'at the very height of his glory' not in any fairy realm but in quotidian locations like the 'Cheesemonger's shop' or 'Mrs Queertable's boarding house', where he creates 'the great fun' of the pantomime by 'taking lodgings which he has not the slightest intention of paying for, or obtaining goods under false pretences', and 'swindling everybody he possibly can'.

However, Dickens contends that 'it is a most remarkable fact that precisely this sort of thing occurs in real life day after day, and nobody sees the humour of it', as demonstrated by the example of the 'Honourable Captain Fitz-Whisker Fiercy'. Fiercy obtains goods from local tradesmen based solely on his name and reputation, which he maintains through performance, as he 'struts and swaggers about with that compound air of conscious superiority and general bloodthirstiness', until he is exposed as an imposter and imprisoned. Dickens implicates the audience in the clown's success, making them complicit in a mutually gratifying relationship with this onstage performer: 'the more extensive the swindling is, and the more barefaced the impudence of the swindler, the greater the rapture and ecstasy of the audience' (*PoL* 504). Outside the playhouse, the confusion of the onstage and the offstage and willingness to believe the captain's performance have left them vulnerable to his deception. Indeed, often only the most disreputable part of the audience can connect onstage events with offstage ones with any sense of knowingness:

> when two young men, dressed in exact imitation of the eel-and-sausage-cravated portion of the audience were being chased by policemen, and finding themselves in danger of being caught, dropped so suddenly as to oblige the policemen to tumble over them, there was great rejoicing among the caps – as though it were a delicate reference to something they had heard of before. (*AYR* 2.44: 418)

As I have described elsewhere, several similar clowns appear in Dickens's early work. In *Sketches by Boz*, the charming Horatio Sparkins turns out to be Samuel Smith the tailor's assistant, Grimaldi himself falls foul of the clownish antics of 'Mackintosh' in the *Memoirs*, and Captain Fitz-Whisker Fiercy is another version of 'Charles Fitz-Marshall', one of Alfred Jingle's many aliases.

However, while such clowns often represent gleeful audacity, Dickens's desire to peep behind the curtain and capture the frown disguised by the greasepaint often uncovers a more tragic struggling figure. The convivial high jinks in *Pickwick*'s early chapters are soon punctured by the tragic inset tale of the starving clown, which echoes the demise of Grimaldi's own son 'JS', and presages Jingle's later incarceration. Dickens repeatedly insisted (through both Mr Sleary and his own journalistic voice) that 'People mutht be amuthed . . . You mutht have uth' (*HT* 35) and Joseph Butwin views this as a 'fairly desperate' acknowledgement that popular entertainers are an inevitable and uncomfortable burden necessary to satisfy an almost primal need for entertainment (1976: 132). According to Butwin, Dickens presents Grimaldi's life according to the popular mythical framework of the public performer eliciting our laughter who is also the private, hidden sufferer eliciting our sympathy. Thus rather than blurring the lines between fantasy and reality, Dickens demonstrates a 'persistent interest in what the clown is and what he pretends to be' throughout his work (1976: 118).

For Butwin, figures like the starving clown and Signor Jupe in *Hard Times* are shameful *loci* of failure, and contrary to Schlicke's view of the warmth in Dickens's treatment of the circus community, Butwin feels that popular entertainers are presented as 'a mixed bag of absurdity wrapped in the inevitably false dignity of modern publicity' (1976: 128). This is epitomised in Gradgrind and son's final humiliation as clowns in the centre of the ring, where Gradgrind Junior's 'comic livery' becomes 'a badge announcing him to be the prince of flops and failures' (1976: 131). In *The Mystery of Edwin Drood*, the debased clown is one of a number of bathetic 'seasonal tokens', alongside 'such a very poor little Twelfth Cake, that one would rather call it a Twenty-fourth Cake or a Forty-eighth Cake' and a 'Wax-Work' displayed 'on the premises of the bankrupt livery-stable-keeper up the lane'; the 'new grand comic Christmas pantomime' is 'heralded by the portrait of Signor Jacksonini the clown, saying "How do you do tomorrow?" quite as large as life, and almost as miserably' (*MED* 153–4).

As the following chapter will show, the *Memoirs* is replete with melancholy reflections on the physical and mental toll that Grimaldi's joyful and exuberant performances took, and the cruel juxtapositions between the two. While Grimaldi's onstage clown silently absorbed endless physical shocks without lasting damage, Grimaldi the human carried the pain and scars forever. Tragic personal events were kept firmly offstage, as Grimaldi remained true to his duty to entertain and amuse, and for all the happy reminiscences in Dickens's opening to the *Memoirs*, the closing thought is a stark reminder of their transitory nature: 'the light and life of a brilliant theatre were exchanged in an instant for the gloom and sadness of a dull sick room' (*MJG* 2: 211). Dickens's opening inquiries which preface the work – 'whether they were born Clowns, or gradually turned into Clowns as they grew up' (*MJG* 1: v) – often turn up tragic answers, as the clowning careers of both Bradbury and Grimaldi's son end in disgrace and madness. In Dickens's account, Grimaldi's prematurely aged body inscribes these mental and physical shocks, just as in Sala's 'Getting Up a Pantomime' the 'once brilliant' clown's costume viewed close up reveals its 'rents and rivings [. . .] rags and tatters', before being made 'new all over' for the next performance (*HW* 4.91: 295).

However, despite these revelations of a sometimes grim reality, the romantic side invariably insists on breaking through the surface. 'Astley's' epitomises this defiant tone; even after its detailed revelation of the bitter knowledge of the offstage reality, when asked to accept that 'our friend in the military uniform' on stage appears elsewhere in 'threadbare attire' and descends 'to the comparatively unwadded costume of every-day life', Boz asserts 'We cannot – we will not – believe it' (*SkB* 134). He chooses to 'believe' the more fantastical option, in the power of pantomime to reveal the wondrous in the everyday, which is Dickens's second major preoccupation in his writing on pantomime.

## Pantomime as Source of Fancy and Wonder

As we saw in the previous chapter, pantomime's primary mechanism for revealing the wondrous in the everyday is the transformation scene. *Drood* opens with one such set-piece, in which the 'well-known massive gray square tower' of an 'ancient English Cathedral' switches to the Sultan's 'long procession', in which 'Ten thousand scimitars flash in the sunlight, and thrice ten thousand dancing-girls strew flowers. Then, follow white elephants caparisoned in countless gorgeous colours, and infinite in number and attendants' (*MED* 1). This resembles spectacles like the 'Grand Turkish Procession' of the 1877 pantomime, *Blue Beard*, which includes 'children with red and white turbans, silver scimitars, and crescent-shaped shields', 'a train of women playing some very Oriental-looking bells [. . .] followed by soldiers clothed in yellow jackets and steel armour and helmets', and finally Bluebeard 'seated on an elephant' ([Anon.] 1877b: 4).

*The Times* called the inclusion of such Eastern 'fable' in pantomimes as 'the very wantoning of an imagination, overwhelmed by its own unconquerable fertility' ([Anon.] 1813: 3), a phrase which neatly correlates with Dickens's own imagination and Walter Bagehot's view of Dickens's style as 'the overflow of a copious mind'

(1858: 464). The 'divine fires of transformation', as Percy Fitzgerald calls them, burn brightly throughout Dickens's work, as a consequence of his mental capacity to see the infinite possibilities latent within a single object, person or situation (*AYR* 12.278: 45). Pantomime's excessiveness also aligns with the excessiveness of Dickens's writing, which Steven Connor describes as 'the problematic overflowing of categories, the blurring of boundaries, and the promiscuous commingling of what official ideologies wish to promote as naturally distinct' (1996: 28). Dickens found in pantomime an art form sympathetic to his attentiveness to such topics as the hyperbolic, the bodily grotesque, the margins between good and bad, alive and dead, mundane and magical. Other traits, such as Dickens's tendency towards exaggeration, magnifying, intensifying and accumulating, find a natural corollary in the practices of the pantomime clown, who supersizes his world and multiplies to excess.

One symptom of this overflow was Dickens's recourse to pantomimic similes and metaphors. The wordless spectacle of pantomime provides a rich store of imagery and in just a well-chosen subclause Dickens reveals the hidden fantastical, often using a clown to complete a sentence and subvert its expected narrative progress. Just as the Astley's clown ventures 'on such familiarities with the military man in boots' (*OCS* 299), Dickens's surprise clowns disregard form, ceremony or dignity to level perceived social differences. As Mr Pickwick anxiously parleys with the stern patriarch Winkle Senior, Bob Sawyer is possessed by Grimaldi's irreverent spirit, three months after his death, to puncture the gravity of proceedings: Sawyer 'whose wit had laid dormant for some minutes, placed his hands on his knees and made a face after the portraits of the late Mr Grimaldi, as clown' (*PP* 671). Grimaldi also possessed Dickens himself in this way when he was particularly excited at his return from America, promising that 'I shall have lost all power of self-restraint, and shall as certainly make a fool of myself [. . .] as ever Grimaldi did in his way' (*LCD* 3: 343).

Elsewhere Dickens bestows the clown's ridiculous, erratic or hyperbolised qualities onto his characters to level social difference. In *Martin Chuzzlewit*, Grimaldi punctures the cultural and literary pretensions of American society as embodied in Mrs Hominy. She wears 'a highly aristocratic and classical cap', but its effect is completely undermined when it is described as 'so admirably adapted to her countenance, that if the late Mr Grimaldi had appeared in the lappets of Mrs Siddons, a more complete effect could not have been produced' (*MC* 353). Even when Mrs Jarley hurriedly transforms her waxwork of Grimaldi into the grammarian Lindley Murray to satisfy the more decorous tastes of the young ladies' boarding-schools, the clown is always lurking beneath the surface of respectability, ready to erupt irreverently at any minute.

Dickens's interest in the presentation of the fanciful behind ordinary life also serves other purposes. As I described in Chapter 1, a number of critics have recently presented valuable politicised readings of Dickens's engagement with popular entertainment in light of his democratic aim to highlight and nurture the 'light of Fancy which is inherent in the human breast' (*HW* 1.1: 1). As Paul Schlicke describes, Dickens associated popular entertainment with a 'release for imagination, escape from dull routine, encouragement to fellow-feeling, [and] remembrance of past pleasures' (1985: 27) and was disparaging of an ailing English theatre not utilised to its full pedagogical potential.

One ameliorative effect of pantomime was its encouragement of the bodily response of laughter, which is enjoyable as both laugher and observer. As Dickens notes in 'Astley's': 'we are far more delighted and amused by the audience, than with the pageantry we once so highly appreciated' (*SkB* 129) a pastime facilitated by the open 'pit, box, and gallery' design of nineteenth-century theatres and the constantly raised house lights. While this site of surveillance could sometimes have sinister implications – Pip is watched by Compeyson while watching a pantomime, and Compeyson in turn is watched by Wopsle from the stage – Dickens more regularly presents its beneficial effects.

Dickens's fictional personae (including Boz) usually inhabit the gallery, the best vantage point from which to observe both play and audience. Kit Nubbles's family sit in the Astley's gallery, from where Barbara's mother comments that it 'was the place to see from' and wonders why 'it wasn't much dearer than the boxes' (*OCS* 299). The illustration for this scene shows the gallery audience engaged in a variety of activities besides watching the play, including watching each other (Fig. 3.1).

In 'Amusements of the People', Dickens similarly praises the gallery at the Britannia, from which spectators are 'thoroughly able to take in the whole performance', and criticises 'the dark gap in the roof' which serves as the gallery at Drury Lane or Covent Garden (*HW* 1.3: 58).

In his 'Astley's' sketch, Boz demonstrates the importance of such a vantage point. From there, he watches the rest of the audience laughing and describes how it thoroughly possesses the laugher, breaking

**Figure 3.1** George Cattermole, 'The Balcony Audience at Astley's Amphitheatre', *The Old Curiosity Shop*. Reproduced by courtesy of Charles Dickens Museum, London.

form and restraint: 'ma' was 'perfectly overcome by the drollery of the principal comedian, and laughed till every one of the immense bows on her ample cap trembled', while 'the governess peeped out from behind the pillar again, and whenever she could catch ma's eye, put her handkerchief to her mouth, and appeared, as in duty bound, to be in convulsions of laughter also' (*SkB* 130–1). For other spectators, watching these laughers becomes part of the entertainment, and begets further laughter in both the supposedly detached observer ('we [. . .] actually join in the laugh which follows the clown's shrill shout of "Here we are!" just for old acquaintance' sake') and the reader of the sketch, involving everyone in the communal experience (*SkB* 132).

Other articles 'conducted' by Dickens in his journals echo this phenomenon. Percy Fitzgerald describes the same involuntary bodily experience when, as a child, he and another boy 'became fascinated, enthralled, bewildered, and drawn into one absorbing devouring gaze towards the stage'. They become part of a larger collective of 'little heads, peering [. . .] just over the edges of the boxes', which 'shook, and were agitated brightly, like silk shot with silver' as 'round us rang out the music of laughter in a high key'. These 'peals of convulsive laughter' cause 'acute spasms of mirth', and 'a sort of agony of laughter', from which the laugher 'dropped back suffering much'. Later the same spectator was 'well-nigh rolling under the seat in hysterical convulsion' (*AYR* 12.278: 43–4).

This abandonment to pantomime's bodily effects, particularly laughter, is a consequence of its alluring sensory immersion: as a child, Dickens 'had no eyes, ears, or corporeal sense but for the pantomime'. Pantomime can 'dazzle one's eyes with tinsel and gold leaf' and is full of 'varied and many-coloured' actions. The Harlequin is 'all glittering with spangles, and dazzling with many colours', 'amid the smell of saw-dust, and orange-peel' (*PoL* 500–1). Similarly, Sala and Spicer (with Dickens) describe the smells as 'an aromatic perfume of orange-peel and lamp-oil' (*HW* 5.112: 191) and 'the old delicious inexpressible fragrance of commingled gas, damp sawdust, and squeezed orange-peel' (*AYR* 15.352: 32) respectively.

As part of this escapist aesthetic, pantomime breaks ordinary time and, like the elastic body of the clown, puts it out of joint. Dickens showed particular interest in the structure and use of pantomime time, primarily through the device of the clock, fulfilling what Matthew Bevis calls a 'secret, long-standing yearning [. . .] for an escape from onward plodding narrative, from plot, from consequence' (2013: 66). Pantomime time has a fixity, through its link with festive holidays, but also a flux, in its suspension of real, purposeful, forward moving time, particularly during the harlequinade: as Bevis observes, 'In "pantomime time", clocks are used to evade the exigencies of the moment', and in fact can 'stop the clock' (2013: 62). During the harlequinade Clown interfered with clocks and their workings in defiance of their regulatory purpose, hanging onto the dial, jumping through the face, or usurping the role of the figures who strike the hour and thus replace useful work with destructive activity. As Charlie Chaplin demonstrated in *Modern Times* (1936), the clown can mock the mechanical regularity of time by embodying it. Bergson's description of the comical as the 'mechanical encrusted on the living' (1956: 84) is epitomised in such Dickensian images as the clown face on the pier-clock, 'red-faced [. . .] with a white rim' (*HW* 13.327: 553), the 'honest little grocer' with the red nose who pops out of a clock, 'knocking everybody down from behind' with a gridiron (*GE* 287), and Wopsle ascending to the clouds 'in a large watch-case' (*GE* 287). This mechanical movement has implications for Dickens's depiction of slapstick violence, which will be the topic of Chapter 7.

Yet privately Dickens was not always so gleeful at pantomime's temporal disruptions. On one occasion, he anxiously enquires after a watch sent for repair, because his borrowed one 'goes like the Clown's in a Pantomime' (*LCD* 10: 156); time has become erratic and accelerated. The rest of the letter discusses the composition of forthcoming numbers of *All the Year Round*, and clearly the exigencies of this moment demonstrate that Dickens cannot use a watch that lacks the same exactitude with which he conducts his business. Time was being systematised and regularised to serve the pressing needs of transport, communication and commerce, and the development of 'railway time' led to the adoption of Greenwich Mean Time in 1847. The mercantile Dombey always carries his 'heavy gold watch-chain' (*DS* 11) and for Florence 'a very loud ticking watch, embodied her idea of a father' (*DS* 13), while Ebenezer Scrooge is a clock-watcher *par excellence*, 'an excellent man of business on the very day of [Marley's] funeral' (*CC* 1), who sees Christmas as a disruption to the regular time of commerce.

However, Scrooge's ultimate co-option into the festive mindset actually reverses time by releasing emotions associated with childhood and triggers childlike actions such as laughing, dancing and playing pranks. Schlicke views the child as an imaginative focus for the values that Dickens associated with popular entertainment, such as 'spontaneity, freedom, fancy and release' (1985: 14), so a primary attraction of pantomime for Dickens was its perennial association with childhood. For Dickens, children are particularly adept at seeing the world in pantomimic terms, able to create magical fantasies from the everyday and observe the everyday within the fantastic.

Dickens's most evocative descriptions of pantomime are firmly entwined with meditations on childhood experience, with pantomime regarded as a mechanism for releasing the inner child. It reminds the careworn adult writer of his 'early imaginations', which were once held 'so full of innocent construction and guileless belief', but have become 'so worn and torn, so much the wiser and so much the worse' through adulthood (*AYR* 3.62: 278). Dickens elsewhere outlines the importance of nurturing and enjoying these childhood feelings as an adult, because 'If we can only preserve ourselves from growing up, we shall never grow old, and the young may love us to the last' (*HW* 6.145: 363). He also encouraged the promotion of such feelings in other writers for his journals; one anonymous writer similarly explained how the thrills of the pantomime should be enjoyed by all:

> It is no harm for the wisest, the gravest, the busiest of us to cultivate and nurture a little feeling of this sort 'for one night only', and on principle, as the writer hereof does, makes a regular boys' holiday of boxing-day, winding up with the ever-welcome pantomime at night. (*AYR* 17.408: 191)

This perception of pantomime as a bulwark of purity against the corruption of maturity continues in Dickens's description of it as one of the only 'innocent tastes of [. . .] childhood' to have 'fairly weathered the storms and buffets of life; to have defied the disenchanting influence of time; and flourish yet, serene and unimpaired, above the ruins of many a far more potent passion' (*AYR* 15.352: 30). Immersion in the pantomime reverses the process of ageing; the grown-up narrator of 'Paradise Revisited' becomes part of 'a crowd of happy children, from six years old to seventy' (*AYR* 15.352: 32), while Andrew Halliday describes how he 'can enjoy [a pantomime] as heartily as any six-year-old home from the holidays' (1865: 229).

Prior to a visit to the Drury Lane pantomime, Dickens told Angela Burdett Coutts that his four-year-old son Sydney was 'in a dreadful state of anticipation' at 'the eventful occasion [. . .] of his first appearance' (*LCD* 6: 574) in a theatre, and in 'First Fruits', a child's first pantomime is one of the seminal and memorable first-time experiences described. The performance may be dismissed as 'stupid, badly acted [and] badly got up', but the clown transcends such rebuke, and is vividly described as 'The funny man (there never was such a funny man) in the red scratch wig, who, when imprisoned in the deepest dungeon beneath the castle moat, sang a comic song about a leg of mutton' (*HW* 5.112: 190). He returns later, amidst

> The admonitions to 'sit up', the warnings not to 'talk loud', in defiance of which (seeing condonatory smiles on the faces of those we loved) we screamed outright with laughter, when the funny man, in the after-piece, essaying to scale a first-floor front by means of a rope ladder, fell, ladder and all, to the ground. (*HW* 5.112: 191)

This rich description outlines the attractions of the pantomime clown for the child-adult (or as Malcolm Andrews (1994) has it, the 'grown up child'): an invitation (also extended to the adults) to defy convention and decorum; a defiant challenge to hardship through absurdity; and the contagious bodily reaction of laughter.

Dickens asserts that 'We have never outgrown' (*HW* 6.145: 362) the theatres of Covent Garden and in 'Astley's', even the older, wiser and more distant observer admits that 'there is no place which recalls so strongly our recollections of childhood as Astley's' (*SkB* 129). This memory is more powerful than that of his governess's strict teaching and is the first episode in a sustained meta-narrative of the imagination's victories over restrictive pedagogy that reaches its apotheosis in *Hard Times*. Other writers in Dickens's circle adopted this theme: in 'Paradise Revisited', the governess Miss Cavalier, usually 'Miss Puritan in the matter of theatres', succumbs to pantomime's regressive thrills. She is spotted in the audience, 'leaning forward, flushed with excitement, and devouring the scene with the interest of a child of ten', attracted by the 'happy faces' she saw there (*AYR* 15.352: 34).

For Dickens, a pantomimic sensibility can also be a child's mechanism for coping with the traumatic exposure to an adult world. In 'Gone Astray', immediately after being terrorised by Merrylegs the dog, Dickens notes how the boy 'wandered about the City [. . .] in a dream, staring at the British merchants, and inspired by a mighty faith in the marvellousness of everything'. These merchants are transformed into 'a compound of Mr Fitzwarren and Sinbad the Sailor', from the pantomime *Dick Whittington*, complete with their 'cross cook', Dame Cicely Suet, who was played by Grimaldi and transformed into Clown for the harlequinade. Other pantomime scenarios and characters are introduced as the boy supposes how 'Barings had seen Rocs' eggs and travelled with caravans', while 'Rothschild had sat in the Bazaar at Bagdad with rich stuffs for sale; and a veiled lady from the Sultan's harem, riding on a donkey, had fallen in love with him'. By asserting that he believed 'In such stories [. . .] as devoutly as in the City itself', he demonstrates how the child's need to make sense of his environment pushes him towards the firmest frames of reference within his imagination, which are pantomime and fairytale (*HW* 7.177: 555).

The fact that these pantomime motifs are used to negotiate through the business world is also significant; Carlyle amongst others had expressed concern for the mortifying effect of the new mercantile 'cash nexus' on human spirit and imagination, lamenting how '*Cash-payment*' has become the 'sole relation of human beings' (1843: 126). The adult Dickens similarly hopes for a pantomime ending to the literary travails of his collaborator Richard Horne in his struggles within the harsh world of commercial publishing: 'His wanderings and climbings will never land him in the castle at the top of the beanstalk, where the Giant keeps his money; I wish they might ever drop him in at some halfway house in the clouds!' (*LCD* 11: 110)

Here the pantomimic is a device for transforming the threatening or unfamiliar into the benign and known. On his travels in the unfamiliar territory of America, Dickens employs a multi-layered pantomime motif to neutralise the foreign and racial other with ridicule: his coach driver at Potomac Creek 'twirl[s] his head round and round like a harlequin, rolling his eyes, shrugging his shoulders, and grinning from ear to ear' (*AN* 150), and evokes 'the late lamented Ducrow', manager and trick-rider at Astley's (*AN* 149). The unknown (America) becomes the homely (Astley's), the potentially threatening racial other (the dangerously fast African-American coach driver) becomes the harmlessly comical (the mechanical Harlequin).

Dickens also employed this method to tranquillise the pain of a domestic accident. When describing Wills's accident with his gas supply, Dickens imagines it to have left him 'upside-down ever since, in some corner, – like the Groom to whom the Sultan's daughter was to have been sacrificed' (*LCD* 7: 616). Malcolm Andrews has read this in relation to its literary antecedent, *The Arabian Nights*, but it could equally refer to its pantomimic counterpart, especially when Dickens then claims he 'went about the streets all next day, laughing like a Pantomime mask', his face becoming fixed in an elaborately exaggerated expression. His next suggestively ambiguous line – 'I never did see anything so ridiculous' – may refer to Wills's topsy-turvy appearance, the Groom in the pantomime, or even Dickens himself, laughing at himself laughing at a comic scene like a pantomime spectator.

This pantomimic sensibility could also enable romantic escapism: after receiving an unexpected letter from the Countess of Lovelace, he declares 'I felt as Aladdin might have done if the Princess Baralbadour had entrusted a familiar communication to the attendant at her Bath' (*LCD* 5: 495). Through his allusion to the world of fantasy, make-believe and performance Dickens temporarily inhabits an alternative, more romantic universe, in which he is the hero and suitor of the heroine. Given the pains he took to maintain his secret affair with Ellen Ternan, his romantic thoughts might well have sought refuge in such a fantastical alternative world.

However, Dickens also makes significant comic capital from the child's perceptiveness to see through poorly executed transformations in which the romantic remains firmly in the shade of the familiar. Pantomime's emphasis on fantasy leaves it particularly vulnerable to this kind of scrutiny, and during these failed transformations, the artifice is perceptible, as when 'His Majesty backed to the side-scenes and began untying himself behind, with his big face all on one side' (*AYR* 2.44: 418) or when the scene pauses, 'suggestive of the coming fairy stopping to tie her shoe' (*AYR* 15.352: 32). A depiction of an ineffective giant's costume 'which but for the peculiarity of the eyes being situated in the chin, and the nose on the forehead, might have been called human' (*AYR* 15.352: 33) is humorous but slightly rueful, as the child's perspective merges with the grown-up's to acknowledge the potential for wonder that has been squandered.

This tone informs *Great Expectations*, when the pantomime Pip watches as an adult is incapable of making him suspend his disbelief and return him to the state of childhood wonder that he desires. He admits that 'it pained me to suspect that I detected Mr Wopsle with red worsted legs under a highly magnified phosphoric countenance and a shock of red curtain-fringe for his hair', a meticulous deconstruction that unravels every part of the pretence. Wopsle's later return is no more successful, for Pip notes that the 'sententious Enchanter [. . .] coming up from the antipodes rather unsteadily, after an apparently violent journey, proved to be Mr Wopsle in a high-crowned hat' (*GE* 287).

Yet one area in which the pantomime illusion must hold firm is in its representation of violence. When the clown in Sala's 'Getting Up a Pantomime' warns that without 'a red-hot poker introduced into the comic business [. . .] the pantomime is sure to fail' (*HW* 4.91: 295), he pinpoints the importance of violent slapstick to pantomime, even in its post-Regency form. Pantomime for Dickens was a world without the pain of ordinary life, but he often appears ambivalent as to whether this rejection of real suffering is an important social salve or a potentially desensitising social corrosive.

In 'A Curious Dance Round a Curious Tree', Dickens calls the 'jocund world' of pantomime a place in which 'no affliction or calamity [. . .] leaves the least impression' and where the only effect of rehearsing the real accidents of life is laughter: 'a man may tumble into the broken ice, or dive into the kitchen fire, and only be droller for the incident' (*HW* 4.95: 385–6). The audience's enjoyment comes from the disparity between their position as 'vulnerable spectators, liable to pain and sorrow' and the position of the pantomime characters (but crucially not the actors) who are 'so superior to all the accidents of life, though encountering them at every turn'. But by describing this enjoyment as 'secret', whereby many spectators 'may not present [it] to themselves', the communal pantomime laughter becomes a selfish Bergsonian pleasure at one's superiority to others' misfortunes

(*HW* 4.95: 386). The laughter may occur publicly, but its underlying cause is so shameful that it cannot be publicly acknowledged.

In 'A Curious Dance' he presents the choice between either observing a real suffering woman in St Luke's, a 'poor creature [. . .] driven mad by an infuriated ox in the streets' or watching a hypothetical 'Pantomimic woman', who could have been 'gored to any extent by a Pantomimic ox, at any height of ferocity' that would have left him with 'the comforting assurance that she had rather enjoyed it otherwise' (*HW* 4.95, 386). By choosing the former compassionate act over the artificial Hobbesian spectacle, he puts the pantomime spectator firmly in his moral place.

For although Dickens often emphasises pantomime's communality, he also regularly asserts this disingenuous and 'secret' pleasure of pantomime. In 'The Pantomime of Life', the 'secret cause of [the audience's] amusement and delight' is how 'pantomime is to [them] a mirror of life [. . .] although they are not aware of it'. This suppressed element is the 'best of the joke' for Dickens, demonstrated by the 'coal-merchant who is loudest in his complaints against the person who defrauded him' outside the theatre but is 'the identical man who sat in the centre of the very front row of the pit last night and laughed the most boisterously at this very same thing' (*PoL* 504). This spectator happily enjoys watching the misfortunes of others within the context of the playhouse but is outraged when he is part of the same comic spectacle in real life.

The primary agent of this impermanent violence is the clown, as demonstrated in this performance at Astley's:

> The clown throws himself on the ground, and goes through a variety of gymnastic convulsions, doubling himself up, and untying himself again, and makes himself look very like a man in the most hopeless extreme of agony, to the vociferous delight of the gallery [. . .] (*SkB* 132–3)

Once again, Dickens depicts such violence ambiguously; the shared humanity that the clown cultivates through his proximity to the audience is counteracted by the other-ness of his superhuman bodily resilience. The audience's laughter hesitates between Rabelaisian and Bergsonian as the clown's routine becomes a mechanical repetition of movement ('doubling himself, and untying himself again'), which distances him from natural bodily movement, and the audience delight in his appearance at 'the most hopeless extreme of agony'. Yet the finale confirms his ultimate invulnerability, as he triumphantly escapes his oppressor, 'making ludicrous grimaces at the riding-master every time his back is turned; and finally quitting the circle by jumping over his head, having previously directed his attention the other way' (*SkB* 133).

## Coda

This chapter has embraced the broad sweep of Dickens's engagement with the pantomime through its manifold forms – its persistent recurrence across the span of Dickens's career and creative output attest to its centrality to his vision. Moreover, front and centre of Dickens's reimagining and reworking of the pantomime was its principal agent during its Regency form, the clown. This figure has already appeared intermittently throughout the foregoing discussion, but as he is utterly central to Dickens's vision of pantomime's imaginative power, the rest of this book will be devoted to a fuller exploration of this figure, beginning with Dickens's creative relationship with the greatest clown of all, Joseph Grimaldi.

# Part II: Dickens and the *Memoirs of Joseph Grimaldi*

Chapter 4

# The *Memoirs* as Nineteenth-Century Biography

## Introduction

Dickens's *Memoirs of Joseph Grimaldi* is a textually entangled artefact. Grimaldi himself threw together a written record of his reminiscences before his death in May 1837, which was shaped, condensed and augmented in consultation with the hack Thomas Egerton Wilks. Wilks continued after Grimaldi's death, but sold an unfinished manuscript to Richard Bentley, who passed it to Dickens in December 1837. Dickens then dictated another version to his father John, and published it as his other self, 'Boz' in February 1838, which was then followed by Charles Whitehead's edition in 1846. This shared act of narration, selection and interpretation creates a complex hybrid of overlaid Grimaldis and speakers, while the editorial asides and footnotes offer evidence and a commentary on the range of texts and genres encompassed within the *Memoirs*, as successive editors have attempted to marshal this material. For the modern reader, this hybridity is compounded by the lack of original manuscripts or explicit textual demarcation, which makes conclusive attribution between contributors impossible – although scholars including myself have indicated sections where Boz's mind (if not his hand) may have been stronger.

When the *Memoirs* was first published, Dickens's earlier literary successes ensured that it was reviewed extensively, but commentators soon disagreed over the extent of Dickens's involvement in the work. *The Idler* identified the humour as Dickens's imprint, claiming that the author is 'as droll as the clown' ([Anon.] 1838e: 66) and a 'wag of the first order' ([Anon.] 1838f: 74), while *The Knickerbocker* similarly felt that much 'of the felicity of thought and language, which is the characteristic of Mr. DICKENS' style, is apparent in parts of these volumes' ([Anon.] 1838i: 463). However, mindful of Dickens's most recent creative success, *The Mirror of Literature* felt that 'barring a few phrases of Pickwickian point, and the alteration of the narrative from the first to the third person, there is little of the expansive craft in these pages' ([Anon.] 1838g: 169). The *Gentleman's Magazine* went even further, asserting that the 'leaden nature of its contents, and the slip-slop quality of the author's style' demonstrate that it is not the work of Dickens at all, but instead that of 'some hack of a scribbler [paid by Bentley] to fill a couple of volumes with melancholy common places and insufferable platitudes "long drawn out"' ([Anon.] 1838j: 416).

Reviewers also queried how accurately and completely the events of Grimaldi's life were presented. At one extreme, *The Gentleman's Magazine* claimed that 'the history of the death of his only son is purposely altered from the truth, without serving the purpose desired' and that 'the account given of the assumed madness of Bradbury, Grimaldi's rival, is incorrect in every particular' ([Anon.] 1838j: 417). However, other commentators suggested a middle ground: *The Literary Gazette* described Dickens as 'a biographer' who had created a 'narrative founded on data, preserved by Grimaldi himself' ([Anon.] 1838b: 97), and reiterated this balanced view a week later, regarding the *Memoirs* as 'imbued with both the comic humour and the fine natural feeling of its editor, Mr Dickens, whilst, at the same time, it is the accurate transcript of poor Grimaldi's own materials and own views' ([Anon.] 1838c: 118). *The Athenaeum* also identified the blend of factual and creative by referring to Grimaldi's own journal and concluding that 'the anecdotes are doubtless grounded in fact, though rendered a little more effectively ornamental by the biographer' ([Anon.] 1838a: 115).

Public reaction was also hesitant, for despite promising initial sales – '1700 *Grimaldis* have already been sold and the demand increases daily!!!!!!!!!!!!!!!!!!!!!!!!!!!!!!!', Dickens excitedly told Forster soon after publication (*LCD* 1: 391) – nearly half of the first edition were unsold. Since then the *Memoirs* has received little critical attention and has been dismissed by Grimaldi and Dickens biographers alike as inferior and careless hack-work rushed out for a quick profit. Forster granted it a couple of pages in his *Life of Charles Dickens* and claimed that Dickens merely reworked certain sections, having a 'most indifferent opinion of the mass of material which in general composed it' and a 'modest estimate' of the final work. He further notes that a 'great many critical faults were found', before quickly proceeding to the happier business of the celebratory dinner for the completed *Pickwick Papers* (1966 1: 80). Peter Ackroyd more curtly dismisses the *Memoirs* as something 'to fill up the empty days' after completing *The Pickwick Papers* and before starting his next major work. The extent of his analysis is to comment that Dickens 'seemed to have warmed to [the] task' after he 'began it unwillingly' and observe that Grimaldi's 'character and temperament bear in many ways striking resemblances to Dickens's own' (1991: 254–5). It is only recently that any positive reappraisals – most notably those of Robert Douglas-Fairhurst and Michael Slater – have appeared at all.

Dickens later attempted to distance himself from his disappointing apprentice creation, describing it as 'a mistake' of which he was 'not very proud' (*LCD* 5: 73), and which was created 'chiefly to please [Grimaldi's friend George] Cruikshank' (*LCD* 6: 97). He never wrote another biography for publication, declined to write the harlequin Thomas Ellar's memoirs and discouraged the actor Richard Nelson Lee from publishing his own autobiography, noting that only 'a mere handful of persons' would be interested in theatrical anecdotes. In his letter to Lee, Dickens indicates an antipathy towards written biography, asserting that 'the life of any persevering, industrious, and honourable man, is a lesson. But it is a lesson to be acted, not written' (*LCD* 8: 571) where 'acted' here can carry nuances of both the performed and the lived out and 'done'.

In an oft-quoted injunction from his will Dickens reasserted this experiential and relational basis for his life, and proposes that his own words and the close relationship he fostered with his readership are the most appropriate source of remembrance of him, rather than any posthumous accounts by another hand:

> I enjoin my friends, on no account, to make me the subject of any monument, memorial, or testimonial whatever. I rest my claims to the remembrance of my country upon my published works, and the remembrance of my friends upon their experience of me in addition thereto. (*LCD* 12: 732)

However, as with any pronouncement from such a prolific writer, these later negative comments should be considered judiciously 'in the round' with his earlier words and actions. This first commercial failure would have deeply stung such an aspiring and self-conscious author, and his later reflections carry both the benefit of hindsight and the need to safeguard his reputation as a great writer. Indeed, the *Memoirs* would not be the only early work that he would repudiate: he similarly described *Sketches by Boz* as 'often being extremely crude and ill-considered, and bearing obvious marks of haste and inexperience' (*SkB* 11).

Moreover, although Dickens claims limited agency in the *Memoirs*' Introduction (calling himself merely the 'editor' who 'has not swelled the quantity of matter, but materially abridged it' [*MJG* 1: xi]), several factors suggest a greater level of imaginative investment than he would have us believe. During the editing process, he indicated in his private correspondence an intimate pseudo-Frankensteinian relationship with an almost organic subject when he told Bentley that the 'Grimaldi grows under the alterations much better than I supposed possible' (*LCD* 1: 340). He also commented to Forster that 'Grimaldi speeds but twaddles' (*LCD* 1: 337), and finally that he had 'finished Grimaldi' (*LCD* 1: 350), and such a close identification echoes other literary biographers of the early nineteenth century, whom Julian North has described as feeling a sense of ownership and investment in the creation of their subject. It also explains his exclamation-mark riddled enthusiasm for the early sales figures.

Dickens indicates a conscious and deliberate deployment of the various discourses within the *Memoirs*: the Introduction describes how he has improved the telling of the story (not the content) and emphasises his intention to tell things in his own way, 'altering its form throughout, and making such other alterations as he conceived would improve the narration of the facts, without any departure from the facts themselves' (*MJG* 1: x–xi). In a letter to Grimaldi's doctor J. A. Wilson Dickens again admits 'telling some of the stories in [his] own way', in direct contradiction of his own more public claim that he had 'merely been editing another account', and describes another organising principle to Wilson when he explains how 'I was very much struck by the many traits of kindheartedness scattered through the book, and have given it that colouring throughout' (*LCD* 1: 373).

However, despite such gestures at control this chapter will argue that the *Memoirs* inscribes the complexity of the multiple overlapping discourses that constitute life writing during the period. It arrived at the end of two significant decades for the genre during which, in the words of Julian North, 'Biographical discourse – and literary *Lives* especially – became part of the daily fabric of reading' (2009: 3). Just as Grimaldi's death in 1837 stands at the watershed between the Regency and the Victorian periods, so the *Memoirs* stand on the border between two epochs of life writing.

These years saw the publication of Thomas Moore's two-volume *Letters and Journals of Lord Byron* (1830), John Croker's new edition of Boswell's *Life of Johnson* (1831), and John Gibson Lockhart's biographies of Robert Burns (1828) and Sir Walter Scott (1837–8). Biography also filled the literary weeklies and monthly periodicals, for example in the 'Sketches of Contemporary Authors' in *The Athenaeum* (1828), 'Gallery of Illustrious Literary Characters' in *Fraser's Magazine* (1830–8) and 'Living Literary Characters' in *The New Monthly* (1831). Thomas Carlyle had initiated his own critical framework for the consideration of life writing in his 1832 essay 'Biography', where he described history as 'the essence of innumerable Biographies' (1832: 254). He further developed this idea in his lectures 'On Heroes, Hero-Worship and the Heroic in History', delivered in May 1840 and published the following year, in which he declares 'Universal History, the history of what man has accomplished in this world, is at bottom the History of the Great Men who have worked here' (1841: 1). Carlyle makes the will and actions of man central to the course of momentous events, rather than merely subject to the inevitable and irresistible tide in the events themselves, but despite this interest in the 'Great Men', he also acknowledges the pedagogic value of the lives of those operating at a less grand level: 'Of these millions of living men each individual is a mirror to us: a mirror both scientific and poetic; or, if you will, both natural and magical' (1832: 253).

By contextualising the *Memoirs* alongside some key examples of life writing from two prolific subgenres – stage biography and domestic relational biography – this chapter argues that the uncertain critical handling of the *Memoirs* is symptomatic of the work itself, which epitomises the nature of contemporary life writing, characterised by Richard Altick as 'an unstable compound' of genres (1966: 181). David Amigoni indicates that early nineteenth-century biography was 'premised on experiments that played restlessly upon [. . .] boundaries', such as those between 'public print and private inscription [. . .], notability and obscurity [. . .], the collective and the individual, the formally polished and the chaotically inchoate' (2006: 17), and the *Memoirs* fully articulates such a play in the generic hinterlands. Dickens's final published version is in tension with Grimaldi's own private account, transcribed and modified by successive editors, which also puts the collective enterprise at odds with the individual's. Grimaldi's notoriety is revealed as a burden within a narrative which relies on his fame for its success; Dickens gives a formal polish to the apparently chaotic mess of the Grimaldi–Wilks manuscript, but at a great cost to Grimaldi's original vision.

However, I will also demonstrate how such plurality and indeterminacy offers rich interpretive possibilities, and the *Memoirs* perfectly demonstrates how not just one but many selves create a life. This complex genealogy of Grimaldi's textual life aptly demonstrates that although the 'I' attempts to create itself by writing its own story, the self is in fact defined by its relations with other selves. Here, this is most emphatically signalled through the erasure of the 'I' of the narrative; Boz changed the text from first person to third, claiming that Wilks's narrative, 'had necessarily lost any original manner which [Grimaldi's] recital might have imparted' to it and thus its subject only speaks directly when Boz allows him (*MJG* 1: x). Instead, Dickens defines a collective narrator, 'we', who appears in the very first line of his Introduction, who can be a combination of the child Dickens and the adult Dickens, or both, plus his readers whom he draws into his confidence.

Thus biography's broad and inclusive framework represented an ideal creative fit for Dickens in 1837, in one of the most indeterminate periods of his career. Still fresh from a number of earlier potential vocations – law clerk, parliamentary reporter and sketch writer – Dickens was beginning to write novels (which in their serial and disparate form still read like sketches), plays and operettas. At the time of the *Memoirs*, Boz was, in Robert Douglas-Fairhurst's words, 'becoming Dickens', and as the apprentice writer Dickens attempts to define his own identity, the text incorporates a variety of overlapping forms (theatrical biography, Newgate novel, travelogue, comic serial and so on).

## The Stage Life

The most obvious genre of life writing that Dickens engages with is stage biography, as he deliberately foregrounds the themes of theatre and performance in his construction of Grimaldi's life. The memoirs of actors such as Sophia Baddeley (1787), Tate Wilkinson (1790), Charles Macklin (1799) and other associated figures such as bookseller James Lackington (1791) and manager Mark Moore (1795) consciously use theatrical forms, metaphors and images to evaluate their lives and draw on a collective pool of theatrical wisdom to formulate morals from their actions. In this context, dramatists become not only life's chroniclers but its teachers as well, which promotes the profession of acting as a superior form of education: James Kirkman regards it as an extensive programme of training for life, through which his subject Macklin was

> steeling his constitution, learning the human heart, storing up in his mind character in all its shapes, familiarizing himself to the caprices of fortune, and laying up a treasure of information which he could not have acquired in any seminary in the course of an age. (Macklin 1799 1: 60)

In Grimaldi's *Memoirs*, Dickens reworks stage biography's key techniques – particularly the overarching *theatrum mundi* theme, structure, concern with the constructedness of identity, and use of dramatic tone – to present Grimaldi's (and by extension everyone's) existence as an inherently theatrical one.

## The theatrum mundi

Many stage biographies incorporated the classical idea of the *theatrum mundi* in varying degrees of broadness. At its broadest, Jaques's well-known 'seven ages of man' speech from *As You Like It* is regularly plundered: Kirkman includes it as part of the title page of Macklin's memoirs, and later calls England 'that great theatre of the world' (1799 1: 55). More extensively, Tate Wilkinson notes how 'acting is not confined to the stage' and 'All men and women are merely players, / They have their exits and their entrances' (1790 2: 241) and scatters further allusions through his memoirs. To Wilkinson, people are 'actors and actresses in the world's drama' (1790 2: 254), while David Garrick is 'the actor on the stage of life' who did not act onstage but rather held 'life's exact mirror [. . .] to public view' (1790 2: 143), until his death – an 'exit from the world's stage' (1790 4: 48).

Stage biographers also demonstrated this precept by exposing the porousness of the boundaries between real life and the stage as well as meditating on the inherent theatricality of real historical events. Macklin describes how George III's coronation in 1761 was immediately restaged at both patent theatres and attributes Covent Garden's greater success to its superior reproduction of the original event's theatricality, particularly its 'profusion of fine cloaths, of velvet, silk, satin, lace, feathers, jewels, pearls, &.c', as well as 'The scenery, music, and other ornaments, [which] were all correspondent to the grandeur of the Ceremony' (1799 1: 425). Other areas of life outside the playhouse are also highlighted for their theatrical qualities, for Macklin, the church is 'the most proper theatre' for religious topics and the clergy are 'the fittest actors in the religious drama of Providence' (1799 1: 185), while Lackington likens his shop to a stage, which presents to him 'some knowledge of mankind' and 'a fine amusement' (1792: 384).

In the *Memoirs* Dickens foregrounds the theatricality inherent in much of Grimaldi's offstage life. During the 'Old Price' Riots at Covent Garden, playgoers protested against increased ticket prices in a manner which removed the distinction between them and the actors onstage. Thus Dickens shows how the audience performed their own acts of protest, including one spectator who 'regaled himself and the company with a watchman's rattle', and another who rang 'a large dustman's bell [. . .] with a perseverance and strength of arm quite astounding to all beholders' (*MJG* 2: 69).

The status of the 'official' performers was negated in other ways that dissolved the boundary between observer and observed. While the theatre manager 'Kemble was constantly called for, constantly came on, and constantly went off again without being able to obtain a hearing', soliloquies from other parts of the playhouse found space in the performance, as 'scarce an evening passed without flaming speeches being made from the pit, boxes and gallery' (*MJG* 2: 70). Such incidents endorse Marc Baer's description of the theatre pit as 'the people's theatre', in which the audience were 'prepared to answer the stage with dramatics of their own' (1992: 63).

Within the *theatrum mundi* framework, the trial scene – those public enactments of private disputes – was a popular trope for biographers, and one which reflects Hamlet's conviction that theatre can provoke and reveal an inner, hidden truth. In his own memoirs, both Macklin's murder trial and his legal dispute against Reddish and Sparks are presented as theatrical dialogues, including dramatic presentations of the alleged events and stage laughter. The participants are entirely aware of this theatricality and the trials become a complex muddle of onstage and offstage, with people interchanging between roles. At one point in the King's Bench trial, the lawyer Bearcroft observes that one of the accused has been 'brought upon the Stage in this Character' and so 'must perform his Part, and when the Court come to see his behaviour, if they don't dismiss him with applause, they will dismiss him at least without any censure' (1799 2: 72). At the end of his other court appearance, the judge observes to Macklin that 'You have met with great applause today – You never acted better', indicating an awareness of this theatricality on both sides of the bar (1799 2: 256).

In Grimaldi's *Memoirs*, Dickens adapts this convention to show how Grimaldi brings his stage life into the courtroom in a manner that counters anti-theatrical prejudice. When Mackintosh's fraud against him is revealed, Grimaldi privately reveals an 'uncontrollable fury' (*MJG* 2: 7) but adopts a very different role in the witness box at Mackintosh's trial, as Dickens explains how Grimaldi wanted to demonstrate that 'the same man who could play the clown upon a public stage could conduct himself with perfect propriety as a private individual' (*MJG* 2: 14). The prosecutor's counsel echo Bearcroft's approach when they designate Grimaldi as 'a common player, a mountebank-stroller' and 'necessarily a systematic liar' (*MJG* 2: 13), but he adeptly deflects the criticism, and as in Macklin's case, the judge commends Grimaldi's conduct. Moreover, in a rare editorial intervention, Wilks notes how Grimaldi was chosen to deliver apologies to theatre audiences, which he did with 'an entire absence of all buffoonery or grimace, [so] that, in spite of his grotesque dress and appearance [. . .] the audience forgot the clown, and only remembered the gentleman' (*MJG* 2: 15n).

However, as befitting pantomime's comic tone Dickens's variant on the *theatrum mundi* theme can also be humorous. He began this approach earlier in 'The Pantomime of Life' (which I explored in the previous chapter) and his practical experiments with this theory are also discernible in other early work. The sketches 'Private Theatres', 'Mrs Joseph Porter' and 'Astley's' dramatise meta-theatrical events (such as people watching or preparing for theatrical performances) in a way that again dissolves the boundary between onstage and offstage. 'Astley's' begins with the admission that 'Boz' is more interested in the performance of the audience than in the players onstage, while 'Private Theatres' narrates the backstage drama ahead of the scheduled performance and closes with the rise of the curtain. The *Memoirs* similarly presents the events of Grimaldi's 'offstage' life as further theatrical performances in which the familiar archetypes of pantomime (the 'mirror of life') have identifiable counterparts in 'offstage' society.

Dickens's technique of rendering action and speech in a theatrical register further shows his appreciation of the stage biographer's method, which had in turn been adopted from the methods of the playwright. Conversations between individuals are artificially transcribed rather than paraphrased, a technique which disregards reasonable powers of memory but makes such passages dramatically effective. Accents were also rendered semi-phonetically to aid recitation in the manner of an actor's script: Kirkman relates Macklin's anecdotes or conversations, 'nearly in the words of the old gentleman, as he told [them]' (1799 1: 138), including pauses, repetitions, confusions and interruptions. Any editor focused on the content would excise such details, but here they create a sense of immediacy and demonstrate the subject's weak mental state to the reader. This technique is regularly used throughout the *Memoirs*, for example for a conversation between the burglars during the Pentonville robberies which no-one else would have heard and for Grimaldi's meeting with his prospective father-in-law.

### Tone

Dickens enhances the theatrical (and often specifically pantomimic) effect of such staged scenes by carefully managing their tone. The burglary episode (Book 2, Chapter 3) is presented predominantly through a lens of pantomime humour and would be recast in *Oliver Twist* as a mild Newgate melodrama. Gestures are exaggerated and action is presented as stage directions, such as when 'Grimaldi beckoned [. . .] Mr. King [. . .] and suggested in a whisper that they should search the garden together' (*MJG* 1: 61). This incongruous and heightened style defuses any potential tension and transforms the search for the felons into a piece of comic theatre: 'It was a dark night, and they groped about the garden for some time, but found nobody' (*MJG* 1: 62).

It reaches a comic *denouement* when Grimaldi discovers one of the burglars and deals him 'a heavy blow with a broadsword' (*MJG* 1: 62), a weapon which stage tutor Leman Thomas Rede calls 'essential' in 'all [stage] melodramas' (1868: 22). The burglar is perfunctorily dismissed, as he 'yelled out loudly, and stopping for an instant, as if in extreme pain, dropped to the ground, limped off a few paces, and was lost in the darkness' (*MJG* 1: 62). This description presents the *performance* of the characters, as the burglar signals his pain to the audience and then exits stage left. In this pantomime's finale Grimaldi is 'stopped in the very outset of his [pursuit], by tumbling over a cow, which was lying on the ground', which extracts him from reality and places him back in the playhouse, and indeed he only avoids cutting off his own head due to an 'involuntary pantomimic feat' and his own 'theatrical practice as a fencer' (*MJG* 1: 62). The combination of tripping over the cow, Grimaldi's theatrical reaction and the black slapstick of the possible self-decapitation moves the scene yet closer to the theatrical.

After another offstage scene when he was compelled to perform in a barber-shop, Grimaldi subsequently decided to integrate it within a stage performance, in a belated attempt to contain its theatricality. Yet its presentation in the *Memoirs* demonstrates its refusal to be contained, as this domestic episode is related as a series of stage directions and stylised dialogue. For example, when Joe returns to the shop a third time to see if the barber had returned:

> The girl was still sitting at work; but she laid it aside when the visitors entered, and said she really was very sorry, but her father had not come in yet.

> 'That's very provoking,' said Grimaldi, 'considering that I have called here three times already.'
>
> The girl agreed that it was, and, stepping to the door, looked anxiously up the street and down the street, but there was no barber in sight.
>
> 'Do you want to see him on any particular business?' inquired [Grimaldi's companion] Howard.
>
> 'Bless my heart! No, not I,' said Grimaldi: 'I only want to be shaved.'
>
> 'Shaved, sir!' cried the girl. 'Oh, dear me! What a pity it is that you did not say so before! For I do most of the shaving for father when he's at home, and all when he's out.' (*MJG* 2: 117)

Everything here is on the level of surface while the gestures and conversation feel more suited to the stage directions and dialogue of a play than to a real exchange. While being shaved by this young girl in the barber's chair, the comic nature of the scene appeals to Grimaldi's compulsive desire to perform: we are told that he felt 'an irresistible tendency to laugh at the oddity of the operation'. He finally gives in to his performing side, and when the real barber returns, he discovers Joe 'with a soapy face and a gigantic mouth making the most extravagant faces over a white towel', and comments that 'that gentleman as was being shaved, was out of sight the funniest gentleman he had ever seen' (*MJG* 2: 117–18).

## *Structure*

Dickens also seems to be working within the theatrical structure of stage biographies, whereby the precepts that actors articulated onstage were increasingly revisited offstage to impose an order and meaning upon the unpredictable events of their offstage lives. Memoirists frequently mapped theatrical patterns of good and bad luck onto the events of their lives, as expressed in Mark Moore's theatrical metaphor for life's vicissitudes: 'Thus fortune likes to shift the scene' (1795: 217). Wilkinson similarly borrows from *Hamlet* when he comments that '"As one woe treads upon another's heels", as Shakspeare [*sic*] observes, so did another misfortune happen to my good friends' (1790 1: 224) while Lackington, who had read Wilkinson's memoirs, prefaces a change in his own fortunes with a similar quotation from *Julius Caesar* describing 'the tide in the affairs of men' (1792: 335).

Dickens similarly structures the events of Grimaldi's life to direct us towards corresponding conclusions; as *The Athenaeum* observed, the *Memoirs* presented 'a sort of pantomime in itself', including 'rapid changes of scene – sudden findings of riches, as sudden losses [. . .] all blended to make an existence!' ([Anon.] 1838a: 115). Dickens directly comments that Grimaldi laid 'great stress' on the fact that there 'always seemed some connexion [*sic*] between his good and bad fortune' (*MJG* 1: 56) and his improved fortunes are immediately followed by unexpected setbacks. After he gains the favour of his future wife he is injured onstage, his happy anticipation of becoming a father is swept away by the death of that same wife, and any money that is made or unexpectedly found on the street is quickly snatched away through misuse or theft, to the extent that this becomes a narrative expectation: 'Of course some unforeseen circumstance was to happen, or some unexpected demand to be made on the money so easily earned' (*MJG* 2: 43). Comical and seemingly whimsical anecdotes, such as the 'guinea wager' or 'the piece of tin' episode, are swiftly followed by scenes of sadness or tribulation, with the cumulative effect of a life constructed around exemplary scenes rather than a more realistic unpredictable unfolding of episodes.

Dickens's chapter division also broadly replicates a theatrical structure. Richard Findlater claims that 'the original division was arbitrary and gimmicky' (1968: 15), but Dickens ends several chapters like scene endings, typically at a moment of dramatic tension, mid-action or before the full outcome has unfolded. However, unlike the more detailed *tableau* 'situations' that closed some of his early sketches, the *Memoirs* uses simpler transitions to carry the action across in nine chapter endings, and three in particular close on strong 'curtains' that forestall the climax of dramatic scenes. After the first attempted burglary at Pentonville, we are told that 'on the third night, after the girl's return, they made a fresh attack, for which we will reserve a fresh chapter' (*MJG* 1: 70). Chapter 7 closes during a description of Grimaldi's great hopes for his stage career, as the narrator comments, 'how far his expectations were borne out by subsequent occurrences, the next chapter will show' (*MJG* 1: 153). Finally, we are given a sense of foreboding about troubles to come when Chapter 10 ends: 'On the conclusion of the night's amusements, he had an interview with the acting manager [at Drury Lane], which, although at first both pleasing and profitable, led in less than six weeks to his departure from the theatre' (*MJG* 1: 199). Martin Meisel has observed that in their presentation of arrested movement chapter endings of this kind often resembled the *tableaux* of the art world, but here Dickens was also adapting his own serial technique which concluded each part at a point to make the reader want to read (and preferably buy) the next instalment.

## Identity

However, the aspect of theatrical life writing that would have the most impact on Dickens's subsequent work is the way that the theatricality of such biographies becomes a lens through which to delineate and evaluate character and identity. The most direct manifestation of this is the use of theatrical sources, particularly direct quotation, as a means to illuminate character and incident. Tate Wilkinson describes this as utilising a corpus of shared stage wisdom whereby 'the learned reader' may 'recognise an old acquaintance' and 'be pleased to meet [the quotation] in a novel and unexpected situation' (1790 2: viii) and Deborah Vlock (1998) has substantiated this high level of stage literacy amongst nineteenth-century readers, for whom the theatre was more affordable than the printed word until the 1830s. Donald Stauffer also recognises how such quotations became 'the touchstones by means of which an autobiographer or memorialist may evaluate the actions of a whole life' (1941: 14), and a point of authority against which to contextualise these actions.

In the hands of the (auto)biographer quotations self-dramatise and often even aggrandise the subject's actions by magnifying 'ordinary' events and stake a claim to Carlylean greatness for a wider range of lives. When Lackington prefaces the narration of his humble birth with a speech from *Thomas, Lord Cromwell*, in which the eponymous protagonist resolves not to let his own low birth curtail his aspirations (1792: 55), he makes his life analogous with a leading statesman to potentially inspire his readers. Lockhart and Wilkinson similarly draw on Portius's rousing words from Addison's tragedy, *Cato*: ''Tis not in mortals to command success, / But we'll do more, Sempronius, we'll deserve it', as they attempt to overcome periods of severe illness and stage fright respectively (*MWS* 7: 282 and 1790 4: 25).

This identification with specific stage figures is a more sustained use of theatrical material which becomes a *leitmotif* in some biographies. Charles Macklin's life is given a wider perspective through his association with one of his most famous roles, Shylock. He is called the 'veteran Shylock', and further linked through Pope's epitaph for him: 'Here lies the Jew / That Shakespeare drew' (1799 2: 428). Kirkman measures Macklin's real character against this fictional one on several occasions; Macklin's generosity with money is contrasted with Shylock's avaricious behaviour, and both Kirkman and Wilkinson draw on the comparison when judging Macklin's lenient conduct towards his detractors during a legal dispute. Kirkman and

Wilkinson both conclude that Macklin never forgot and indeed acted up 'to his great master Shakespeare: – when he says – "And earthly power doth then shew likest God's / When mercy seasons justice"' (1799 2: 432; 1790 2, 66).

But if (auto)biographers could designate identity as a series of changing theatrical roles, so could audiences and other less benign observers, who regularly indulged in restrictive 'typecasting', and fixed performers in roles according to their own needs and desires. So while Macklin appeared onstage prior to a performance of *Macbeth* 'in his own Character' (1799 2: 61) to report his grievances against his accusers, they ensured that regardless of his chosen role, 'the only Character in which Mr Macklin in future was to be seen, was that of a Delinquent, or condemned Malefactor, at the Bar of the Public, who were to be collected to be judges upon him' (1799 2, 158). Even when he played Shylock onstage, his audience persisted in recasting him as Macklin the villain, demanding that he removed his Shylock costume – even the nefariousness of Shakespeare's villain was an insufficient measure by which he could be properly judged.

The *Memoirs* also examines this conflict between self-projection and audience determination, as the same failure by spectators to distinguish between the performed and the real that Macklin suffered has profound consequences for Grimaldi's sense of selfhood. The volatility of the ever-present and judgemental audience often transforms them into the mob, who insist on an immutable notion of his identity even when offstage. Dickens had offered an initial view of this uneasy relationship between performer and audience in 'The Pantomime of Life', when the elderly Pantaloon is violently attacked onstage, and in the *Memoirs* Dickens demonstrates further how easily such a slippage can occur, as the audience regard a real onstage beating of a young Grimaldi as 'a most capital joke' and feel that it was 'perfectly wonderful to see [him] perform so naturally' (*MJG* 1: 16). Later, his father dresses him for the role of '"a gentleman"' when visiting relatives, but on the street the public misread this performance, jeering and threatening him with violence.

Grimaldi's identity thus becomes fixed according to the demands of the audience and he is regularly coerced into performing outside the playhouse. In perhaps the most sinister episode, Grimaldi is late for a performance one night and so must travel to the theatre in his clown's costume and makeup but is pursued by an adoring yet intimidating mob, who trap him in a carriage and force him to perform outside the theatre's official space and time. Such incidents expose a troubling tension within the identity of the biographical subject: by locating its origin within external performances and effects rather than interior feelings and emotions, Dickens and other stage biographers indicate that identity is an ephemeral outward projection, rather than a durable inward quality.

In several stage (auto)biographies, the subjects themselves are implicated in transporting their acting talents from the formal stage to public/private life, for various levels of personal gain. Macklin played a prank on tour by dressing in the character of Emilia from *Othello* ('a part he occasionally filled') and then trying to get a night's lodgings at the hostel in which he was already staying. He is given space in the landlady's bedroom, with predictably farcical consequences when she retires for the night; thus life imitates art (1799 1: 170). Macklin also encouraged his fellow Irish actor Barry to 'perform' offstage as 'the Earl of Munster' on his first visit to London to confound social expectations (1799 1: 299).

Such ruses hint at the figure most suited to this *milieu* of 'social theatre', the confidence trickster, and by the time he took up the Grimaldi manuscript, Dickens had already started developing just such a character, who would persist throughout his career. In *Sketches by Boz*, Horatio Sparkins, Theodosius Butler and Captain Waters all assume roles within a society willing to be deceived in order to preserve its own pretences, and represent early prototypes of the more developed figure of Alfred Jingle in the *Pickwick Papers*, who in turn is echoed in the *Memoirs* by the character of John Mackoull (or Mackintosh). All these figures play with assumptions of various kinds; as actors they put on or 'assume' roles, and their audiences are directed towards making assumptions of their own. Mackintosh may only assume the role of country gentleman, but Grimaldi accepts this performance to feel part of a social group, while the Pickwick Club make similar assumptions about Jingle in order to be associated with such an interesting and well-connected person.

Adopting the most appropriate character to perform in a given situation is Grimaldi's primary mode of existence in the *Memoirs*, even when it is an unwelcome choice. When Grimaldi was a young boy, his father staged his own death to elicit the true feelings of his two sons (echoing the larger public trials of Macklin's life in which the truth was sought through theatricality). However, Joseph cleverly spotted the deception and responded with his own performance, 'bursting into a roar of the most distracted grief' and rolling on the floor 'in a seeming transport of anguish', which his father assumed to be true distress (*MJG* 1: 28).

Grimaldi is often engaged in reading the social performances of others, correctly interpreting them with the acuity of a fellow player. Hamilton the highwayman's 'great coolness and self-possession' in front of his accusers is viewed by Grimaldi as a theatrical act; 'The practised eye of an old actor was not so easily deceived' as Hamilton makes 'a desperate effort to assume an easy confidence of manner' to escape the gallows (*MJG* 2: 63–4). Earlier his 'somewhat disordered' mind was revealed to Grimaldi in such visual cues as 'a nervous restlessness of manner, an occasional incoherence of speech' and 'a wildness of look' (*MJG* 2: 50). Grimaldi similarly decodes Byron's varying states of mind through gesture and action: when he 'appeared lost in deep melancholy' Byron 'really looked the picture of despair, for his face was highly capable of expressing profound grief', whereas at other times his exhibition of 'his white hands and teeth with an almost ludicrous degree of affectation' characterise him as 'a complete fop' (*MJG* 2: 106).

Dickens's presentation of easily readable external expressions similarly follows contemporary stage practice, whereby outward and observable gestures and motions formed an index to internal feelings. Martin Meisel describes how this 'iconography of emotion' developed within nineteenth-century culture through the work of stage tutors like Rede, where 'interior experience was conveyed through a conventionalised language of facial expression, pose, and gesture' (1983: 5). Thus young Grimaldi's aforementioned enactment of filial mourning resembles Rede's description of the inherently theatrical emotion of grief. It is 'a passion, which admits, like many others, of a great deal of Stage trick' (1868: 34) and expressed through a variety of gestures, including 'beating the head or forehead, tearing the hair, and catching the breath, as if choking' (1868: 32). On this occasion, Grimaldi's performance is rewarded by his father, who praises him as the son who 'truly and sincerely loved him' (*MJG* 1: 29), while his naïve younger brother John who performs inappropriately (celebrating their father's death) is beaten for his hurtful honesty.

Ultimately, the perspective of the *theatrum mundi* is so internalised that even when such displays are not deliberate and may be based in uncontrolled emotion, the *Memoirs* draws on the appropriate stage gestures to describe them. When Grimaldi finds a purse of money he worries that he will be accused of theft and in this 'state of turmoil and agitation', 'his legs trembled beneath him so that he could scarcely walk, his heart beat violently, and the perspiration started on his face' (*MJG* 1: 93). When the beadle comes to arraign him later, Grimaldi 'was quite petrified, and stood rooted to the spot, looking from one to another [of his companions] with a face in which dismay and fear were visibly depicted' (*MJG* 1: 114), as if the emotion could be physically drawn onto his features.

## The 'Relational' Life

Although Dickens works most closely within the themes and conventions of stage biography, other forms are at work in the complex hybrid of Grimaldi's memoirs. Virginia Woolf characterised the typical Victorian biographical subject as a wax effigy that has 'only a smooth superficial likeness to the body in the coffin' (1981: 121) and remains a polished and impenetrable subject standing apart from his social milieu. Here in working through the relation between Grimaldi's public and private lives, Dickens challenges the apparent superficiality of his performed life by depicting the complex relationality of his life as a whole. In his introduction Dickens immediately declares his intent to place Grimaldi within society rather than apart from it, expressing his desire to uncover 'what [clowns] did with themselves [. . .] off the stage', and determine 'at whose expense' their appetite for sausages was maintained (*MJG* 1: v). All those who surround and interact with Dickens's Grimaldi contribute to his construction and create what Donna Loftus calls 'a self [. . .] constituted by social narratives' (2006: 68).

The relation between private and the public selves was a key tension within auto/biographical writing during the Romantic period. Recent studies have shown how some Romantic biographers domesticated, materialised and humanised their chosen subjects, writing against the developing Romantic figure of the autonomous artist-subject who is aloof from the wider world and inhabits a *Spiegelkabinette* constructed from their own words. These domestic biographers recalled the previous methods of Johnson, which advocated the primacy of the domestic space to the biographer, urging them to focus on 'domestick privacies' and the 'minute details of daily life' (1750: 33); Boswell similarly felt that 'nobody can write the life of a man, but those who have eat and drink and lived in social intercourse with him' (1934 2: 166).

This section will use John Gibson Lockhart's *Life of Sir Walter Scott*, a work that Dickens knew well, as a prism through which to view how Dickens uses the methods of the relational biographer to broaden and enrich his life of Grimaldi. Lockhart's *Scott*, which Dickens read during its serial publication, provides an instructive comparison with the *Memoirs* in several ways. While Dickens's governing method of condensation and selection differs from Lockhart's limited editorialising of seven (and later ten) solid volumes of letters, journals, personal reminiscences and other material, both writers focus on the relationality of their subject in a very similar manner.

Although Lockhart operates at one remove from the shared physical social space of Boswell and Johnson, he adopts three mechanisms which Julian North attributes to 'domestic' biographers of the 1820s and 30s: using the poet's home as a recurrent trope; presenting eyewitness testimonies; and including intimate forms of address (such as private letters and conversations) within the work. Indeed, Lockhart himself asserts the greater value of interrelations recorded in the specific moment rather than detached introspection, claiming at one point that the inclusion of two letters from 1814 will give 'the history of the completion of Waverley' in that year 'in more exact detail that the author's own recollection could supply in 1830' (*MWS* 3: 125).

These strategies inform Dicken's approach to bringing the life of Grimaldi into a more familiar and intimate *milieu*, as he similarly interrogates the notion of the remote and interiorised artist-genius, and echoes Lockhart in, as North puts it, insisting 'upon the connection between public/historical and the private/domestic worlds' (2009: 6). This democratising approach is wholly suitable for its subject – a popular entertainer – and anticipates Dickens's mode of engagement with the popular cultural figure of the clown that I will trace in later chapters. To discover the private life, Dickens turns away from the public persona of Grimaldi's art, but as Dickens's treatment of the *theatrum mundi* theme has demonstrated, the private life reveals itself to be another version of public one.

To unpack the various layers of relationality contained within these works, Paul John Eakin's three relational lenses provide a useful theoretical framework. These lenses explore how the subject is connected within 'identity-shaping environments' (1999: 85), how the subject relates to certain principal figures, or 'proximate others' (1999: 86), and finally, how the self comprises a series of 'dynamic, changing and plural' selves (1999: 98). The *Memoirs* (and to some extent Lockhart's *Scott*) not only operate across and interweave all three levels, but also explicitly foreground the extent to which their subjects' lives are relational.

## *Environment*

One of the most direct ways in which Scott engages with his wider social environment is through the constant domestic improvements that he describes in his correspondence, and the 'great delight' (*MWS* 4: 367) which he takes from his 'household gods' (*MWS* 5: 306), such as his drawing room and his gaslights. These home comforts are explicitly linked to Scott's art via his own recognition that the public art is the material enabler of these private effects: to create space for a 'handsome library', drawing room and 'bedrooms for company', Scott admits that 'It will cost me a little hard work to meet the expense' (*MWS* 4: 367). He populates this social environment with friends and intimates and Lockhart regularly reports of Scott's enjoyment of informal Sundays spent at home, with just a few close friends and 'never any person with whom he stood on ceremony' (*MWS* 4: 158).

Lockhart suggests how Scott's private domestic demands took precedence over any public artistic ones, claiming that 'Perhaps no great poet ever made his literature so completely ancillary to the objects and purposes of practical life' (*MWS* 7: 415), but also acknowledges Scott's own recognition of a symbiotic relationship between them. Scott believed that 'literature, worthy of the name, was more likely to be fed and nourished by the converse' of 'men engaged in the active business of the world' rather than 'so called, literary people' (*MWS* 4: 195). Therefore his work becomes an extension of his self, socialised among his friends before and after publication, and given its own autonomous existence in a domestic environment: novels such as *Guy Mannering* were 'seen on every table, the subject of every conversation' (*MWS* 3: 333).

While Scott is humanised through his attention to hearth and home, in the *Memoirs* Grimaldi's primary domesticated space is the theatre, which is both a place of work and a central support network that replaces traditional familial relations. Accounts of assistance and generosity towards Grimaldi are threaded throughout the early part of the narrative; for example, after his father has cruelly swung him around the stage on a chain 'the famous rope-dancers, Mr and Mrs Redige' were among 'the many persons who [. . .] behaved with great kindness to him' (*MJG* 1: 19–20). Similarly, when Grimaldi senior dies and the family are bankrupted, 'offers of assistance were heaped upon [them] from all quarters' (*MJG* 1: 32).

Due to their emphasis on the subject's social environment, biographies that privilege the relational such as these foreground different personal qualities from those in traditional male biographies emanating from a climate of heroes and hero-worship. Rather than facilitating success through attributes such as bravery, single-mindedness and perseverance, alternative qualities such as sensitivity and generosity engender reciprocal goodwill and a collective confrontation to individual problems. As Loftus indicates, the notion of success in such relational lives is predicated less upon individuals enacting great deeds and more upon managing the competing demands of varying social relationships in both private and public spheres. Lockhart particularly notes Scott's adaptability between social spheres (although, as Scott's son-in-law, he is not the most disinterested of observers). At Ashestiel, Scott 'was the cherished friend and kind neighbour of every middling Selkirkshire yeoman, just as easily as in Edinburgh he was the companion of clever youth and narrative old age in refined society' (*MWS* 4: 195).

In such narratives, collective support overwhelms obstacles that are insurmountable individually. As we saw earlier, when Grimaldi is falsely accused by the corrupt beadle 'Old Lucas', he becomes a spectacle of fear and inaction, but while he may lack individual fortitude his congenial interpersonal manner ensures that his close colleagues promise him that '"we will prove ourselves your friends, and support you against this old rascal"' (*MJG* 1: 115). They confront his accuser as 'a general chorus' (*MJG* 1: 116), while Grimaldi as a separate entity temporarily disappears. Similarly, Scott's public management of his personal misfortunes (especially his financial problems and wife's death in 1826) encourages a spirit of reciprocity that supports and sustains him through these difficulties. His relations rally round him at often great cost to themselves, to the extent that Lockhart feels 'I must note how greatly I admired the manner in which all his dependents appeared to have met the reverse of his fortunes – a reverse which inferred a very considerable alteration in the circumstances of every one of them' (*MWS* 7: 80).

In Grimaldi's case, the material benefits of this support are most clearly realised in his final fundraising performances. When he is too 'ill and depressed' (*MJG* 2: 176) to organise them himself, his actress friend Frances Kelly obtains the free use of Sadler's Wells and Drury Lane, and the *gratis* services of numerous performers who agree to '"put their shoulders to the wheel, on behalf of poor old Joe"' (*MJG* 2: 177). This is both a vindication of the personal qualities so lauded in Grimaldi himself and a direct contradiction of the anti-theatrical prejudice that regarded the theatre business as ruthless and indolent, akin to the later defences of the profession within Dickens's journals that we saw in Chapter 2.

In his farewell speeches, Grimaldi acknowledges the symbiotic relationship between himself and his audience, observing that 'By strict attention, perseverance, and exertion, did I arrive at the height of my profession, and proud I am to acknowledge, have ofttimes been honoured with your smiles, approbation, and support' (*MJG* 2: 179).

Dickens later develops this by reiterating this balance between public effort and public support that sustained Grimaldi's life, commenting how Grimaldi's 'exertions were fostered by public indulgence, and stimulated by public applause' (*MJG* 2: 186). His final profit of £895 is the tangible appreciation of a network of private donors, fellow performers and audience members which goes a little way to making his final years 'peaceful and contented' (*MJG* 2: 195), but ultimately proves to be a poor substitute for human relations. After his son and second wife die, Grimaldi is described as wholly unsuited to an autonomous existence, as his 'solitary desolation' pushes him towards 'a state of melancholy madness', only held at bay by 'old friends [who] came from time to time to cheer him with a few minutes conversation' (*MJG* 2: 202–3).

Significantly, the *Memoirs* contains no deathbed scene, even though for Altick, this is 'the one obligatory scene in nineteenth-century biography' (1966: 210), serving as a key locus for the biographer's religious and ethical inspiration for his readers but also a final expression of relationality. Thus at Scott's end, Lockhart reports that 'It was a beautiful day [. . .] and so perfectly still, that the sound of all others most delicious to his ear, the gentle ripple of the Tweed over its pebbles, was distinctly audible as we knelt around the bed, and his eldest son kissed and closed his eyes' (*MWS* 7: 394). Yet while Grimaldi's own reminiscences obviously lacked such a conclusion, Dickens deliberately chooses not to invent one either. Instead, Grimaldi's death is briefly reported in a few paragraphs with the objectivity of a coroner's report, and rather than hearing his dying words we hear only 'an unusual noise, similar to loud snoring' (*MJG* 2: 206) heard from his room. The fact that Grimaldi dies alone, rather than in company, does not fit the *Memoirs*'s overarching framework of relationality, and so we are not given a deathbed set-piece, fabricated or otherwise. The reader is left with a final impression of a man reliant on the company of others for his existence. Without his family and wider public audience, Grimaldi has no life of which to speak.

## *Proximate others*

Dickens's telling of Grimaldi's life also reflects Eakin's second layer of relationality, whereby the subject's life is put into relief against significant 'proximate others'. When measuring the relative presences of mothers and fathers in middle-class Victorian biographies, Loftus notes that paternal relations occupy greater space, but although the *Memoirs* follows this pattern, it is without the associated privileging of masculine agency in the subject's positive development. In fact, like Loftus's examples, paternal masculinity in the *Memoirs* often undermines the subject's claim to independence.

Grimaldi ambivalently describes his father as his '"severe, but excellent parent"' (*MJG* 1: 14) and Dickens follows this lead by noting that he 'bore the reputation of being a very honest man, and a very charitable one, never turning a deaf ear to the entreaties of the distressed', who 'was never known to be inebriated' (*MJG* 1: 7). Furthermore, Dickens's dismissal of Grimaldi's regular beatings as 'the little traits' of 'a very singular and eccentric man' (*MJG* 1: 7) somewhat justifies the claim of rival biographer H. D. Miles that Dickens shows 'a determination to blink the question' of Grimaldi senior's cruelty, and hides 'moral turpitude behind a cloak of "eccentricity"' (1838: 17–18).

However, despite the exculpatory tone of Dickens's editorial summarising, his presentation of individual events shows much more concern with parental influence. As I described earlier in this chapter, two incidents involving his father – Grimaldi senior's feigned death and his presentation of his son as a 'gentleman'– were formative in the development of Grimaldi's character, as they revealed both the value and danger of 'offstage' performance and the constant search for a role suitable for the social situation.

Moreover, Dickens draws further parallels by making Grimaldi's own son an increasingly significant figure at the end of the *Memoirs* and a key touchstone by which to measure Grimaldi's own character. Scott's benevolent treatment of his children had been similarly underscored by Lockhart through editorial comment and the presentation of their correspondence. While Scott's letters during his son's service in the Irish Hussars sometimes include Polonius-like advice ('In buying your horses you will be very cautious' [*MWS* 4: 290], 'I like very much your methodical arrangement as to expenses [. . .] it is highly necessary and enables one to see how the money actually goes' [*MWS* 4: 299]), they also articulate a sense of the subject's absence and a concern for his wellbeing while away from home and family. Dickens emphasises Grimaldi's emotional and financial investment in his son, to whom he was 'devotedly attached' and 'for whom he had always entertained the most anxious solicitude, whom he had educated at a great expense, and upon whom a considerable portion of the earnings of his best days had been most liberally bestowed' (*MJG* 2: 164).

However, the comparative consequences of these two models of positive paternalism are starkly different. Lockhart demonstrates how Scott is repaid through Walter junior's later conduct; on one occasion, he describes how he proudly promoted the work within his regiment, receiving 'nightly invitations to *evening parties!* to read and illustrate passages [of *The Lady of the Lake*]' (*MWS* 2: 348). By contrast, J.S. negates the symbiotic generosity of Grimaldi's fellow performers by not reciprocating his father's fond feelings. J.S. runs 'a reckless and vicious course', 'to the heart-rending grief of his father and mother'; the 'heavy shock' of J.S.'s rejection, 'in Grimaldi's weak and debilitated state, almost broke his heart' (*MJG* 2: 170). J.S. finally dies in dissipated circumstances, but in this story of genealogies (realising Terry Eagleton's assertion that 'the structure of biography is biology' (1993: 12), he is not repeating any sins of his father, but rather rejecting his father's moral inheritance.

Dickens also uses other theatrical figures as proximate others, and – notwithstanding those more general examples of generosity we saw earlier – such figures often appear in a less positive light to make Grimaldi shine brighter. Jack Bologna, who played Harlequin to Grimaldi's Clown, is presented offstage as a parsimonious foil to Grimaldi's generosity. Bologna knows the price of everything but the value of nothing, and his refusal to stay at a supposedly expensive hotel gives Grimaldi the narrative space to explain his own preference for a first-rate house over a second-rate one. At dinner, Bologna orders a simple Welsh rarebit while Grimaldi entrusts the landlady to provide appropriately, as the two men trade insults regarding their respective 'shabbiness' and 'extravagance'. This battle between Carnival and Lent ends with Carnival triumphant as Bologna discovers that dinner is the same price regardless of the choice, and pays up, 'to his own great wrath and his friend's unspeakable amusement' (*MJG* 2: 124–5).

Grimaldi's fellow clown Robert Bradbury is another yardstick for appraising his character, and Dickens describes Grimaldi's clowning as 'more composed and subdued' than Bradbury's reckless acrobatic antics (*MJG* 2: 28). This again correlates with their offstage activities when Bradbury must feign madness to protect a gentleman's reputation during a convoluted intrigue involving a gold snuff-box. The ruse succeeds but Bradbury confuses playing the madman onstage and offstage with dire consequences: during an official performance he is 'impelled by some strange and sudden whim' to commit 'a disgusting piece of irreverence and impertinence', which offends his audience and ends his career (*MJG* 2: 33).

Grimaldi becomes acquainted with several criminals, and Dickens also uses these relationships to further enhance, rather than compromise, Grimaldi's reputation. As described earlier, Grimaldi's conduct when dealing with the roguish Mackintosh puts Grimaldi's own honesty into sharp relief rather than diluting it. Moreover, Grimaldi can also deploy the 'pious fraud': when the novice highwayman George Hamilton robs him, Grimaldi has such a strong 'desire to save this young man, whom he strongly suspected to be but a beginner in crime', that he deliberately fails to recognise his assailant in court (*MJG* 2: 65). Dickens's postscript to the episode indicates that such benevolence is well-placed, as Hamilton lives to bear 'the reputation of an honest man' for another twenty years, before heroically dying in a neighbour's house fire (*MJG* 2: 66).

## *Multiple selves*

Eakin's final relational dimension is that between multiple selves, in refutation of the notion of a single, continuous identity (which Eakin calls 'the primary fiction of all self-narration' (1999: 93)). As Laura Marcus describes, although autobiography 'offered a private occasion, and subsequently a public forum, for attempting to resolve the problematics of identity' (1994: 16), the results often only confounded the premise of an original, solid and unitary 'self', and broke down binary positions such as masculine and feminine, individual and society. This is instantiated in the generic confusion of the *Memoirs* as its various components and fragmented narrative reflect the similarly diffuse and hybrid nature of its subject's identity – neither the *Memoirs* as a text nor Grimaldi as a subject is a single, continuous entity. As we saw earlier, this was a key strand of the *theatrum mundi* theme, as 'real life' becomes just another pantomime, and is the point at which stage biography and relational biography intersect.

Despite his initial intention to observe clowns 'out of pantomime time' (*MJG* 1: v), Dickens presents Grimaldi's life as a complex interplay between public 'outside' and private 'inside' selves, which leaves both the subject and those around him with a confused sense of his identity. Lockhart similarly describes the interaction between the author's different selves – the gentleman, the gardener and so on – as the journal of his yachting voyages presents 'according to the scene and occasion, the poet, the antiquary, the magistrate, the planter, and the agriculturalist' (*MWS* 3: 278). Scott himself indicates how he plays multiple discrete but interchangeable roles when he tells Lockhart, 'Author as I am, I wish these good people would recollect that I began with being a gentleman, and don't mean to give up the character' (*MWS* 2: 185–6).

But despite these attempts at self-determination, both men are vulnerable to the perceptions of others. When Scott works publicly 'among the active citizens of his native town' for charities and educational institutions, popular perception creates two separate Scotts, 'one the miraculously fertile author [. . .] another some retired magistrate or senator of easy fortune and indefatigable philanthropy' (*MWS* 5: 64). The *Memoirs* demonstrates the difficulty of sustaining the serious private individual and comic public performer as separate identities within the *theatrum mundi*, by starkly juxtaposing scenes in real life with scenes in the theatre. After the death of his wife, Grimaldi switches between mournfully haunting 'the scenes of his old hopes and happiness' and appearing at 'the theatre to set the audience in a roar'. His fragile greasepaint mask simultaneously projects the comic self and attempts to insulate the grieving self, 'chalking over the seams which mental agony has worn in his face' as he is 'hailed with boisterous applause in the merry Christmas pantomime' (*MJG* 1: 137). This trope is replicated when his brother-in-law Richard Hughes dies and Grimaldi 'was compelled to rehearse part of his Clown's character on the stage' then 'run to the funeral', 'get back from the churchyard to the theatre to finish the rehearsal, and [finally] exert all his comic powers at night' to again 'set the audience in a roar' (*MJG* 2: 94). The recurrence of the roaring audience transcends a benign expression of collective laughter to become the insatiable demand for constant satisfaction of the pursuing mob.

Earlier in this chapter we saw how Grimaldi as a boy was required to perform as a 'gentleman' on the streets, when he also performed clownish stunts for visitors to the green room (a space intended for actors to inhabit outside the performance). Throughout his career, others cannot separate private individual from performer, like a Bath clergyman who invites Grimaldi to dinner expecting him to sing for the assembled guests, and guests at Byron's house who similarly assume that his clownish identity is a fixed constant rather than a temporary role, as they trick him into eating apple pie with soy sauce. The delineation of these broader and more superficial public personas makes it extremely difficult for Dickens to delineate a single, discrete sense of Grimaldi, since his identity is consistently predicated upon one kind of performance or another.

Nonetheless, both Lockhart and Dickens attempt to unify their subjects by including the more regular and recurring role of a sensitive and more feeling self within this cast of alternative selves. Dickens thus describes Grimaldi as 'a feeling, sensitive man' (*MJG* 1: 108), 'a man of the kindest heart, and the most child-like simplicity' (*MJG* 2: 209), and 'a man of great feeling and sensibility [. . .] who suffered most severely from the afflictions which befel [*sic*] him' (*MJG* 2: 210). Grimaldi is further revealed to be a 'feeling' subject in more direct, corporeal ways. Jennifer Wallace, drawing correlations between Keats's body and readings of his life and work, asserts that 'Biographies are about bodies' (2003: 139) and bodies are also biographies in themselves, which physically encode the meaning of their subject's life. This physical encoding becomes a more permanent and lasting record of the history of a life and points to a more stable marker of identity that persists through the other changing roles.

In the *Memoirs*, the actor's body inscribes the pain and suffering that accompanies his life within the theatre, as Dickens documents the physical toll extracted by the multiple blows inflicted on the supposedly indestructible clown. By narrating each broken or burned limb that Grimaldi suffered on stage, Dickens uses Grimaldi's body as a text through which to tell his life, in a mirror of the corporeal semiotics of Grimaldi's mimed clown performances onstage.

Moreover, Dickens's observation that:

> [t]he spectators, who were convulsed with laughter while he was on the stage, little thought that while their applause was resounding through the house, he was suffering the most excruciating and horrible pains (*MJG* 2: 159)

further acknowledges how this self is a separate, hidden and suffering one that only becomes revealed in the act of (auto)biography. After falling through a trapdoor at Manchester he 'was terribly shaken and stunned by the fall, but quickly recovering himself' went on stage and 'played as though nothing had happened to discompose him', as the agony and 'pain wholly left him as he went on, in the excitement of the part'. After a similar accident in Liverpool, the 'excessive pain' is temporarily overcome as Grimaldi, 'warming with his exertions and kindling with the great applause he received [. . .] rallied successfully, and got through the part with flying colours' (*MJG* 2: 46–7). His professionalism as an indefatigable comic performer requires him to conceal his pain from the audience and play on through his injuries, and such an endurance is also wholly relational, since it requires constant positive affirmation to sustain this.

Lockhart shows how Scott reconciles his multiple identities, revealing that the public affairs of the world and the private concerns of his art are mutually dependent. Like Dickens, Lockhart inscribes

Scott's body within his biography by showing how Scott marked his illness on the pages of his journal and entwined the corporeal with the textual. This is done both directly, when he marks the pages with, for example, 'R. for Rheumatism, or RR. for Rheumatism Redoubled' (*MWS* 7: 12), and indirectly, as the legibility of his handwriting deteriorates with his failing health: after transcribing a diary entry recording a stroke of April 1831, Lockhart notes that 'The preceding paragraph has been deciphered with difficulty. The blow which it records was greatly more severe than any that had gone before it' (*MWS* 7: 277).

However, Lockhart only occasionally records any notion that Scott's weakening physical existence was a potential obstacle to his poetical one, and more often links Scott's suffering and his art in a positive way. This is seen in Scott's own creative and imaginative depictions of his illnesses and physical pains, which underscore the connection between the artist and the man, the poetic and the physical. In one visceral image, he describes 'my old enemy the cramp in my stomach' as similar to 'the process by which *the diel* would make one's *king's-hood* [a ruminant's 2nd stomach] into a *spleuchan* [a Highlander's tobacco-pouch]' (*MWS* 7: 305). The alternating conditions brought upon by conflicting medication produce 'a most disagreeable see-saw – a kind of pull-devil, pull-baker contention, the field of battle being my unfortunate *praecordia*' (*MWS* 4: 233).

Scott's physicality and creativity are also associated through the juxtaposition of his bodily state with his artistic one. In one letter, he immediately follows the miserable news of his physical condition ('a whoreson thickness of the blood, and a depression of spirits arising from the loss of friends') with ideas for a new literary project: 'a Scotch archer in the French King's guard, *tempore* Louis XI, the most picturesque of all times' (*MWS* 5: 237). After Scott had previously related a 'miserable catalogue of losses' (*MWS* 4: 332) to his son Thomas, including the death of his mother, his close friend Dr Rutherford, and Rutherford's sister, Lockhart adds the observation that 'On the 18th [December], in the midst of these accumulated afflictions, the romance of Ivanhoe made its appearance' (*MWS* 4: 336).

Scott's continuation of his work during periods of pain and illness also has a theatrical quality to it: we are told that 'spirit seemed to triumph altogether over matter – he arose from his couch and walked up and down the room, raising and lowering his voice, and as it were acting the parts' (*MWS* 4: 258). Indeed, Scott regularly adopts a role to conceal his private woes from his public appearances, and Lockhart repeats his theatrical metaphor when he tells us that Scott 'always exhibited great self-possession, and acted his part with wonderful power whenever visited, though he relapsed the next moment into the stupor from which strange voices had roused him' (*MWS* 7: 383–4). However, Lockhart is keen that this adoption of a suitable countenance for the occasion is not taken for a lack of real feeling on Scott's part; he points out that 'My meaning will be misunderstood if it be imagined from this picture that I suspected any hypocrisy, or an affectation of grief in the first instance' (*MWS* 6: 316), and always ensures that despite any multiplicity of the selves, the feeling self is seen to co-exist with the performing self. He justifies his inclusion of Scott's private journals within his *Life* as a means to reveal this more relatable, feeling self; for Lockhart, Scott's diary reveals that 'the dignified equanimity which characterised all his conversation with mankind' was actually a mask to hide 'the delicate sensibilities, the mysterious ups and downs, the wayward melancholy, and fantastic sunbeams of the poetical temperament' (*MWS* 7: 81) from many of his closest friends.

Both life narratives reach similar conclusions. Scott asserts that 'I am too much of a philosopher to be anxious about protracted life, which, with all its infirmities and deprivations, I have never considered as a blessing' (*MWS* 4: 105) and after acknowledging his own severe (and similar) misfortunes – illness, the loss of numerous friends and family, and bankruptcy – he reflects that 'if you compare me to Brutus in the harsher points of his character, you must also allow me some of his stoical fortitude "no man bears sorrow better"' (*MWS* 6: 273). Lockhart thus suggests the life provides as many morals to be read as Scott's art: 'the more the details of his personal history are revealed and studied, the more powerfully will that be found to inculcate the same great lessons with his works'; Scott's life teaches us how 'prosperity may be extended by beneficence, and adversity confronted by exertion', in a manner that rebukes the 'follies of the wise'. Thus Scott's character is 'beautifully purified and exalted in the passage through affliction to death' (*MWS* 7: 417).

While the pessimistic final line of the *Memoirs*, reminding the reader that 'the light and life of a brilliant theatre' can be 'exchanged in an instant for the gloom and sadness of a dull sickroom', is at variance with the Introduction's childlike revelry in the joy of the clown, the *Memoirs* as a whole celebrates the durability and resilience of more feeling selves over the artificial and contrived ones. Grimaldi constantly encounters figures that live *entirely* based on performance and impersonation, who must have seemed attractive to someone whose true feelings were regularly tested by personal tragedy, but his adherence to other, more persistent feeling selves ultimately prevails. In his Conclusion, after enumerating Grimaldi's principal misfortunes – the death of two wives, his son's reckless decline and premature death, his own physical decline – Dickens casts Grimaldi in one final role, that of a stoic and proto-existential Beckettian hero, who was 'patient and resigned under all these trials' and 'lived to recover his cheerfulness and peace'. Dickens finally offers Grimaldi's 'strong endurance of griefs so keen, and reverses so poignant' as proof that 'there are no afflictions which time will not soften, and fortitude overcome' (*MJG* 2: 211).

## Conclusion

Dickens's only previous pantomime clown, the drunken clown of 'The Stroller's Tale', is Grimaldi's antithesis, exhibiting a miserable, *anti*-relational life, beating his family who then desert him in his final dying moments, while his few sympathetic acquaintances toss him a few coins before turning away. Consequently, his final reminiscences are not of the kindness and support of others as Grimaldi's are, but are nightmares of 'the faces of men he knew, rendered hideous by gibing and mouthing', 'searing him with heated irons, and binding his head with cords till the blood started' (*PP* 53). He fundamentally misunderstands the place of the clown, whose method is not the soliloquy, but the to-and-fro repartee with the crowd, and who does not shun relationships, but seeks them out.

The relationality of Grimaldi's auto/biography thus mirrors the communal nature of his clown act, as both aim to create a shared, intimate space for audience and artist to co-exist. Like the figure of the clown, the biographical form is well situated to cultivate close bonds between itself and its reader, as the text simultaneously introduces the subject into the reader's home and draws the reader into the domestic space of the subject. Thus the biographical form was not only attractive to Dickens due to its experimental and generic inclusivity, but was also conducive to Dickens's own sense of his relationship with his readers, that 'personal and confidential position with them' that I described in Chapter 2. As *Household Words* aspired 'to live in the Household affections, and to be numbered among the Household thoughts, of our readers' (*HW* 1.1: 1), so the biographical project strove to reciprocate the reader's introduction into their homes. The relationality that Dickens emphasises so regularly here, then, is thus both a fully integrated mechanism employed to tell the life of Grimaldi in the most appropriate way for its subject, and a suitable vehicle for Dickens's own desire for a relational existence with his readers.

As this chapter has demonstrated, the *Memoirs of Joseph Grimaldi*, despite its commercial failure and critical neglect, deserves its place both within Grimaldi studies and Dickens studies. Sitting on the very edge of the cultural epochs of the Regency and Victorian periods, it embodies a transitional moment, by both acknowledging prior forms and adapting their conventions to reflect the intellectual cross-currents of the present moment.

Dickens moulds the themes and conventions of the stage memoir (as exemplified by Macklin and Lackington) to tell the life of a specialised theatrical performer in a manner that reflects his own deep interest in clowns and pantomime, but also in his own status as an artist. He also draws on the more recent, revisionist genre of domestic biography, the most familiar model being Lockhart's *Life of Scott*, to make his subject not a man apart from the world, but one deeply engaged within it.

This framing of events within a persistent commentary on the spiritual (and sometimes material) rewards of hard work and perseverance point towards a final biographical model operating within the *Memoirs*. Altick terms such life narrative 'the literature of success', whereby 'the biographer dedicated himself not merely to honouring a luminous memory, but also to turning his subject's character and achievements into an exemplum' (1966: 147). As other Dickens scholars have briefly noted, such lessons of course have clear significance for Dickens's own life, and the *Memoirs* becomes, to adopt Janet Beizer's term, 'bio-autography' (2008: 3), that is, a biography that is written with the author's own autobiography in mind, anticipating the more overt narratives of improvement, such as Samuel Smiles's, that the later nineteenth century would provide.

Chapter 5

# George Cruikshank as Co-Biographer of the *Memoirs*

## Introduction

Cruikshank's pictorial contribution to the *Memoirs* has divided critics as much as Dickens's. The *Monthly Magazine* called the twelve illustrations 'some of the most felicitous in design and perfect in execution that have ever emanated from the pencil of that well-known artist' ([Anon.] 1838h: 435) and William J. Thoms in *Bentley's Miscellany* described these 'sketches' as 'admirable' (1838: 623), recalling their earlier successful collaboration. For the *Athenaeum* they were 'capital, full of character, spirit and fun' ([Anon.] 1838d: 165) and Dickens offered his own tribute in his Introduction, perhaps inevitably asserting that 'the good right hand of GEORGE CRUIKSHANK [. . .] has seldom been better exercised' (*MJG* 1: xi). However, the unstintingly critical *Gentleman's Magazine* declared that, due to Dickens's mediocre text, 'the inimitable Cruikshank [. . .] has not produced a single illustration worthy [*sic*] his abilities' ([Anon.] 1838j: 416). More recently David Mayer has called them 'second rate and of small theatrical interest' (2003: 54), a comment which epitomises the tone of those few recent studies that even consider the illustrations at all.

The previous chapter described how Dickens presented Grimaldi's life as 'relational', based on his subject's interaction with his immediate environment, his interdependence with others, and the multiple related 'lives' that he led. In this chapter, I want to present George Cruikshank as another 'significant other' and moreover the co-biographer of Grimaldi's life, developing the link that Robert Patten makes between Cruikshank's graphic art and the practice of life writing, as he describes 'the growth of caricature' as 'another manifestation of the Romantic movement, [and its] exploration of individuality and difference' (1992: 70). Cruikshank's accompanying plates reflect his long creative and personal relationship with the subject, which began in the early 1800s. Grimaldi was both his Islington neighbour and fellow member of his 'Crib' drinking club, and he had already depicted him in the satirical song heads 'Me and My Neddy' and 'All the World's In Paris', and as Napoleon in a sketch lampooning the events of the Napoleonic Wars ('The Narrow Escape, or Boney's Grand Leap a la Grimaldi').

I will argue that his *Memoirs* illustrations merit equal status to Dickens's text, with which they interact in a meaningful dialogue that not only reflects the period's looser delineation between the written and pictorial (Cruikshank was one of *Fraser's* 'Literary Characters' in 1833), but also the symbiotic relationship between theatrical and pictorial traditions, as Cruikshank supports Dickens's textual motif of theatricality (as he had in *Sketches*). An instructive approach for interpreting and contextualising these plates is suggested by Martin Meisel, whose *Realizations* (1983) explores the interplay between word and image. Meisel feels that the nineteenth century saw an 'extraordinary dialogue of literary and pictorial forms' moving between these twin impulses of 'interpretive re-creation' (illustration) and 'giving concrete perceptual form to a literary text' (realisation) (1983: 32). Cruikshank's figures draw on a range of literary, graphic and theatrical representations, which form part of a shared vocabulary of signs exchanged and understood by artists, actors, novelists, playwrights and poets. This vocabulary is used in what Deborah Vlock calls the 'cultural text upon which popular culture consumers drew in processing their aesthetic experiences' (1998: 19).

Such close interrelations also complicate the notion of authorship and further support the role of Cruikshank as co-biographer. Both Dickens and Cruikshank had been co-authors before – Dickens was initially engaged on *Pickwick* as textual illustrator of Seymour's sporting plates and Cruikshank had provided pictorial material to accompany Pierce Egan's text in *Life of London* (1821). For *The Tower of London* (1840) he suggested storylines and provided the writer W. H. Ainsworth with salient details of plates so that he could write complementary text, and controversially claimed greater credit for *Oliver Twist* than traditionally ascribed to him. While I will not evaluate those claims here, his pictures undoubtedly make a significant contribution towards the overall meaning of these works.

It is also worth remembering that while Boz's name appeared largest on the title page of the *Memoirs*, Cruikshank's name carried the greater weight in early 1838. He was a veteran of around thirty years of published illustrations, while Dickens's literary career amounted to less than five years. To the *Monthly Magazine*, he was the 'well-known artist', in the *Gentleman's Magazine*, it was Cruikshank who was billed as 'the inimitable' rather than Dickens and *The Spectator* in December 1836 could offer no greater praise for Dickens than by defining him as 'the CRUIKSHANK of writers' ([Anon.] 1836: 16).

In his contemporaneous work with 'Phiz' on *Pickwick Papers*, Dickens – as the more established partner – had been more prescriptive in his expectations of the illustrations, but his work with Cruikshank operated according to a different dynamic. For the *Sketches*, Cruikshank would read the complete text and then choose the most interesting to illustrate; as he outlines in an unsent letter of complaint to the publishers, he fully expected 'to have the choise [*sic*] of a quantity of "Sketches" to select subjects from – & not to be *compeled* [*sic*] to *illustrate those only which might be sent as a matter of course*' (Patten 1996: 30). Richard L. Stein characterises their working relationship as an entwined one, as 'writer and illustrator collaborated with some care on the drawings, Dickens advising and, in some cases, revising, Cruikshank reading and perhaps even attempting to rewrite' (1980: 28) and Patten feels that this became a 'tug-of-war between the author's sensibility and the artist's'. The final plates became 'not *representations* of the text, but *responses* to it', and to other stimuli, specifically: 'the conventions shaping verbal and visual *mimesis*' and 'the phenomena of London by which Dickens and Cruikshank were differently affected' (1996: 38). However, what made this relationship work was not what made the two men different, but what they had in common.

## Correspondences

The *Memoirs* was one of Dickens's four collaborations with the artist, and while their working method on the *Sketches* might have been more combative in nature, the conjunction of Grimaldi, Cruikshank and Dickens was a harmonious one. Four key commonalities in style and approach – a radical spirit, a broad audience, a theatrical sensibility and an interest in animism – merit brief exploration here, as they will be significant in what follows.

*Blackwood's Edinburgh Magazine* felt that Cruikshank 'will do anything he is paid for' and 'is quite contented to dine off the proceeds of a "George IV" today and those of a "Hone" or a "Cobbett" tomorrow', but this general impression of political opportunism belies Cruikshank's often radical sensibility (['Christopher North'] 1823: 18). Sally Ledger (2007) has comprehensively outlined Dickens's debt to the radical literature and culture of the early nineteenth century, and Cruikshank acts as an important bridge between this Dickensian radicalism and the sort of radical imagination that Grimaldi shared with figures such as Leigh Hunt (as I described earlier). Cruikshank also worked with Hone on the principal propaganda wars between 1815 and 1821 and at the height of their popularity, their co-authored pamphlets sold over 100,000 copies. Like other radical forms, Cruikshank's pictures combined physical comedy with a more intellectual humour and operated in a liminal space between low and high culture – just like pantomime.

As principal caricaturist on the satirical magazine *The Scourge, or Monthly Expositor of Imposture and Folly* (1811–16) Cruikshank devised graphic responses to the same concerns that Grimaldi was contemporaneously exploring in the theatre, ranging from the local (profiteering brewers, the Four-in-Hand Club and spiritual hoaxers) to the international (the Napoleonic wars and diplomatic relations with America). Outside of *Scourge* work, their work cross-fertilised elsewhere, as both explored through print and performance such topics such as comically grotesque 'frenchified' fashions, the craze for velocipedes and the disruption caused by the installation of new gas lighting. It is therefore unsurprising that Thackeray describes the effect of Cruikshank's prints in the same bodily terms used to explain the effect of Grimaldi's humour:

> There must be no smiling with Cruikshank. A man who does not laugh outright is a dullard, and has no heart [. . .] there are some of Cruikshank's designs which have the blessed faculty of creating laughter as often as you see them. (1840: 7)

There were also clear correspondences in the way that Cruikshank and Dickens circulated their work to reach a broad audience. At one end of the social scale, Cruikshank sold copies of prints through dealers' shops in the West End, which catered, in Patten's words, 'to all the nobs', who bought individual prints or sets, or rented 'circulating portfolios' for country house entertainment (1983: 332–3). At the other end, more accessible public exhibitions were held for a small fee at the larger dealers' premises, whose large shop windows also provided free displays for people on the street (as memorably captured in James

Gillray's *Very Slippy-Weather* [1808]). Thackeray describes the operation of such mechanisms when he observes how '[t]here used to be a crowd round the window in those days of grinning, good-natured mechanics, who spelt the songs, and spoke them out for the benefit of the company, and who received the points of the humour with a sympathising roar' (1840: 6–7) and also how a series of prints might 'purchased by a joint stock company of boys, each drawing lots afterwards for the separate prints, and taking his choice in rotation' (1840: 5).

As Thackeray's experiences attest, Cruikshank's great successes with Hone derived from his blending their politics with more popular sources of entertainment, such as the theatre and comic songs, and childlike devices such as nursery rhymes and toys. His images were also reproduced on other commercial products, such as broadsides, lottery tickets, posters, pottery and walking sticks. From nobs to mobs then, Cruikshank's prints reached the same wide audiences that Dickens's serials would reach during their publication, and became so prominent in the popular consciousness that, as Patten has argued, they became part of the animus for a range of popular agitation, such as the disruption of ministerial elections, arrests on parliamentary authority and the O. P. Riots of 1809.

Patten describes how Cruikshank's lifelong interest in the theatre shaped his illustrative style, as he 'cast his political and social commentary in dramatic terms' and became 'a dramatist in pictures' (1992: 35). This supports Meisel's description of the nineteenth-century play as the 'meeting place of story and picture' (1983: 3) and can be extended to include Grimaldi's *Memoirs*, which is the meeting-place of theatre and picture. In terms of pantomimic effects specifically, Cruikshank shared an interest in animism with Grimaldi and Dickens, which belies G. K. Chesterton's observation that no illustrator other than Phiz 'ever created the true Dickens atmosphere, in which clerks are clerks and yet at the same time elves' (1909: 74). Louis James identifies in Cruikshank's prints a 'fertile, at times overburdening, inventiveness [. . .] a romantic imagination that constantly animates objects, a dramatic energy that flows round his best designs making them dance into life' (1978: 109). This is evident in illustrations such as *London Going Out of Town or The March of Bricks and Mortar* (1830); described by William Feaver as 'animism running amuck' (1974: 5), the tools and materials of construction are formed into nightmarish composite figures to launch an assault on the English countryside. Similarly *The Triumph of Cupid: A Reverie* (1845) depicts, *à la Dickens's Dream*, the self-aware illustrator surrounded by the products of his imagination, including living tablecloths, and anthropomorphic fire tongs, shovels and pokers. Such 'animated' images, whereby one object is used to evoke a similar one for comic effect (a hod of bricks for a human face, the metal 'legs' of fire tongs for human ones and so on) creates a pictorial analogue for Grimaldi's method, but as Patten suggests, also offers up the rich creative possibilities that come from such a conflation of multiple discourses:

> the similarity of [a landlady's] gown to [a] cabbage might suggest some unflattering things about the landlady, since 'cabbage' – the scraps of cloth (cut away when making a garment) that tailors traditionally claimed as their property – had become schoolboy slang for pilfering or cribbing. Sociological, narratological, visual, and moral implications are thus fused by the artist's design to be deciphered by the knowledgeable observer. (1992: 279)

## The *Memoirs* Illustrations

Cruikshank created the twelve main illustrations of the *Memoirs* in January 1838, based on the main body of Dickens's text that he received at the start of the month. Five of these illustrate scenes from the text by emphasising the theatrical and performative nature of offstage life ('Master Joey Going to Visit his Godpapa', 'A Bit of Pantomime off the Stage', 'Appearing in Public', 'The Wager' and 'The Barber's Shop'), and are supported by another four that directly realise actions on the stage ('Joe's Unexpected Visit to the Pit at Sadler's Wells', 'A Startling Effect', 'Live Properties' and 'The Last Song'). The remaining three also maintain the theatrical theme by comfortably lending themselves to *tableaux* ('Mr Mackintosh's Covey', 'Like Master like Man' and 'Grimaldi's Kindness to the Giants'), although the last two contribute relatively little here.

The first group is the most interesting, occupying an intermediate position neither of the stage nor entirely apart from it. In these pictures Cruikshank both realises the incidents described in Dickens's text and extends the work's overarching theme of the *theatrum mundi*. Examining Cruikshank's pictures for *Sketches by Boz*, such as those for 'The Tuggs's at Ramsgate' and 'Mr Minns and his Cousin', Hillis Miller identifies a tension between this theatricality ('the pantomime violence of gesture, expression, and movement' and its associated stylised poses) and the desire for mimesis, whereby Cruikshank's figures are 'caught frozen in unstable gestures or poses' within *tableaux*, adopting 'a gesture or pose that could last only an instant and then would pass, never to return' (1971: 57).

This use of the *tableau* is something that Cruikshank refined through the course of his career as an illustrator. Jonathan Hill characterises Cruikshank's work with Dickens as in a 'vignette' style based around 'small scale, graphic minutiae, comic or grotesque mood, [and the] lack of any clearly delineated border', and – although Cruikshank's illustrations for *Oliver Twist* had already been realised in the *tableaux* of three separate dramatisations (Charles Zachary Barnett's, George Almar's and Thomas Hailes Lacy's) – feels that he only establishes a '*tableau*' style more directly derived from theatrical devices and aesthetics when he later worked with Ainsworth (1980: 433). However, I will show that there are clear precedents in his *Memoirs* work, which represents a proving ground for this new technique and an important transition point between these two distinct styles.

One of the earliest pictures in the *Memoirs*, 'Master Joey Going to Visit his Godpapa', underscores the themes of the formative childhood episode I explored in the last chapter, in which he goes to visit his grandfather dressed as 'a gentleman' but is treated with derision rather than admiration by the passing public. The small figure of Joe strikes an attitude appropriate to his gentleman's costume, and which distinguishes him from the general crowd. He holds his head upright, looking straight forward and showing off his outfit, lavishly described in the text as a 'green coat, embroidered with [. . .] artificial flowers', 'a little cane in his hand, which he switched to and fro as our clowns may do now', along with accessories such as 'a small watch set with diamonds – theatrical, we suppose' (*MJG* 1: 20–1). This costume marks him off from the other figures, just as his decorative cane contrasts with the artisanal tools carried by the more proletarian boys (Fig. 5.1).

The pavement forms a stage on which he is observed by the mingled audience of people and is the first example of Cruikshank's technique of heightening the sense of theatricality by registering the presence of an audience. James has suggested how, in *Sketches by Boz*, Cruikshank complemented Dickens's textual perspective of the distanced observer by including groups of onlookers (including himself) and also portraits or statues which subtly act as silent, still observers, and Cruikshank continues this method in the *Memoirs*.

**Figure 5.1** George Cruikshank, 'Master Joey Going to Visit his Godpapa', *Memoirs of Joseph Grimaldi*. Reproduced by courtesy of Charles Dickens Museum, London.

The audience here is heterogeneous, including a woman clasping her hands together, two taller and more well-to-do figures towards the rear reviewing the spectacle before them, and the central, largest observer, whose jaunty hat, coloured nose and slightly irregular eyes all suggest inebriation. In isolation, Joe's stance denotes control and strength, but when read as part of the larger scene – his central position enclosed on all sides by the mob, railings, closed door and even a brick wall in the background – he is imprisoned within this public space at the mercy of his audience's interpretation.

Cruikshank had produced a similar illustration a few months earlier, for Part 7 of *Oliver Twist* in September 1837's *Bentley's Miscellany*, and when viewed as a pair one can see how both support the shared interests of these contiguous texts – the development of character through performance and the interpretation of this performance in the ensuing interpersonal relations. In Dickens's text, one of Brownlow's earliest acts to gentrify Oliver is to dress him in 'a complete new suit, and a new cap, and a new pair of shoes' (*OT* 96). But this performance fails like young Joey's, as the crowd (led by Sikes and Nancy) incorrectly interpret his role and cast him as a 'young wretch' and a 'little brute' (*OT* 107). Oliver is overcome both physically and by 'the conviction of the bystanders that he really was the hardened little wretch he was described to be' (*OT* 108).

Comparing Cruikshank's accompanying image, 'Oliver Claimed by his Affectionate Friends' with the *Memoirs* illustration, the composed posture of young Grimaldi is replaced by a frightened child desperately clutching Brownlow's books, which are another symbolic prop of a more 'gentlemanly' life. The genteel suburbs of the *Memoirs* are replaced by the squalid doorway of a beer-shop (whose gaudy signage provides the overarching frame) and the figures are more tightly closed around the boy. This time the threat of the audience becoming the mob is realised as Oliver is seized by Nancy and the heavy-drinking Bill Sikes – a distortion of the gentler drunken figure of the *Memoirs* illustration (Fig. 5.2).

Dickens and Cruikshank return to this idea of Grimaldi's dependence on the audience-mob and their interpretations in a later scene (also described earlier), when Grimaldi is recognised in the street and must satisfy the mob by performing 'in character'. In 'Appearing in Public' Cruikshank develops these textual themes by conflating the audience for a performance and the crowd in the street into a single group. Within his 'stage'-coach, Joe is framed and narrowly constrained once again, with the stage formed by the window from which he leans out. This is the focal point for every other figure, from

**Figure 5.2** George Cruikshank, 'Oliver Claimed by his Affectionate Friends', *Oliver Twist*. Reproduced by courtesy of Charles Dickens Museum, London.

the 'groundlings' running alongside to the more privileged spectators seated either side of the coach (Fig. 5.3).

Another example of Grimaldi performing for an audience offstage is seen in 'The Barber's Shop', which illustrates the scene in which Grimaldi visits the barber for a shave (and appears on the front cover

**Figure 5.3** George Cruikshank, 'Appearing in Public', *Memoirs of Joseph Grimaldi*. Reproduced by courtesy of Charles Dickens Museum, London.

of this book). Here Cruikshank reworks the tropes of 'Appearing in Public', as Grimaldi is the sole focus of the laughing onlookers' attention and the cut-away view creates the outline of a proscenium arch and stage set.

This double structure of spectatorship, whereby we observe within Cruikshank's picture one or more other observers, creates what Baudelaire calls 'the absolute comic', whereby we see 'in a single consciousness or structure both the laugher and the object of his laughter' (Miller 1971: 65). This became a particularly significant and emblematic scene for both Grimaldi and Cruikshank: Grimaldi reworked it into a pantomime routine, while Cruikshank extended and amplified its meaning in a contemporaneous watercolour.

This was pantomime outside the theatre, then, a theme which directly informs the title of another illustration, 'A Bit of Pantomime off the Stage', in which the gravity of life is leavened by the revelation of an underlying humorous theatricality. It captures the moment at which, during a pursuit of several burglars from his Pentonville home, Grimaldi 'set off at full speed' into the chase, but 'was stopped in the very outset of his career, by tumbling over a cow, which was lying on the ground'. As I described in Chapter 4, we are told that during this 'involuntary pantomimic feat' 'he would most probably have cut his own head off with the weapon he carried, if his theatrical practice as a fencer had not taught him to carry edge tools with caution' (*MJG* 1: 62).

While Grimaldi here utilises his stage skills offstage to survive in the real world, he is presented upside down in a typical 'topsy turvy' clown position; coupled with the alarmed look on his face, this contrasts humorously with the sedateness of the cow. The darkness of the picture is only alleviated by the lightness of Grimaldi's head, which in its unusual position close to the ground appears to be separated from his body. Dickens elsewhere uses the spectacle of a disembodied head to suggest hauntings: the Ghost of Christmas Past transmutes from 'being now a thing with one arm, now with one leg, now with twenty legs, now a pair of legs without a head, now a head without a body' (*CC* 55), while in *Our Mutual Friend* Eugene Wrayburn's tormented pursuer Bradley Headstone undergoes a similar transformation as 'looking like [. . .] a haggard head suspended in the air; so completely did the force of his expression cancel his figure' (*OMF* 534). Here, however, Cruikshank's illustration supports the text's overall tenor of a potentially serious scene comically deflated by a slapstick beheading of the clown.

Even 'The Wager', which illustrates one of Grimaldi's entertaining escapades in the countryside in which he 'lost a guinea wager in a somewhat ludicrous manner', underscores the theme of performance (*MJG* 1: 126). In the text, Grimaldi's travelling companion prevents a horse-rider from passing their carriage (thus winning the guinea) by putting on another stage-coach show. He adopts the appropriate appearance and attitude to generate the required reaction of fear in the rider by 'assuming a ferocious countenance and menacing air' (*MJG* 1: 128) and waving his pistol at the rider to keep him at a distance behind them.

'The Wager' and 'Appearing in Public' also echo the Pickwick Club's transformation of coaches into mobile theatres, as passengers took their licence to perform from their freedom of movement and separation from the means of motion. Cruikshank occasionally indulged in such performances himself: Dickens once described how, after a party in Greenwich celebrating his return from America, Cruikshank stood on his head on the cab ride home, singing comic songs 'to the great delight of the loose Midnight Loungers in Regent Street' (*LCD* 3: 264). He further elaborated how 'after singing all manner of maniac songs' Cruikshank 'wound up the entertainment by coming home (six miles) in a little open phaeton of mine, *on his head* – to the mingled delight and indignation of the metropolitan police' (*LCD* 3: 292).

Cruikshank's final picture for the *Memoirs*, 'The Last Song', firmly re-establishes Grimaldi as a theatrical performer, but its clear visual correspondences with 'The Barber's Shop' – the amused members of the front row throwing their heads back in laughter, and his positioning of his hands and legs as he sits centre stage – also reasserts the porous line between onstage and offstage, and suggests that Grimaldi could perform on a variety of stages (Fig. 5.4).

'The Last Song' also neatly bridges those illustrations that reinforce the themes of theatricality in a non-theatrical setting and those that specifically realise action onstage. It creates a circularity with the first illustration of the *Memoirs*, 'Master Joe's Unexpected Visit to the Pit' (Fig. 5.5). This picture accompanies Dickens's description of Grimaldi's early childhood performances in which he was led onto stage on a chain by his father, who then swung him round his head. However, on one occasion the chain snapped, and Grimaldi was 'hurled a considerable distance into the pit' (*MJG* 1: 19). This picture symbolically represents Grimaldi's literal irruption from the stage world into the real life and the breaking through the 'fourth

**Figure 5.4** George Cruikshank, 'The Last Song', *Memoirs of Joseph Grimaldi*. Reproduced by courtesy of Charles Dickens Museum, London.

**Figure 5.5** George Cruikshank, 'Master Joe's Unexpected Visit to the Pit', *Memoirs of Joseph Grimaldi*. Reproduced by courtesy of Charles Dickens Museum, London.

wall' which dominates Dickens's depiction of his life. It also captures the moment at which the connecting cord between the infant Grimaldi and his more significant parent is severed: as a partially formed and featureless figure in the centre of this composition, he is a *tabula rasa* on which his audience's reactions and impressions will be written, establishing and modifying his identity throughout his life. By contrast, in 'The Last Song', Cruikshank registers Grimaldi's achievements by giving him greater control of the scene, placing him composedly in the centre of the stage rather than flying off it, and in the presence of a larger audience, packing more figures into the boxes and in the wings.

'Live Properties' depicts Grimaldi onstage at a midpoint between these illustrations and subtly marks the progress of his career by 1808. It illustrates the humorous consequences when the mischievous manager of a provincial theatre provides Grimaldi with live animals – a pig, two ducks and a goose – rather than prop ones. Although initially surprised, Grimaldi demonstrates his improvisatory powers by successfully incorporating them into his act.

As Cruikshank shows, despite the manager's attempt to 'upstage' him, Grimaldi occupies centre front stage, with the other three characters positioned in a manner that foregrounds the clown's role. As well as indicating Clown's role in the narrative, standing between the two lovers, this configuration renders the others as slight figures in the background, making them subordinate 'live properties' as well – the diminutive Harlequin lurks in the wings behind a tree, while Columbine and Pantaloon are turned away from us.

The final theatrical picture, 'A Startling Effect', may seem an unusual topic for a plate in Grimaldi's *Life*, since it does not include him at all, but it does give us another demonstration of the role of the clown in undermining more serious treatments of life. It illustrates a further 'ludicrous anecdote' (*MJG* 1: 145) from Grimaldi's reminiscences in which the comic actor 'Jew Davis' upstages the main star Kemble in a production of *Hamlet*. Kemble had earlier criticised Davis for his levity and grimace-making during their 'serious' scenes, but on this occasion Davis replaces his 'comic grimaces' for 'mock terror' and 'an expression of intense terror', which cause similar amusement and deflate Kemble's earnestness (*MJG* 1: 147). Kemble was in fact one of Cruikshank's regular targets, and the main subject of his Hogarthian series of prints *The Stroller's Progress* (1809). Cruikshank also worked with his father on at least fourteen satirical prints unsympathetic to Kemble during the O. P. Riots between October and November 1809, and the inclusion of this picture in the *Memoirs* is a clear indicator of Cruikshank's influence on the work.

In 'A Startling Effect', Cruikshank divides our attention between serious and comic acting, and realises contemporary theatre's visual aesthetic through the postures of its protagonists. Actors were trained to form triangles through deliberate positioning of their bodies and heads, and while Kemble demonstrates the classical form, Davis mockingly mirrors it with an inverted triangle. In a further reflection of the text's wider themes, the picture also operates along the fine margin between the real world (including the dirt, tomb, skull and so on) and the performing (the curtains, the proscenium arch and the neatly cut hole representing the grave). What we see is 'staged' (in other words, occurs on a stage) but Davis's action (and Kemble's reaction to it) are both extemporised, blurring distinctions again.

Distinctions are also blurred in the final illustration I will consider here, 'Mr Mackintosh's Covey', which elaborates on the themes of social play-acting, the 'assumption' of roles, and the dangers of this assumption. One day, Grimaldi and his acting friend Bologna are invited to the countryside by the con-man Mackintosh. While there, they are fooled into shooting birds on another man's estate, mistakenly believing they are Mackintosh's (Fig. 5.6).

This was a popular scenario for sporting sketches of hapless city types playing at countrymen for the day and mocked their folly in attempting to play an inappropriate role. The slyly grinning Mackintosh points out his assumed game birds from a safe distance to the two incredulous gulls. Bologna's stance, clutching his gun tightly to his chest, and standing nervously on tiptoe, carries strong visual resonances with one of Seymour's *Humorous Sketches,* 'I'm Dem'd if I Can Ever Hit 'em', which also includes a field of birds and an amused farmer within its composition. In presenting a scenario by which the city dwellers are duped by the countrymen, this episode represents an inversion of the typical scenario of Grimaldi's urban comedy, in which the country bumpkin is deceived by the streetwise clown, as Clown's offstage existence echoes his onstage life once again.

## Conclusion

When Dickens sent John Britton a copy of the *Memoirs* in June 1850, he told him that he was not 'very proud' of the work and wrote it 'chiefly to please Cruikshank' (*LCD* 6, 97). While this should be read cautiously within Dickens's later strategy of distancing himself from

**Figure 5.6** George Cruikshank, 'Mr Mackintosh's Covey', *Memoirs of Joseph Grimaldi*. Reproduced by courtesy of Charles Dickens Museum, London.

his earlier unsuccessful apprentice work, it nonetheless acknowledges the instrumentality of the man who should be regarded as his co-biographer.

Thackeray (who had auditioned for the role of *Pickwick*'s illustrator) similarly privileged illustrator over writer in his 1840 encomium on Cruikshank, in which he recognises that while one can appreciate 'the works and genius of Mr Dickens', 'we are sure he would admit as readily as any man the wonderful assistance that he has derived from the artist'. According to Thackeray, Cruikshank 'has given us the portraits of [Dickens's'] ideal personages, and made them familiar to all the world' so that they 'remain impressed on the memory, which otherwise would have no hold upon them' and 'become personal acquaintances with each of us' (1840: 53). For Thackeray, Dickens may conjure the originating image or outline sketch, but it is Cruikshank who fills in the detail, vivifies the figures and leaves us our lasting impression of them, and this is certainly true in the case of the *Memoirs*. Not for the first (or indeed last) time, the veteran Cruikshank makes a complex and visually sophisticated response to the work of this promising young writer, in a manner that both enriches the meaning of the text but also provides Cruikshank with a means to provide a multi-layered tribute to his friend Grimaldi's career.

# Part III: The Clown at Large

Chapter 6

# The Gluttonous Clown

## Introduction

The *Memoirs* serves up a number of culinary anecdotes, including one proto-absurdist episode in which Grimaldi orders the same dish of Newcastle 'pickled salmon' in his hotel every night, only to be served a different dish – a mutton cutlet, a rump-steak and a veal cutlet – each time. The manager explains that as all pickled salmon came from London, his waiter had no idea what was wanted, and so 'determined not to confess his ignorance, had resolved to try all of the dishes in the general request until he came to the right one' (*MJG* 2: 135). As we saw in Chapter 4, on another trip his parsimonious companion Bologna tries to save money by ordering 'Welsh rare-bit' every night, only to be billed the same price as Grimaldi's 'warm dish of game or poultry', as the hotel's rule was to charge the same price regardless of the dish.

Such episodes support the text's wider themes: when Grimaldi dines with Lord Byron, he is tricked into eating more than he can manage, including a bizarre dish of apple pie with fish sauce, in a narrative that continues the recurrent theme of the *theatrum mundi* but also parallels both the excessive and unusual consumption of Grimaldi's performances. These onstage and offstage gustatory performances rely on the phenomenon of the bodily grotesque for their effect. Philip Thomson describes the grotesque as 'a clash between incompatible reactions – laughter on the one hand, horror or disgust on the other' (1972: 2) and the scene at Byron's provokes amusement and revulsion in equal measure. The comic incongruity of the meal itself (sweet apple pie and sour soy sauce) and the image of Grimaldi gamely working through Byron's endless dinner are held in a delicate balance with the repellent taste of the pie and sauce, Grimaldi's nausea and bloatedness, and our sympathy at his manipulation by a powerful host.

Mikhail Bakhtin notes that 'eating and drinking are [. . .] significant manifestations' (1968: 281) of the bodily grotesque and during what he calls the 'formalization of carnival-grotesque images' (1968: 34), such manifestations migrated from the street spectacles of folk culture into a variety of more formal arena including theatre and literature. This chapter will show how the performances of Grimaldi and the works of Dickens embody this formalisation: Grimaldi's comically excessive consumption was a popular mainstay, articulated through both the predictable rhythms of harlequinade set-pieces and more widely through the medium of popular print, while Dickens makes the clown's grotesque body a tangible presence within the 'clownish' characters and comic situations of a number of his works.

Dickens's association with the grotesque (particularly grotesque realism) has proved to be a popular and engaging line of study with Michael Hollington's *Dickens and the Grotesque* (1984) as the landmark study. William Axton's discussion of Dickens's theatricality is founded on his contention that the 'grotesque style is marked by a host of techniques identical with those of the nineteenth-century theater and of Charles Dickens' works' (1966: 28), but although Axton acknowledges Dickens's debt to the pantomime for this sense of the grotesque, he gives insufficient consideration to the centrality of Clown. Moreover, most studies focus on the 'shock effect' of the grotesque, whereby its conflicting feelings engender a sense of alienation that forces the spectator or reader to re-examine their world afresh. Consequently, the negative effects of the grotesque have been privileged over any positive ones, yet Bakhtin conceives the bodily grotesque as a primarily celebratory form, which Thomson also supports when he calls eating and drinking an expression of 'the body and bodily excesses [. . .] in an uninhibited, outrageous but essentially joyous fashion' (1972: 56).

In fact, both Grimaldi and Dickens use it to strike a more ambiguous tone, reflecting the complexity of grotesque humour from a split position that replicates the broader ambiguousness of pantomime comedy. On the one hand, they use the bodily grotesque quasi-satirically, to demonstrate the economic consequences of unpaid consumption and provoke our derisive laughter from a position of superiority. As Leigh Hunt's 'practical satirist', Grimaldi uses the licence of pantomime performance to push 'the national vice of stuffing' to extreme and ridiculous limits as he 'gulped down a tray of tarts, or made a

Gargantuan meal of pies, or crammed more food into his capacious pockets' (Findlater 1978: 158–9). This deployment of the grotesque accords with Bergson's view of comedy as a corrective instrument, whereby laughter is 'a social gesture that singles out and represses a special kind of absentmindedness in men and in events' (1956: 117) and the means by which 'society avenges itself for the liberties taken with it' (1956: 187). Arthur Clayborough similarly observes how Dickens's grotesque humour operates in a Bergsonian manner to flatter the reader 'into feeling an effortless sense of superiority' (1965: 233) as we view his imperfect figures from our 'Olympian height' (1965: 221). For Clayborough, Dickens's comic grotesquerie is 'a symptom of detachment' (1965: 232), which echoes Bergson's insistence on an emotionless state as a prerequisite for laughter. While Bakhtin and Wylie Sypher have noted the limits of Bergson's analysis, when supported by readings such as Clayborough's he offers a persuasive interpretation of the grotesque comedy of both Grimaldi and Dickens.

However, on the other hand, 'The Pantomime of Life' also warns us of adopting a wholly Bergsonian interpretation when Dickens notes that those who laugh the loudest at the gullible dupes onstage are the same people who show the most indignation when they are (inevitably) fooled in real life. Here Grimaldi and Dickens can be said to generate Bakhtin's 'carnival laughter' which is 'universal in scope [. . .] directed to all and everyone, including the carnival's participants', and is both 'triumphant' and 'deriding' (1968: 11–12). Their presentation of food and its excessive consumers prompts us to laugh in a more inclusive way as we embrace their comic everyman figures in all their gustatory glory, and the 'unquenchable vitality of man gushes up from the lower strata' in Rabelaisian style (Sypher 1956: 208).

In *The Stones of Venice* (1851–3) John Ruskin divides the grotesque into the 'pure' or 'noble' and the 'false' or 'ignoble', whereby the pure grotesque is 'the expression of the *repose* or play of a *serious* mind' while the false grotesque is 'the result of the *full exertion* of a *frivolous* one' (1907 3: 158). Dickens's association with satirical writing leads Ruskin to place him in the latter category, yet the celebrations of bodily appetites that both Grimaldi and Dickens present are far from frivolous and positively articulate what it is to be fully human, in a manner that rebukes Ruskin's categorisation, whereby the pure artist focuses on 'man's tragic and imperfect nature' (Thomson 1972: 15).

In this chapter I will explore a number of different perspectives and discourses through which both Grimaldi and Dickens examined food and the bodily grotesque, and identify significant correspondences between the two creators. This chapter will build upon my previous work on the gluttonous clown: in *Dickens and the Imagined Child*, I explored a number of the exaggerated feats of eating and drinking performed by Grimaldi's Clown and Dickens's clownish characters, and focused on Christmas as one of the central confluences of the ideas of gluttony, pantomime and Dickens.

Section 2 of this chapter positions the significance of excessive consumption within popular conceptions of Grimaldi and the wider meaning of his act as a cultural commentary. This provides the framework through which I will delineate Dickens's presentation of the greedy clown. Section 3 then analyses the exaggerated and fantastical feats of eating and drinking performed by Grimaldi's Clown and Dickens's clownish characters. Here I demonstrate how figures like Quilp, in depicting the bodily grotesque, extend their bodies beyond their normal limits and by pushing boundaries and celebrating the bodily also move towards a sexualisation of the act of eating, as a different kind of flesh becomes desirable.

Section 4 returns to the excesses of Christmas, and the bodily grotesque's association with the festive and carnival tradition, describing how both Grimaldi and Dickens work within this tradition of public bodily display and celebration by using scenes in market places and other common spaces to similarly celebrate the grotesque.

The final section moves from the celebratory to the admonitory to initially show how the excessive consumption within Grimaldi's act can also be situated within other contemporary debates around the wasteful consumer, which include correspondent visual depictions of the grotesque. Finally, I show how Dickens adapts this theme to explore the alternative value of food as communal celebration, in opposition to corrosive effects of selfish wastefulness.

## The Importance of Clownish Consumption

The centrality of excessive consumption to Grimaldi's art, and its pervasiveness in the reception of his work is aptly illustrated in *The Drama*'s aforementioned catalogue of Grimaldi's repertoire, in which around a third of his accomplishments are related to ingestion of some kind. Grimaldi steals and eats the wares of a pieman, opens oysters, eats puddings and takes snuff, and all 'in so admirably humorous and extravagantly natural a manner' ([Smith] 1822: 59); this epithet epitomises the grotesque's marriage of the fantastic and the real, whereby Clown only disorients us, rather than abandoning us entirely to fairytale.

He consumed his food and drink during the harlequinade, which incorporated numerous food-related images, characters and locations. For example, in *The Astrologer or Harlequin and Moore's Almanack* (Sadler's Wells, 1810), the harlequinade scene in 'A Pastry Cook's Shop' included set-pieces called 'Toad in a Hole', 'Cherry Bounce' and 'Raspberry Brandy', while a later scene in Pantaloon's house involves 'Curds and Whey' and 'Rare Pippins' (C. Dibdin 1810a: 15–16). Similarly, the harlequinade of *Harlequin and Fortunio* (Covent Garden, 1815) presented the scenes of 'Strawberries and Saloop', 'A New Dish', 'the Pleasures of an Inn', 'the Joys of Bottle' and 'Nothing to Eat' ([Anon.] 1815a: 13–14). The harlequinade of *Bang Up! or Harlequin Prime* (Sadler's Wells, 1810), set in an 'English Kitchen' (C. Dibdin 1810b: 11), includes Grimaldi's song 'Tippity Witchet', which narrates a catalogue of excessive consumption; one verse runs 'This very morning, handy, / My malady was such, / I in my tea took brandy, / And took a cup too much' (C. Dibdin 1810b: 8). The language used in accounts of Grimaldi's stage makeup further develops this central motif of consumption, noting that he 'painted some red patches on his cheeks, so as to give the idea of a greedy boy who had smeared his face with jam in robbing his mother's pantry' (Wilson 1949: 27), and in another variation his 'white face [was] larded with red like a schoolboy's that has been dipped in a surreptitious jam-pot' (Murray 1930: 125).

While in one sense feats and pranks based on eating and drinking were a timeless part of the stage clown's act (for example in the routines of Falstaff or *Macbeth*'s Porter), Grimaldi's gluttony and drunkenness also spoke to the very specific material and cultural conditions of his own time. Both the consumer and the consumed were topics of a national debate during Grimaldi's performing life: as Timothy Morton outlines, food in the Romantic period was 'not simply an empirical reality [. . .] but a mixture of ideas, practices, figures, debates, and philosophical speculations' (2004: xv). Penny Bradshaw further notes how 'political moments of the period relate to questions concerning food and consumption and in particular to the dichotomy between the absence of food and excessive consumption' (2004: 59). Grimaldi's antics became absorbed into this wider web of food-related motifs and associations, making Clown a key operator within what Morton calls 'the theatre of consumption' inside which the emerging 'economic consumer' could adopt 'various consumer and literary positions' (2004: 2–3). These positions operate across a series of binaries such as excess and discipline, production and consumption, and in the next section I examine some specific manifestations of the bodily grotesque, to reveal how Grimaldi's clown rehearses some of the debates around these binaries. Moreover, I will show how Dickens's early writing emanates from such manifestations, as he adapted these elements from the clown's repertoire in his own comic characters.

## Supersized Appetites: Clown's Amazing Feats of Digestion

For Jane Moody, pantomime is a 'spectacular, corporeal' form of theatre, with Clown as the principal signifier within its 'corporeal semiotics' due to his emphasis on 'bodily excrescences and uncontrollable consumption' (2000: 24). This accords with Bakhtin's description of the 'fundamental attributes of the grotesque style' as 'exaggeration, hyperbolism [and] excessiveness' (1968: 303), which are primarily mediated through 'the body as a whole' and 'the limits of this whole' (1968: 315). The mouth is the most important part within this, being the largest point of interface between the body and the world, and the means by which 'the world enters the body'; for Bakhtin it stands in for the entire body, as the 'wide-open bodily abyss' (1968: 317).

Clown filled himself with all manner of substances during superhuman acts of consumption that expanded his body's boundaries beyond their natural limits in defiance of any rational laws of measurable human capacity. In their stage bouts of eating and drinking during *Peter Wilkins, or Harlequin in the Flying World* (Covent Garden, 1800), Grimaldi and Dubois (as the characters of 'Guzzle' and 'Gobble' respectively) transcended regular corporeal bounds as 'Dubois grew fatter and more flatulent, Joe drunker and more incoherent' (Stott 2009: 98). It was not just regular foodstuffs that were taken in excess either: as the comical Tartar 'Munchicow' in *Harlequin and Fortunio* Clown saves the kingdom from the villainous Tongluck by consuming not only 'all the bread of the city' but also 'all the water of the Fountain of Seven Lions' ([Anon.] 1815a: 3–5). In *London, or Harlequin and Time* (Sadler's Wells, 1814) the hero of Clown's song steals the London Monument and then swallows it in 'one gulp' to escape detection (C. Dibdin 1814: 5), while in *Harlequin in His Element* (Covent Garden, 1807) Clown is so used to the *taking in* of substances that when blowing glass, he sucks in the hot air until he 'has both his cheeks blown to an enormous size' (T. Dibdin 1808: 10).

These pantomime stunts were comical, burlesque versions of sensational sideshow acts like that of the Signora Girardelli and Ivan Ivanitz Chabert. Girardelli performed in rooms on Bond Street in 1818, and in what Paul Youngquist describes as a 'public ordeal of female embodiment' (2004: 253) she dropped a variety of molten substances (wax, oil and even lead) into her mouth and cooked eggs in boiling oil that she held in her hands. Chabert also visited London and was similarly observed to swallow 'nearly two table spoonfuls' of boiling oil, 'put several small pieces of burning charcoal into his mouth' and take 'a lighted torch and [ate] it as a sallad' ([Anon.] 1818: 170). While their audiences may have recognised that such acts were as artificial and contrived as the pantomime, they briefly offered a tantalising suggestion of the superhuman transcendence of bodily limits.

Dickens particularly revelled in the fantastically gluttonous side of Grimaldi's Clown. In the *Memoirs* Grimaldi relates how, as a child, he would 'pester [his] relations and friends' with questions about the clown's diet, wondering 'whether [Clown's] appetite for sausages and such like wares was always the same, and if so, at whose expense they were maintained' (*MJG* 1: v). In his *paean* to eating and drinking, *The Pickwick Papers*, several clownish characters exhibit these superhuman powers of consumption. Jingle regularly drinks in excess with no effect while his drinking companions succumb to drunkenness around him and during the dinner at the Blue Lion Inn he exhibits the appetite of 'half-a-dozen ordinary men at least' (*PP* 104). In the same novel, which Steven Marcus calls a 'robust celebration of food and drink' (1965: 71), there are others with similar appetites: at the 'festive occasion' (*PP* 730) of reading Mrs Weller's will, everybody enjoys the lunch of 'porter, cold beef, and oysters', at which 'the coachman with the hoarse voice' 'evinced greater powers' than the rest when he 'took an imperial pint of vinegar with his oysters, without betraying the least emotion' (*PP* 731). In detailing the exaggerated quantity of vinegar and control of his facial expression, Dickens defines this moment as a fantastical sideshow stunt like those of Girardelli, Chabert or Grimaldi.

Such figures appear in other works: Mr Grimwig in *Oliver Twist* also threatens a particularly pantomimic spectacle of extreme eating, in which his head becomes a detachable comestible. He regularly threatens to eat his own head and on one occasion threatens to eat Oliver's too: '"If that's not the boy, sir, who had the orange, and threw this bit of peel upon the stair-case, I'll eat my head, and his too"' (*OT* 100). On this occasion, Dickens pauses to consider the rational implications of Grimwig's threat, which he describes as

> the more singular in [Grimwig's] case, because, even admitting for the sake of argument, the possibility of scientific improvements being brought to that pass which will enable a gentleman to eat his own head in the event of his being so disposed; Mr. Grimwig's head was such a particularly large one, that the most sanguine man alive, could hardly entertain a hope of being able to get through it at a sitting. (*OT* 99)

As the rational observer Dickens renders Grimwig's threat doubly impossible, but in allowing the repetition of the threat Dickens generates a tantalising moment of possibility, which could only be possible through the laws of the pantomime.

These robust celebrations of bodily appetites also encompass the sexualisation of food and the act of eating it, something to which popular prints of Grimaldi were attuned. In Dyer's famous image of 'Mr Grimaldi, as Clown', a clown loaded with consumables stands with his legs wide apart, as a dead goose swings suggestively from his pocket. Food's sexual allusiveness is also evident in Cruikshank's print from *Harlequin and Friar Bacon* in which Clown stands stiffly upright: his large knife and a partially opened oyster (with its tantalising contents partially on display through the orifice) draw attention and focus to his 'lower bodily strata' (Fig. 6.1).

This illustration is a manifestation of Grimaldi's recurrent and multivalent association with oysters, also described in *The Drama*'s list of accomplishments: one of his popular routines involved singing to 'an oyster crossed in love' (Findlater 1978: 10) and as noted earlier, in his farewell speech he announced that he had 'filched [his] last oyster'. Aside from the oyster's ubiquity in the contemporary urban diet (Sam Weller observes that in Whitechapel there is 'a oyster stall to every half-dozen houses' [*PP* 294]) they carried a figurative meaning that explicitly associated them with the bodily grotesque's conflation of eating and sex. According to Rebecca Stott, the eighteenth-century woman oyster seller was 'a figure of erotic play, something like the oyster to be consumed, part of the sensuous fruit of the London street for the male urban voyeur' (2004: 157). Moreover, her wares in isolation represent 'a nudge-nudge euphemism for sexually available female flesh' (2004: 163) made even more pointed in pantomime scenes like the one depicted in the *Friar Bacon* print.

**Figure 6.1** George Cruikshank, 'Harlequin and Friar Bacon' (1820), © Victoria and Albert Museum, London.

Dickens's presentation of oysters similarly embraces what T. W. Hill calls 'its gustatory, figurative, social, sociological, and decorative aspects' (1940: 139). When they are served up in *Pickwick* and *Oliver Twist* they both enact a pantomimic transformation to make their consumers clown-like and suggest a more eroticised reading of the bodily grotesque. In his description of the Christmas morning breakfast, Sam Weller gives shape to a constellation of associations for oysters: vigorous physical activity, exaggerated consumption, bodily lower stratum and a comical prank at the expense of the slumbering Joe. He relates how Bob or Ben

> has got a barrel o' oysters atween his knees, vich he's a openin' like steam, and as fast as he eats 'em, he takes a aim vith the shells at young dropsy, who's a settin' down fast asleep, in the chimbley corner. (*PP* 391)

They have a similar effect at the footman's 'swarry', transforming usually professionally dignified individuals into capering buffoons. Mr Tuckle finds oysters 'so extremely exhilarating' when combined with 'three quarters of a bowl of punch' that he becomes a clown who performs one of Grimaldi's own routines: 'dressed out with the cocked hat and stick, [he] danced the frog hornpipe among the shells on the table'. However, these antics take their toll on poor Tuckle who departs from the narrative in a slapstick *denouement*: 'Mr Tuckle no sooner got into the open air, than he was seized with a sudden desire to lie on the curb-stone' (*PP* 503).

Noah Claypole's comic routine with oysters, as he partakes of some home comforts while Sowerberry is absent, draws on the oyster's sexualised relationship with the bodily grotesque. Noah's digestive centricity echoes Clown's own indolence and gluttony, as he is described as 'not being at any time disposed to take upon himself a greater amount of physical exertion than is necessary to a convenient performance of the two functions of eating and drinking'. Dickens further frames this feasting scene as an observed performance by having Bumble watch it through a window 'at the back of the shop' and presents Bumble's observations through stage directions. Noah strikes a languid pose, like an actor's 'attitude' in Rede's acting manual, with exaggerated bodily gestures and appropriately grotesque props, 'loll[ing] negligently in an easy-chair, with his legs thrown over one of the arms; an open clasp-knife in one hand, and a mass of buttered bread in the other'. Following Rede again, he adopts a suitable facial expression in harmony with his bodily pose, exhibiting 'a more than ordinary redness in the region of [his] nose, and a kind of fixed wink in his right eye' (*OT* 184–5).

Noah devours the oysters with 'remarkable avidity' (*OT* 184) and 'intense relish' and his insatiable appetite is underscored by his dismayed comment to Charlotte that he cannot gorge on them too much as 'a number of 'em should ever make you feel uncomfortable'. He also alternates between (and conflates) those linked appetites: after finishing his oyster feast, he offers to kiss Charlotte and is only foiled by Grimaldi's perennial authoritarian nemesis, the beadle. Bumble's sudden appearance precipitates a display of clownish cowardice as he 'gazed at the beadle in drunken terror' and in his 'blubbering' state accuses Charlotte of making 'all manner of love' with him (*OT* 185). These themes are also resonant in Cruikshank's illustration (Fig. 6.2).

In a similar manner to his 'Barber-Shop' illustration from the *Memoirs*, Cruikshank's picture is framed like a stage set watched by an unseen omniscient audience in which Bumble is a participant rather than an observer. One of Cruikshank's alternative titles for

**Figure 6.2** George Cruikshank, 'Mr Claypole as he Appeared when his Master is Out', *Oliver Twist*. Reproduced by courtesy of Charles Dickens Museum, London.

his original pencil sketch further amplifies its themes of the bodily grotesque: 'Mr Claypole Indulging . . .' draws immediate attention to Noah's enjoyment and consumption without specifying its precise object, leaving the oysters and Charlotte as equally valid options (Jones 1978, Plate 63).

This interchange of food and love also occurs in a dining scene from *Pickwick* involving Grimaldi's namesake, Joe ('the Fat Boy') and the servant girl Mary. When Mary takes Joe to the kitchen to feed him, a scene of grotesque excess ensues, during which Joe mentally and verbally confuses Mary with his food. Like Noah, Joe divides his time between eating and wooing, and so conflates two different fleshly pleasures in a manner that combines a latent cannibalism with a grotesque eroticism.

He is surrounded by eatables and consumes them as their flirtatious discussion progresses, starting by helping himself to 'a great deal' of the pie and 'a long draught of the porter' (*PP* 717). Joe's food fixation becomes evident when he cannot separate Mary from associations of food: he expresses his dismay that she is not staying, for 'how we should have enjoyed ourselves at meals, if you had been!' and when she asks a favour of him he 'looked from the pie-dish to the steak, as if he thought a favour must be in a manner connected to something to eat' (*PP* 719). He attempts to woo her between mouthfuls, switching focus between his plate and his dinner companion, so it becomes unclear to which he refers.

Mary's presence is such a distraction to Joe's feasting that he even contemplates eating her: before starting to eat the pie he pauses, knife and fork in hand, to tell her how nice she looks, a compliment unsurprisingly regarded as 'a doubtful one' because 'there was enough of the cannibal in the young gentleman's eyes' as he offered it (*PP* 717). According to Thomson's characterisation 'the grotesque is extravagant', with 'a marked element of exaggeration, of extremeness about it' (1972: 22–3) and here Joe's hyperbolic appetite is pushed to its furthest limit. Phiz's illustration, 'Mary and the Fat Boy' subtly integrates these elements to support the underlying grotesquerie. The pie on the table is of exaggerated proportions, and there are further visual echoes of Cruikshank's *Friar Bacon* print in Joe's upraised knife pointing towards the suggestive orifice of the opened pie.

The balance of power in both the Noah–Charlotte and Joe–Mary pairings ensures that a comic tone prevails: Claypole is left a frightened wreck who submits to Charlotte's power and Mary leaves Joe consoling himself with food as he eats 'a pound or so of steak with a sentimental countenance' (*PP* 719). However, another of Dickens's erotic consumers is a more threatening presence, as suggestive playfulness slips over to sexual aggression: Kincaid describes Daniel Quilp's antics as 'strongly sexual and always extraordinarily physical' (1971: 96), and these elements sometimes combine in his superhuman feats of consumption.

Quilp puts on several quasi-demonic, 'horrifying and uncommon' displays of extreme eating including 'hard eggs, shell and all', 'gigantic prawns with the heads and tails on', as well as drinking 'boiling tea without winking' (*OCS* 47). Quilp uses this feast as a means of intimidating his wife and her friends, and later uses it for the same purpose when plotting with Sampson Brass: Quilp drinks boiling rum directly from a saucepan 'in quantity about half a pint, and had been but a moment before, when he took it off the fire, bubbling and hissing fiercely' (*OCS* 465), and then bullies Sampson into drinking some himself, which of course he is unequal to, crying 'burning tears' which turn 'the colour of his face and eyelids to a deep red [. . .] giving rise to a violent fit of coughing' (*OCS* 466). Schlicke does not include Grimaldi's clown in sources for Quilp's character, but the latter's performances clearly embody the fundamental corporeality of Clown's act: as S. J. Newman notes, Quilp's eating and drinking is depicted as 'hugely carnal', as love is 'solidified into appetite' (1981: 79).

During the all-night vigil he uses to punish his wife, he incessantly drinks and smokes, and his 'deep fiery red' cigar-end becomes a threatening phallic presence in the dark room. This effect is accentuated by Phiz's accompanying illustration, 'Quilp in a Smoking Humour', with Quilp's cigar pointing suggestively upwards, in a miniaturised prefiguration of his death scene at the wharf. In the illustrations of Noah and Joe feasting, Charlotte and Mary are the dominant figures, depicted as larger than their suitors, and standing rather than sitting. Here, however, Quilp fills up more of the picture and thrusts aggressively towards his wife who is seated and shying away from him. Quilp also verbalises this physical threat: he warns his wife 'If ever you listen to these beldames again, I'll bite you' (*OCS* 43), and in a particularly Swiftian retort to Kit's mother, he declares that 'I don't eat babies; I don't like 'em' (*OCS* 166). These elements are the counterbalancing forces to the more celebratory aspects of Quilp's consumption, such as his showman's besting of the cowardly Brass.

## The Festive Quality of Clownish Excess

Pantomime's scheduling as an Easter and Christmas entertainment firmly aligns it with other festive spectacles, and also with Bakhtin's aforementioned 'formalisation of the grotesque and carnivalesque'. However, both Grimaldi and Dickens resist a complete and potentially calcifying formalisation, as their portrayals of festive excess defy outright enclosure or containment within their respective settings of theatre and home. The combination of the seasonal scheduling and the other public spaces that were recreated 'onstage' in his performances allowed Grimaldi to celebrate both the festive and the marketplace, a method adopted by Dickens in his own fiction to present similar scenes of Christmas feasting and streetside revelry. Both exemplify a Bakhtinian sense of the carnival, which has no footlights to divide onstage and offstage because 'it does not acknowledge any distinction between actors and spectators' and is not an objectively observed event but something the audience 'live in', as 'everyone participates because its very idea embraces all the people' (1968: 7).

By devising scenes in locales such as 'A View in a Market Town', 'A View of Golden Square', 'Vauxhall Gardens' (T. Dibdin [1860?]: 4), 'Castle Square, Brighton' ([Anon.] 1815a: 13), 'Outside of the New Auction Mart', 'Exeter 'Change' (C. Dibdin 1810a: 17), 'Charing Cross', 'The Monument, Fish St Hill', and 'Highgate Archway' (C. Dibdin 1814: 4), Grimaldi's harlequinades sought to break any distinction between private performance space and public marketplace. Moreover, many of the other characters with which Grimaldi interacted were the typical inhabitants of these public spaces, as he stole from the pieman and wooed the flower girl. He could also rely on members of the audience to participate in the public gourmandising for, as we have seen, the boundary between eighteenth-century player and audience was highly porous: spectators 'not only drank, but ate on a large scale' (Findlater 1978: 19), whether consuming food served to their seats or their own brought from home. Playgoers also engaged in other public activities within the playhouse, such as fighting, gambling and romancing, as well as engaging in a dialogue with the performers. These were both bidden, in call and response repartee with comic players, but also sometimes unbidden, as they offered a real-time critique of the performance – a form of participation that reached its apotheosis during the O. P. Riots (see Chapter 4).

Grimaldi and Dickens contribute to this deprivatisation of the carnivalesque and realisation of the lower bodily stratum through their presentation of festive eating, which fits into Bakhtin's category of 'symbolically broad kitchen and banquet scenes' (1968: 184). Garrick's corralling of pantomime into the confines of holiday entertainment aligned the pantomime seasons with the two most significant feasting-points in the Christian calendar, Easter and Christmas, and this is reflected in the extensive use of eating and drinking within the performances, which dramatise the triumph of the carnivalesque over 'abstemious Lent' (Stott 2009: 98). Food carries the same great significance in Dickens's Christmas stories, whether it be in depictions of its presence (for example, the Cratchits' Christmas dinner) or its absence (Scrooge's meagre repast).

However, both worked within periods for which Christmas held different meanings. During Grimaldi's career, Christmas was a larger public celebration, but by Dickens's middle adulthood the Christmas carnivalesque had been curtailed into a more modest and private family spectacle. In works such as *A Christmas Carol*, a nostalgic Dickens balances these two models of Christmas in a manner reflecting what Tara Moore calls 'an ideological feasting paradox' (2007: 143), which balanced these competing versions of Christmas through nostalgically enjoying depictions of the former mode while actually practising the latter mode. The scenes at the clownish Fezziwig's party represent Christmas as a boisterous public and communal spectacle: after the first set of dances comes a hyperbolic run of food and festive activities:

> There were more dances, and there were forfeits, and more dances, and there was cake, and there was negus, and there was a great piece of Cold Roast, and there was a great piece of Cold Boiled, and there were mince-pies, and plenty of beer. (*CC* 63)

By contrast to the dizzying superabundance of this huge gathering comes the Cratchits' homely feast, which replaces the jigs and reels with a 'bustle' of co-operative and productive industry:

> Mrs Cratchit made the gravy (ready beforehand in a little saucepan) hissing hot; Master Peter mashed the potatoes with incredible vigour; Miss Belinda sweetened up the apple-sauce; Martha dusted the hot plates; Bob took Tiny Tim beside him in a tiny corner at the table; the two young Cratchits set chairs for everybody[.] (*CC* 80)

Although Dickens notes that there is 'nothing of high mark in this' (*CC* 84), the festive grotesque persists in other details in Dickens's breathless description of the family, which includes the children as fully engaged and enthusiastic participants, and delivers a domesticated form of hyperbole in describing the 'hissing hot' gravy, the 'incredible vigour' of the mashing and even the chairs set for 'everybody'.

This paradox was also present in a nascent form earlier in the century, when the Prince Regent's immoderate behaviour forced his subjects to count the cost of his excessive consumption. Bradshaw notes 'the versatility of dietary metaphors' (2004: 68) during the Regency period and shows how depictions of excess in a range of media were typically poised between two competing consumer attitudes: in Gillray's cartoons for example, the Prince Regent's corpulence denoted gross and selfish excess, but John Bull's similarly ample frame was a defiant symbol of the healthy well-fed citizen.

Images of eating and food were an important bridge between these competing conceptions of Christmas, with the pantomime clown forming one of its key-stones. According to a Bakhtinian reading of the grotesque, Grimaldi's festive overeating and drinking are a celebratory manifestation of abundance and a healthy appetite. However, following Gail Turley Houston's view of Dickensian dietetics, such scenes are acts of displacement, whereby the guilt of over-consumers is projected onto scapegoats such as the pantomime clown and Joe the Fat Boy. Houston describes the latter as 'a mythic embodiment of the Pickwickians' unlimited appetite and leisure' and 'a carnivalesque imitation of the general Pickwickian credo of unlimited leisure and consumption' (1994: 22).

For Houston, *The Pickwick Papers* as a whole is symbiotically engaged with his second novel, in a representation of both sides of the feasting paradox: 'the starvation of *Oliver Twist* retroactively implicates the aggressive satiation that is the undercurrent of jovial Pickwickian gusto' (1994: 15), but more widely, *Pickwick* establishes the link between clownish eating and Christmas within Dickens's work. For example, there are strong pantomimic overtones in the gluttonous performance of Bob Sawyer and Ben Allen at the Christmas Day breakfast, in which Bob observes that 'Nothing like dissecting, to give one an appetite,' and the pair's repartee conflates surgical practice with eating (*PP* 392). While this episode sits uncomfortably with Houston's wider reading of Dickens's reconciliation of Christmas with early Christian feasts, its presentation of a Bakhtinian '"carnival and culinary" anatomy' (1968: 196) reconciles it perfectly with the formalisation of the carnivalesque. Bakhtin observes how Rabelais's feast scenes often position images of dismembered bodies adjacent to descriptions of food in order to suggest a contiguity between them and a sense that one had metamorphosed into the other, and Dickens employs a similar method here.

This process reaches its apotheosis in *A Christmas Carol*, in which Dickens measures the positive aspects of excess against a socially corrosive meanness epitomised in the dietary habits of Scrooge. He rejects his nephew's offer to share a meal with him on Christmas Day, and refuses to make a charitable donation for 'some meat and drink' for the poor. Scrooge continues his Lenten resistance to Bakhtin's rule that 'No meal can be sad' (1968: 283), as he 'took' (rather than 'enjoyed') a 'melancholy dinner in his usual melancholy tavern' (*CC* 41) and later a 'little saucepan of gruel' (*CC* 43). However, these are the final parsimonious meals, as 'Abundance' and Excess triumph in Dickens's elaborate descriptions of food, which evoke the enchanted properties of the clown's meals in the harlequinade. When describing the Christmas marketplace, Dickens's similes lead us to envisage human-sized chestnuts and onions, or even people in vegetable-shaped costumes, like supernumeraries in a pantomime or 'the gigantic sausages and buns that were solemnly carried' (1968: 278) in the carnival processions that Bakhtin describes:

> There were great, round, pot-bellied baskets of chestnuts, shaped like the waistcoats of jolly old gentlemen, lolling at the doors, and tumbling out into the street in their apoplectic opulence. There were ruddy, brown-faced, broad-girthed Spanish Onions, shining in the fatness of their growth like Spanish Friars; and winking from their shelves in wanton slyness at the girls as they went by, and glanced demurely at the hung-up mistletoe. (*CC* 75)

These busy urban scenes are placed firmly within a festive pantomimic tradition, as 'Poulterers' and grocers' trades became a splendid joke' and 'a glorious pageant' (*CC* 40).

## The Unpaid Cost of Consumption and Consumption as Waste

For Bakhtin the grotesque body's association with labour elevated its owner: food was the 'crown of glory' which 'concluded work and struggle' (1968: 281). People worked together and then feasted collectively to celebrate their (temporary) existential triumph over the world, as their bodies grew 'at the world's expense' (1968: 283). Bakhtin contrasts this productive and industrious figure (who is the 'soul of the people') with 'the private, limited, greedy body' (1968: 292), an archetype who has often been depicted in straightforwardly critical terms. However, in accord with the bodily grotesque the selfish consumers of both Grimaldi and Dickens are more ambiguous. They participate in the same activities as productive consumers, for as Bakhtin puts it, 'Bread stolen from the people does not cease to be bread, wine is always wine, even when the Pope drinks it' (1968: 291), and although the audience response is partly derisive it carries a residue of the celebratory.

Grimaldi presents this double-edged clownish wastefulness in *Harlequin and Friar Bacon* (Covent Garden, 1820) where, in a topical hit at modern science Harlequin exploits Clown's excessive appetite by transforming the Aldgate Pump into a 'gazometer'. When the greedy Clown attempts to gulp down the local water supply he is instead inflated with gas and has to be deflated, after which he is presented with a bill for £100 for 'having gorged 10,000 cubic feet of their vapour' ([Anon.] 1821: 68). The economic consequences of Clown's gluttony have a tangible monetary cost here, but we cannot fully condemn him because we are initially invited to laugh at the more comical consequences of his consumption, as his body puffs up like a giant balloon and triumphantly transcends its regular human limits.

Such greedy irresponsibility was a repeated trope: Clown never paid for the food and drink that he consumed and rarely provided any service in return, preferring instead to subsist on the fruits of others' labours. Wilson notes how he 'would steal all sorts of articles from the shops', particularly food stuffs: 'geese, legs of mutton and strings of sausages' (1949: 35), and Mayer summarises Clown's ethos as 'if there was food he would eat it gluttonously; if the food were someone else's he would first steal it' (1969: 262). Thus in *Harlequin and Mother Goose* (Covent Garden, 1806) after the selfless hero Harlequin relieves the poverty of a woodcutter with 'golden favours' from Fortune's cornucopia, Clown 'enters and as usual plunders from the Wood-cutter's WIFE' (T. Dibdin [1860?]: 14). In a later scene outside St Dunstan's Church he robs a pieman and then joins Pantaloon in the 'Grocer's Parlour', where 'they drink wine with the magic bottle' without any concern for the expense that they incur (T. Dibdin [1860?]: 17). In another pantomime Clown audaciously steals drink from two porters while hiding in a box that lies between them. Each porter mistakenly thinks the other is drinking more than his share, and so a fight ensues, leaving Clown to steal the bottle and declare 'I fancy I shall drink the rest' (C. Dibdin 1807: 9–10). In all these examples Clown sabotages Bakhtin's socialist model of production followed by consumption by stealing the food of people who are explicitly identified as workers themselves – woodcutters, piemen, grocers and porters.

As well as disrupting the labour of others, Grimaldi's Clown also indulges in this wasteful and unproductive consumption by abandoning any work he is engaged in (such as the pursuit of Harlequin and Columbine) to follow the lure of food and drink. In *Harlequin and Mother Goose* Clown is diverted into an inn, and immediately 'sits down at the table and drinks wine', before to Clown's 'gratification' a live duck flies out of the pie on the table, which he greedily chases. The notion that Clown has put his own desires before the task in hand is made evident when he locks the door after Pantaloon has left so that he can 'regale' uninterrupted (T. Dibdin [1860?]: 12).

A similar distraction occurs in *Harlequin in His Element* when Harlequin attempts to rescue Columbine. Clown offers his captive a meagre repast of bread and cheese which she refuses, at which point Harlequin transforms it into a roast fowl: 'Clown intimates that he will [eat this]' and while he is 'enjoying the luxuries of the table' Harlequin is able to liberate Columbine. He then diverts Clown's attention again by magically transporting 'the roast fowl to another table, and when Clown goes to fill wine, one glass disappears, and the other throws wine back in his face' (T. Dibdin 1808: 6). Harlequin later turns Clown's greed against him once more by turning a stolen orange into a large wasp while he is sucking it.

Moody views this kind of wasteful over-stuffing by Grimaldi's Clown as a reflection of Georgian habits rather than mere abstract fooling: Clown's gluttony 'seems to mirror the city's greed in its consumptive, competitive excess [and] offers a physical corollary for oversupply, mimicking the uncontrolled character of purchase and desire in the modern city' (2000: 219). Moreover, this part of Grimaldi's repertoire seemed to hold a particular attraction for the king: the comedian J. S. Munden recalled how George III 'laughed almost to suffocation' at Grimaldi's 'mimic exhibition of swallowing a quantity of long puddings' (1846: 77), while Thackeray comments that the King laughed 'outrageously [. . .] when clown swallowed a carrot or a string of sausages' (1869: 82). Findlater sees this as proof of Grimaldi's universal appeal, observing that 'this was the kind of acting which Farmer George understood and enjoyed' (1978: 89), but in keeping with the double appeal of the pantomime to the body and mind, such articulations of the bodily grotesque operate multivalently. Here, Grimaldi's greedy Clown offered the King and his subjects a satirical outlet for a national concern, namely the consuming excesses of George III's son the Prince Regent.

The Regent is described by Timothy Morton as 'the consumer of the 1790s' (2004: xvi) and the nation's antipathy towards this consumption was depicted in cartoons and prints of the period. James Gillray's *A VOLUPTUARY under the Horrors of Digestion* (1792) provides a pictorial complement to Grimaldi's living form of the bodily grotesque, with the Regent as Bakhtin's 'private, limited, greedy body' who contributes no effort to the labour struggle and is not located within the marketplace but instead removes himself to the isolation of 'the house and private chamber' (1968: 302–3).

Aside from the swollen and hulking figure of George himself, the grotesque is suggested in a variety of details. His *credo* of consumption is embedded in the ensign of a knife, fork and plate mounted on the wall, and he is surrounded by waste – bottles on the floor, half-gnawed bones on the golden plates and an overflowing chamber-pot behind his chair. Like Grimaldi's Clown he is unwilling to pay for his consumption – the unpaid bills are symbolically tucked under the chamber-pot. Gillray also links the Prince's body with what he eats: his legs are displayed like joints of meat or two giant chicken drumsticks, with his white stockings giving his lower legs the appearance of bones and his beige breeches the cooked skin at the top.

However, it is George's facial expression that pushes Gillray's print firmly into the realm of the grotesque. Morton notes the careless attitude that the Prince exhibits here, looking more like a 'Romantic poet' in 'contemplation' than a 'tyrannical gourmand' suffering from 'dyspepsia' (2004: xvi). The 'Horror' of the title is entirely absent from his face, for what one sees in his expression is not 'the triumph of the people as a whole' but instead 'the contentment and satiety of the self individual' (Bakhtin 1968: 303) – the horror is entirely in 'the eyes of the middle-class consumer' (Morton 2004: xvi) who views the print.

Dickens acknowledges the ambiguous treatment of consumption in 'The Pantomime of Life', where he calls Clown's 'obtaining goods under false pretences, or abstracting the stock-in-trade of the respectable shopkeeper next door', as the 'great fun' of the performance, because of (rather than despite) its criminal and irresponsible connotations (*PoL* 503). Through his depictions of apparently wasteful and unproductive consumption, Dickens questions whether such consumers serve a more human value beyond economic pragmatism, as, like Clown, they often promote excessive consumption as a communal imaginative act. Conversely, he also questions the motives of those who make a virtue of their gustatory parsimoniousness, regularly exposing this as a hypocritical stance, and suggests these figures are the real wasters, as they requisition food from those who – in Dickens's view – are more deserving.

Sometimes such contrasts are briefly sketched, but all the starker for it. The workhouse diet in Mudfog is 'three meals of thin gruel a day, with an onion twice a week, and half a roll on Sundays' (*OT* 26), which is clearly not what the members of the parish board subsist on, given that they are 'eight or ten fat gentlemen' led by a 'particularly fat gentleman with a very round, red face' (*OT* 24). Outside on the cold marshes of *Great Expectations* Magwitch is reduced to eating like a dog, 'gobbling mincemeat, meat-bone, bread, cheese, and pork pie, all at once' (*GE* 20), while the likes of Pumblechook and Wopsle patronise Pip by means of 'a superb [Christmas] dinner, consisting of a leg of pickled pork and greens, and a pair of roast stuffed fowls' and a 'handsome mince-pie' (*GE* 23). Even as they enjoy the choicest cuts, while Pip is 'regaled with the scaly tips of the drumsticks of the fowls' and 'obscure corners of pork' (*GE* 26), these two hypocrites warn Pip to be grateful. Had he been born a pig, they aver, he would not be 'enjoying himself with his elders and betters, and improving himself with their conversation, and rolling in the lap of luxury' and would instead be slaughtered by Dunstan the butcher (*GE* 27).

The double-dealing of the avaricious landlord Casby is also expressed through the manner of his consumption: at 'the disenchanted feast' with Arthur, Flora, Mr F's aunt and Pancks, we are told that 'The last of the Patriarchs had always been a mighty eater, and he disposed of an immense quantity of solid food with the benignity of a good soul who was feeding some one else' (*LD* 173). In this act of public dining, Casby performs as the selfless consumer, while secretly being a glutton himself, which finds a corollary in his outward pose of benevolence towards his tenants, while privately he urges Pancks to squeeze and drive them to their financial limits.

Dickens's reference to 'a good soul' imparts a religious element to this, and he links excessive consumption and religious cant elsewhere in his work, highlighting the hypocrisy of those unrestrained consumers who preach restraint to others. Pumblechook's Christmas sermonising carries a note of this, but the Reverend Stiggins is a lengthier exposition of this figure: his red nose immediately signals that he has overindulged on 'hot pine-apple rum-and-water' and he eats with 'fierce voracity' (*PP* 354), pausing only to groan and exclaim his disapproval of the male Wellers' moral conduct. After everything has been eaten, he can only be induced to stay with more pine-apple rum-and-water, and finally leaves as he displays 'several most indubitable symptoms of having quite as much [. . .] about him, as he could comfortably accommodate' (*PP* 359). When he later takes to the stage of the Temperance Association he still performs as the drunkard 'staring with a wild eye, and a fixed smile, at the extreme top of the wick of the candle on the table: swaying his body to and fro, meanwhile, in a very unsteady and uncertain manner'. There he accuses someone else of drunkenness and attempts to physically remove this same Brother Tadger from the stage, due to his 'praiseworthy desire to promote the sobriety of the meeting' (*PP* 443).

This public display is not the last example of Stiggins's hypocrisy being revealed through his habits of consumption; cunningly led by

Sam Weller, Stiggins admits that he officially despises all alcoholic 'vanities' before conceding that 'if there is any one of them less odious than another, it is the liquor called rum'. A sense of how much he actually despises this least odious of the vanities is given when he discovers that *The Marquis of Granby* does not serve it: he rails against publicans who do not stock it as 'the hardness of heart of these inveterate men' and 'the accursed cruelty of these inhuman persecutors' (*PP* 600).

Stiggins, then, is diverted from his useful offices as a clergyman by his bodily appetites, and in the same novel, food is also used as a comical but disruptive distraction. Joe the Fat Boy has the chance to fulfil the traditional clown's function as disruptor of the love plot, by informing the Pantaloons – Mr Wardle and Emily's father – of the *amours* of Snodgrass and Emily. However, the lovers exploit the fact that his appetite is his governing motivation to thwart his plan: when a monetary bribe fails, Emily's accomplice Mary relates to Joe in gustatory terms, remarking that he 'had better have something to eat immediately' (*PP* 716). He is taken to the kitchen, where, as we saw earlier, he succumbs to a different kind of appetite. This consumption wastefully distracts Joe from the job in which he is employed and threatens to make him the ultimate symbol of the selfish 'private' consumer, the cannibal. Food is no longer a shared celebration of society but one which places the very constituents of that society in danger; as in 'A Voluptuary', the boundaries between who eats and what is eaten have been dissolved. Bakhtin's conception of the celebratory body of triumphant man devouring the world is inverted to become the body threatened by the world, as humanity demonstrates the potential to devour itself.

While Joe's eternal quest to fill his stomach is predominantly presented as entertainment to the reader only, elsewhere Dickens allows others to enjoy it, to demonstrate its broader social utility. David Copperfield encounters William the waiter on his stopover at Yarmouth, where his Grimaldian appearance and boisterous manner signal the antics to come: he is 'a twinkling-eyed, pimple-faced man, with his hair standing upright all over his head' (*DC* 78), who 'came running out of a kitchen' (*DC* 76) and removes his dish-covers in 'a bouncing manner' (*DC* 76). In their comical exchanges, William inventively employs a gluttonous deception to satisfy his own appetite rather than his customer's. After tricking David into giving him his glass of beer (claiming that the last drinker dropped dead) he eats David's dinner on the pretext that it will offset any ill effects from the beer:

> he took a chop by the bone in one hand, and a potato in the other, and ate away with a very good appetite, to my extreme satisfaction. He afterwards took another chop, and another potato; and after that, another chop and another potato.

The rhythmic and hyperbolic accumulation of David's description reads like pantomime business, as does the finale of an eating competition with 'a batter-pudding' in which David's teaspoon is comically (mis)matched against William's tablespoon (*DC* 79). Crucially, however, David observes the whole incident as a spectacle of fun and rather than feeling dismay at the loss of his meal, he comments that 'it was quite delightful to me, to find him so pleasant' (*DC* 78). The relish of David's account registers that, like the pantomime spectator who is willingly deceived, enjoyment is taken from the deception, even when the victim is a younger self.

Dickens also uses other strategies to offset the direct criticism of such excessive consumers. Sometimes he leavens the less palatable elements of these figures by making them buffoons: Stiggins's ridiculousness certainly outweighs his moral import, a fact underscored by his exit from the narrative in a 'splosh' scene, as Mr Weller senior 'immers[es] Mr Stiggins's head in a horse-trough full of water, and holding it there, till he was all but suffocated' (*PP* 698).

In *Bleak House*, the careless consumer Harold Skimpole presents a direct parasitical drain on the economy, but his portrayal is similarly tempered with some of these elements of Clownish gluttony and the Regent's more Romantic sense of excess. Skimpole is immediately aligned with Romanticism when John Jarndyce describes him as being composed of '"sentiment, and – susceptibility, and – and sensibility, and – and imagination"' (*BH* 522). Moreover, the reactions of others towards him register the simplicity of both the Romantic child and the clown: Esther Summerson notes his 'helpless kind of candour', 'the light-hearted manner in which he was amused by his innocence' and 'the delightful ease of everything he said' (*BH* 526), while Richard Carstone describes him as '"such a cheery fellow"', '"fresh and green-hearted"' with '"No worldliness about him"' (*BH* 459). However, this combination of Romantic and clownish innocence precipitates Skimpole's irresponsible consumption: John Jarndyce warns that these traits are problematically excessive because they '"are not regulated"' or '"balanced and adjusted"' (*BH* 522).

Throughout the narrative Skimpole is an eloquent spokesman for his own dissolute nature and makes numerous pronouncements on his careless attitude to life, which directs all his actions toward his personal gratification; '"When I go anywhere, I go for pleasure. I don't go anywhere for pain, because I was made for pleasure. Pain comes to *me* when it wants me"' (*BH* 726). Skimpole proclaims that '"I covet nothing [. . .] Possession is nothing to me"' (*BH* 66), while another of his mottos is '"Let us live upon you!"' (*BH* 527); he is honest in his admission that '"I don't intend to be responsible. I never could do it. Responsibility is a thing that has always been above me – or below me"' (*BH* 727). He also professes an ignorance of basic economics, claiming that '"I know nothing of the value of money"' (*BH* 184) and '"[i]f I did have any money, I don't know anything about it"' (*BH* 525). Like Grimaldi's Clown, who had no intention of paying for anything he took, Skimpole attempts to absent himself from the process of economic circulation, while still enjoying its bounty.

On one occasion he describes a notable incident that reads like a thoroughly clownish prank from the pantomime. Having borrowed a couple of armchairs from his baker neighbour ('"a rough kind of fellow – a sort of human hedgehog rolled up"') the Skimpole family carelessly wear them out. Therefore when Skimpole returns them, rather than being '"contented [the baker] objected to their being worn"'. Here the angry neighbour is refigured in Skimpole's mind as '"the absurd figure of an angry baker"', echoing one of Grimaldi's perennial targets, the duped tradesman, whom Skimpole describes to us as '"ridiculous"' while wearing a typically Grimaldian expression, 'raising his laughing eyebrows in playful astonishment'. By further noting that this 'was so old a story to all of [Skimpole's family] that it had become a matter of course' (*BH* 528), Dickens makes it clear that such an event is a regular occurrence, like the predictable routine of the pantomime clown.

Skimpole's regular visits to Bleak House follow a similar pattern and rehearse Dickens's description of Clown in 'The Pantomime of Life'. Esther notes that all Skimpole's appearances consist of arriving 'without notice, and never bringing any clothes with him, but always borrowing everything he wanted' (*BH* 384). As a result, Jarndyce can never consider Skimpole as '"an accountable being"' (*BH* 386), which later Skimpole echoes: '"I am a child among you worldly grumblers, and not called upon to account to you or myself for anything"' (*BH* 460).

As the narrative progresses, Dickens develops Skimpole's grotesquerie by juxtaposing his repugnant side alongside his light-hearted one: for example, when Esther later confronts him and politely suggests he faces his obligations he admits that he is quite willing to '"owe as much as good-natured people will let me owe"', justifying this by asking '"If they don't stop, why should I?"' (*BH* 467). However, the carelessness expressed in the early part of the narrative inexorably becomes subject to economic forces, particularly the principle that someone must bear the cost of what he takes even if it is not Skimpole himself, and over the course of the novel a variety of people pay for his consumption, whether directly or indirectly – Richard, Jo and even Jarndyce himself.

The practical Mr Bucket commentates on Skimpole's actions and views them as a calculated theatrical performance. As a police inspector, he is familiar with deception in all its forms and so is not taken in by the '"bounds of [Skimpole's] childish innocence"', and warns Esther that people like Skimpole '"who claim to be innocent as lambs in all concerning money [. . .] are dead certain to collar [your money] if they can"'. He also recognises Skimpole's attempt to extricate himself from the economic nexus as disingenuous, noting that those that claim to be a 'child' in 'worldly matters' are only '"a crying off from being held accountable"' (*BH* 682). Gradually Esther comes to recognise this element of performance in Skimpole's nature herself when she comments that 'I could not satisfy myself that [Skimpole's behaviour] was as artless as it seemed' (*BH* 460).

As a counterpoint to this type of careless consumer, who play one role but then are revealed to be quite another, Dickens also portrays figures who appear to be careless consumers, but in fact serve a social purpose. Although he is financially unproductive and wholly reliant on something 'turning up', Mr Micawber performs the function of social consumer through the communal spectacle of punch-making, something he performs regularly through the narrative even when forced to improvise with a wash-jug. Indeed, even his choice of 'vanity' carries connotations of wholesome heartiness and traditional English values, described as 'that Beverage which is peculiarly associated, in our minds, with the Roast Beef of Old England' (*DC* 810). This merry concoction and the ritual of making it becomes a kind of social cement, building positive relations between characters, and grants Micawber the status of purveyor of genuine geniality, in contrast with the selfish hypocrisy of Heep.

Punch's effect on Micawber is described on several occasions, and its keynote is a warm inclusivity: it makes him 'uncommonly convivial' and David

> never saw him such good company. He made his face shine with the punch, so that it looked as if it had been varnished all over [. . .] As the punch disappeared, Mr Micawber became still more friendly and convivial. (*DC* 273)

Later we are told that Micawber wore an 'expression of perfect joy' when engaged in 'that congenial employment, or the making of punch' which it imparted 'in full completeness to his shining face' (*DC* 787). This alchemical effect is deliberately exploited by David, who uses punch-making as a distracting restorative when Micawber's spirits dip:

> His recent despondency, not to say despair, was gone in a moment [. . .] he stirred, and mixed, and tasted, and looked as if he were making, instead of punch, a fortune for his family down to the latest posterity. (*DC* 419)

By drawing this final correlation between making punch and making a 'fortune for his family' David not only indicates the care and dedication which Micawber brings to the task, but also directs us towards the important societal value of Micawber's mixological demonstrations: like the clown's performance, it unites both the actor and the audience in its fun.

An illuminating contrast to this can found in another demonstration of punch-making in *Little Dorrit*. The circumstances and effect of Mrs Clennam's punch-taking could hardly be more different: at an appointed time, her servant Flintwinch brings in a tray 'on which was the greater part of a bottle of port wine [. . .], a lemon, a sugar-basin, and a spice box', and prepares the punch with a clinical and joyless efficiency entirely at odds with Micawber's approach:

> [H]e filled a tumbler with a hot and odorous mixture, measured out and compounded with as much nicety as a physician's prescription. Into this mixture Mrs Clennam dipped certain of the rusks, and ate them; while the old woman buttered certain other of the rusks, which were to be eaten alone. When the invalid had eaten all the rusks and drunk all the mixture, the two trays were removed [. . .] (*LD* 51)

The sparseness and lack of excess here – nothing is allowed to accumulate or spill over its bounds – drains this ritual of any pleasure, and this emotional abstinence is later signalled by another instance of alimentary abstinence, when Flintwinch serves her eight oysters. They 'looked tempting [. . .] circularly set out on a white plate on a tray covered with a white napkin, flanked by a slice of buttered French roll, and a little compact glass of cool wine and water', but even this meal, which is wholly devoid of warmth and colour, is too much for Mrs Clennam to enjoy: she 'resisted all persuasions, and set them down again' (*LD* 67).

Such meals lack the kind of pantomimic transformation that can turn Micawber's punch into 'a fortune for his family', a transformation fuelled by the imagination. In the gaol at Marseilles, the selfish consumer Rigaud economically devours his large and elaborate meal without emotion or enjoyment, while his cell-mate John Baptist indulges in a protracted ludic performance as he eats his much smaller and simpler meal: 'placing three hunks of coarse bread before himself, and falling to upon a fourth, [he] began contentedly to work his way through them as if to clear them off were a sort of game'. By means of his imagination and a small knife, he transforms a single plain loaf into a variety of courses: '"I can cut my bread so – like a melon. Or so – like an omelette. Or so – like a fried fish. Or so – like Lyons sausage"' (*LD* 22).

Such imaginary play also transforms a basket of tripe into a lengthy and entertaining banquet in *The Chimes*, when Meg devises a guessing-game with Toby to mentally prolong the sensory pleasure of this most archetypally prosaic of meals. This mental exuberance is contrasted with the meanness of Alderman Filer, who evaluates food with the same mathematical exactitude as Mudfog workhouse's political economists. Filer's calculation of the 'wastefulness' of tripe, whereby '"the waste on [a year's production] of tripe, if boiled, would victual a garrison of five hundred men for five months of thirty-one days each, and a February over"' (*Ch* 166) echoes the board's formula that wastefulness was represented by anything more substantial than 'three meals of thin gruel a day, with an onion twice a week, and half a roll on Sundays'. Toby is consequently directed towards productive labour rather than tripe-eating by Sir Joseph, who erroneously regards it as a binary system: '"Now, the design of your creation is – not that you should swill, and guzzle, and associate your enjoyments, brutally, with food"; Toby thought remorsefully of the tripe; "but that you should feel the Dignity of Labour"' (*Ch* 182).

Toby's experience is far removed from this utilitarian view of consumption – there is no brutality, swilling or guzzling, but instead food serves a social function in the manner of Micawber's punch. Toby takes some sensory gratification from food, as he 'sniffed the savour of the hissing bacon' and 'looked lovingly down into the depths of that snug cauldron [of the tea-pot]', but prizes food more as a creator of communality and shared enjoyment, as he watches his guests Will and Lilian enjoy the food he gives to them, in the manner of 'spectators at a city dinner or court banquet' watching 'a monarch or a pope' (*Ch* 193–4).

## Leftovers

As a final example of food as social 'cement', when Mackintosh's pretence of being a landowner is uncovered, the genuine gamekeeper for the estate plays a trick of his own on Grimaldi and Bologna. He puts on a public show of angrily pursuing the men who shot his master's game, and thus tricks them into settling the matter by standing him a 'rumpsteak dinner and a bottle of wine' (*MJG* 1: 113). That he chooses to resolve their differences over the dinner-table is emblematic of the social function of food in which both Grimaldi and Dickens believed. As we saw, to Boswell eating and drinking with someone was the only means by which you could truly understand them, and this perhaps has a part to play in Byron's motivation, testing Grimaldi's character with apple pie and fish sauce. Grimaldi's self-effacing reaction is the measure of the man, and Byron's admiration – not easily won – is later reflected in his gift of an engraved silver snuff-box.

As we have seen throughout this chapter, the revelation of character can be negative, too, and not all Dickens's eaters are worthy exempla: in fact, given food's precious communal utility, some figures appear all the more reprehensible for their abuse of it. But the greedy pantomime clown is never far away from Dickens's mind, and his influence ensures that Dickens's bodily grotesquerie is ultimately celebratory – those who have too much are lampooned and derided, and those who have little are admired, in a true Bakhtinian spirit.

Chapter 7

# The Slapstick Clown

## Introduction

When assessing the audience-reader's experience of comic violence in the work of Grimaldi and Dickens, an apt motif is supplied by *The Old Curiosity Shop*. When Kit Nubbles is falsely imprisoned, his family visit him in jail, and collapse into tears as the cell bars prevent Little Jacob from touching his brother. The scene carries strong elements of pathos, as we are meant to feel the injustice of Kit's situation and his painful exclusion from familial contact. However, one observer is unmoved:

> During this melancholy pause, the turnkey read his newspaper with a waggish look [. . .] until, happening to take his eyes off it for an instant [. . .] it appeared to occur to him for the first time that somebody was crying.

The turnkey's 'waggish look' is prompted by his comic reading matter, which, while maybe a welcome respite in such a place of misery, seems to have conditioned him into a lack of empathy for the victims around him. Later Kit's mother asks for his help, and he seems paralysed within his alternative, comic world, and incapable of a feeling response:

> The turnkey, being in the very crisis and passion of a joke, motioned to her with his hand to keep silent one minute longer, for her life. Nor did he remove his hand into its former posture, but kept it in the same warning attitude until he had finished the paragraph, when he paused for a few seconds; with a smile upon his face, as who should say 'this editor is a comical blade – a funny dog', and then asked her what she wanted. (*OCS* 459)

This issue of the alienating or numbing effect of comedy is particularly pertinent to the source of laughter that I will explore in this chapter. Both Grimaldi and Dickens generate great comic effect from violence and slapstick, a strategy which risks leaving their audiences with the same attitude as the turnkey, a particularly Bergsonian reader; if they are taught to laugh at suffering on stage, and Dickens concomitantly cultivates a sense that we are all living in the *theatrum mundi*, what prevents the audience laughing at suffering off the stage?

The trope of slapstick violence is the most troubling part of pantomime, and its most important. Baudelaire called it 'the distinguishing mark of this type of the comic', and in noting how it was played with 'excess', in a 'giddy round of hyperbole' (2006: 155–6), acknowledges it as a further manifestation of pantomime's grotesque overabundance. T. A. Nelson has suggested how the cruellest deeds provoke the strongest laughter: 'the most hilarious laughter is that which comes closest to the point where the joke is indeed taken too far. The prospect, at least momentary, of mutilation or death [. . .] arouses the wildest hilarity' (1990: 109). This is palpable in Miles's description of Grimaldi as the embodiment of 'clown atrocity' or 'crimes that delight us' (1838: 1992), a sentiment that is echoed in a later epithet for the pantomime as 'brutal buffoonery' ([Anon.] 1877a: 365).

Although Jacky Bratton has indicated that the taste for such routines was receding by the 1850s, as the 'rational adult' chose to 'repudiate an entertainment which is violent, immoral and altogether vulgar' (2010: 96), Dickens gleefully continued to populate his fiction with these violent clowns. However, while this was an accepted (and indeed demanded) element of Regency pantomime theatre, its position within the Victorian novel was less assured. Consequently, Dickens's inclusion of 'brutal buffoonery' in his work creates morally fractured texts which, in another reflection of the disruptive chaos caused by the Grimaldian clown, invite us to both laugh at and pity the beaten child simultaneously.

In the first section of this chapter, I draw on theories of slapstick and physical comedy to sketch a framework for understanding such violence. I then consider several key characteristics of the slapstick form to show how its tropes operate in the work of Grimaldi and Dickens. I will argue that through the agency of seemingly indestructible 'clownish' characters and their slapstick set-pieces, Dickens grants himself brief 'holiday' periods within his wider narratives to generate a relentless cycle of violence within which he suspends his renowned philanthropic views to indulge momentarily in the violent fun of the harlequinade. In the central part of this chapter I consider the consequences of such a moral suspension when the targets of the violence are society's most vulnerable groups – women, the elderly and the young. Unlike the harlequinade, which is detached from the sketchy 'plot' of the pantomime, Dickens's enjoyable slapstick violence complicates the themes of the wider work in which it exists and turns the reader's moral compass round 'topsy-turvy'.

## Slapstick in Theory and Practice

The genre term 'slapstick' derives from the theatrical equipment of the same name, a wooden bat with hinged slats that generates a loud noise when struck against another object. Tom Gunning's analysis of the slapstick's mechanics indicates how it gives the impression of striking a painful blow via an exaggerated noise, which simultaneously announces the falsity of that blow:

> The hinged slats allow energy to be displaced from the apparent purpose of striking a victim to the creation of a sound effect [. . .] Part of the amusement the slapstick offers lies in the exaggerated noise it generates, making the viewer aware that the slaps are not really painful, but are nonetheless intense in their sensual effects. (2010: 141)

Dickens swings his verbal slapstick in a similar fashion, as the displacement of energy occurs when he expands his creative effort in a comical flourish of language rather than in a description that registers physical pain. This flourish is the loud noise which amuses the audience and provides an intense sensual effect, but its exaggerated nature distances the observer from any contemplation of suffering.

This method is encapsulated in Dickens's description of the Game Chicken's boxing match with 'the Larkey Boy' in *Dombey and Son*. Initially, the Game Chicken's physical appearance seems to preclude humour, with 'his visage in a state of such great dilapidation, as to be hardly presentable in society with comfort to the beholders'. But Dickens immediately defuses any concern we might have for the battered Chicken with his report of the fight, within which his language provides the noisy slap:

> The Chicken himself attributed this punishment to his having had the misfortune to get into Chancery early in the proceedings, when he was severely fibbed by the Larkey one, and heavily grassed. But it appeared

> from the published records of that great contest that the Larkey Boy had had it all his own way from the beginning, and that the Chicken had been tapped, and bunged, and had received pepper, and had been made groggy, and had come up piping, and had endured a complication of similar strange inconveniences, until he had been gone into and finished. (*DS* 675)

This grotesquely superabundant accumulation of the amusing slang of the boxing world holds the reader at arm's length from the bloody spectacle of early nineteenth-century prize-fighting.

Millie Taylor feels that the 'interruption' of slapstick violence into the pantomime show serves a number of dramatic purposes, as it 'changes the pace, changes the relationship of audience to performance, and entertains', and although it is 'a moment of disruption', it is also a 'moment of danger and involvement of the liveness of each individual performance' (2007: 35). For Taylor, rather than alienating or shocking the audience, slapstick violence draws the audience closer in to the show and forces them to identify with the main protagonist:

> that status between the performers or between performers and authority figures is challenged in competitive routines and sequences; [and] the audience is involved in the comedy by a complicitous look [. . .] or the physical presence of performers within the auditorium. (2007: 48–9)

This significantly indicates that slapstick laughter carries a range of possible motives, and can be variously retributive, normative or democratic. Its challenge to the status between performers and authority figures promises iconoclasm, but the audience's engagement could be either normative (if the clown causes suffering in others) or democratic (if the clown suffers himself).

Grimaldi's slapstick routines align him with another exponent of humorous violence from popular culture, Mr Punch, as Dickens was aware. In the *Memoirs*, he describes how in *Harlequin Amulet, or the Magic of Mona* (Drury Lane, 1799) Grimaldi 'had to perform Punch, and to change afterwards to Clown' (*MJG* 1: 139). Punch and Clown often shared the stage at other shows, such as Richardson's, and Dickens may have seen such a 'double-header' performance himself as part of 'the pantomime which came lumbering down in Richardson's waggons at fair-time' described in the *Memoirs* (*MJG* 1: vi). The porous division between different popular entertainments made the relationship between clown and Punch symbiotic, as the Grimaldian clown in turn became a popular figure within the Punch and Judy show. Robert Leach feels that the Joey character contributed 'a dimension of fast-moving comedy which highlights without diminishing the violence' (1985: 75). In Henry Mayhew's *London Labour and the London Poor* (1851), a Punchman gives a detailed description of the role of Joey 'the merry clown' puppet, who dances around Punch until he is knocked down, helps Punch steal sausages and burns him with a red-hot poker, before 'he sits down on it himself and burns his breeches' (1968 3: 51).

Commentators on the performances of both Grimaldi and Punch register the audience's complicity in this temporary amorality as they legitimise the crimes of our (anti-)heroes and suspend their own belief in laws that commonly regulate society. Miles claims audiences 'were quite blind to the moral delinquency of Mons. Clown's habits' and 'rejoiced in his successes' even when 'multiplied up to murder' (1838: 6–7). As mentioned in Chapter 2, a *Times* reviewer similarly questions society's moral values when he admits that 'If [Clown] took up a red-hot poker to anybody, we could never interfere – though it had been to save our own father – and when he stole apples, we really doubted whether common honesty was not a kind of prejudice' ([Anon.] 1823: 3).

Punch's crimes are similarly excused in terms that cause introspection in the observer:

> It may be that his mood is hasty, that he is too violent and pugnacious, and that he has a Turkish disregard of mortality; but then – his buoyancy of spirit, his boldness, and his wit, are not these redeeming points [. . .]? Punch is certainly not a very moral personage; but then was there ever one more free from hypocrisy? ([Anon.] 1828a: 83)

Clown has successfully inverted moral norms, for when Punch 'beats out the brains' of his many opponents, the audience wonder 'who even thinks that beating out brains is, *per se*, wrong?' ([Anon.] 1827: 91).

The alteration in the power dynamic that slapstick violence enacts can also be observed in the later reminiscences of Walter Freewood in the *Theatrical Journal*, which explicitly link the audience's enjoyment to Grimaldi's anti-authoritarian pranks:

> You might have heard the laughter miles off when Clown stole the sausages and tried to put the baby in his pocket, and wasn't it capital fun when the policeman tumbled over the butter-slide Clown had just made before the doorstep, and then got pelted with flour bags conveniently pilfered from an adjoining baker's? (qtd in Wilson 1949: 35)

Freewood classifies this lengthy charge-sheet of offences – encompassing theft, kidnap and assault – as 'capital fun' and 'the best fun of all', and A. E. Wilson calls them merely 'boisterous pranks and practical jokes' (1946: 28).

In Chapter 3, I briefly delineated the attraction of violence within the pantomime form, but it will be helpful for what follows to explore this further here. The problematic nature of slapstick laughter stems from its operation on two contrary impulses, broadly defined as 'normative' and 'retributive'. For David Mayer, the 'normative', corrective impulse primarily reaffirms 'the conservative position from which [it] operates' by presenting aberrations from the perceived norms of society and directing the audience to 'compare the aberration that he sees on the stage with the norm as he understands it'. By laughing 'at the disparity between the two', the audience confirms their 'allegiance to the norms' (1969: 52).

The effectiveness of such laughter requires the suspension of moral law: for Bergson, comedy has 'no greater foe than emotion', and thus its audience 'must, for the moment, put [their] affection out of court and impose silence on [their] pity' (1956: 63). While slapstick laughter carries a universality that transcends class, gender and age, it also suspends the laugher's humanity; as Muriel Andrin notes, 'Slapstick laughter plays on the spectator's insensitivity by allowing no time for healing or commiserating' (2010: 229).

One possible consequence of this can be a feeling of superiority over the victim, which forms the basis of Thomas Hobbes's theory of comedy articulated in *Human Nature* (1650). Hobbes asserts that 'the cause of laughter is the exaltation at a triumph of our own or an indignity suffered by someone else: we laugh when we feel superior to others' (qtd in Nelson 1990: 5). Moreover, both Bergson and Hobbes agree that this is a shared experience: for Hobbes, if laughter is to be 'without offence', it 'must be at absurdities and infirmities abstracted from persons, and where all the company may laugh together' (1994: 55); and to Bergson, laughter 'always implies a kind of secret freemasonry, or even complicity, with other laughers, real or imaginary' (1956: 64). Laughter becomes 'a sort of *social gesture*' (1956: 73) which 'singles out and represses' (1956: 117) things regarded as undesirable and damaging to society such as absentmindedness or inelasticity. To Bergson, then, 'laughter is, above all, a corrective. Being intended to humiliate, it must make a painful impression on the person against whom it is directed' (1956: 187).

By contrast, Mayer also traces a strand of what he calls 'retributive' comedy, which aligns with Bakhtin's more democratic view of laughter. In retributive comedy, scenes of order shift towards chaos, and solemn occasions become moments of merriment. As Mayer explains:

> Grave and stately persons are knocked into undignified positions, magistrates and policemen are assaulted, elegant clothes are dirtied and torn, valuable merchandise is deliberately broken, orderly silence is turned into bedlam. (1969: 56)

Such actions enact 'a vicarious release from society's strictures and taboos', and represent a further subversion of 'law', this time the civil laws of society. Retributive comedy makes mutiny 'harmless and even pleasurable' and enables protest to occur 'without injurious consequences to the protester' (1969: 56). Consequently, it reverses the direction of normative comedy by being directed by the governed against those who govern. This shifts it away from conservatism to radicalism, and explains Grimaldi's attractions to the likes of Hazlitt and Hunt, who, as Moody describes, saw the 'episodic violence' of the harlequinade as enacting 'the pleasures of a delicious political retribution' (2000: 14). This parallels Andrew Stott's characterisation of Bakhtin's carnivalesque comedy as 'the vehicle of an authentic proletarian voice answering the ascetic oppressions of the ruling classes' (2005: 33). Grimaldi's Clown is seen to be operating in this mode when Mayer defines him as 'a happy criminal, who knew neither shame, nor guilt, nor repentance' (1969: 47), who acted as the audience's surrogate for the violation of social codes and excessive bodily pain, inviting 'spectators to feel and to experience with him, without the exertion or pain or ridicule of doing so, and encourag[ing] them to participate in his wildest misdeeds and wittiest jests' (1969: 48).

The audience's knowing implication in the onstage violence is partly explained by the perceived constitutional illegitimacy of the pantomime form, based on its position outside the prevailing licensing laws and its association with carnivalesque holidays. The 'illegal' acts that are performed onstage, particularly during the anarchic harlequinade are, as Moody puts it, 'allowed to exist because of pantomime's perceived status as a theatrical genre beyond rationality' (2000: 215) which 'made possible the theatrical defeat of beadles and constables, or the self-aggrandisement of military men' (2000: 225). The clown thus becomes 'a precious symbol of social licence' (2000: 14), who 'was presumed to inhabit an imaginary space outside ordinary human morality' (2000: 215).

For the rest of this chapter, I will trace the uneasy balance between these two kinds of comedy that slapstick violence tries to traverse in Dickens's work. It is notable that Dickens makes this particularly difficult for himself, since – given his public persona of social reformer and humanitarian – it is significant that a large portion of his slapstick violence is directed towards three of the most vulnerable groups within Victorian society: women; the elderly; and the young. As T. A. Nelson suggests, because our 'response to [such] comedy' is often 'two-faced', perhaps inevitably the 'work of Dickens betrays a conflict of impulses' (1990: 63–4).

## Violence against Women and the Elderly

Although pantomime's miniaturised counterpart *Punch and Judy* often has Punch's assault on Judy as its centrepiece (indeed, Marlene Tromp opens *The Private Rod: Marital Violence, Sensation, and the Law in Victorian Britain* with one such scene), Grimaldi's slapstick violence is never directed towards women. The harlequinade was a male-dominated spectacle, in which the sole principal female character Columbine functioned specifically as a passive object of desire – controlled by Pantaloon, wooed by an inappropriate suitor, chased by Clown and protected by Harlequin. However, Dickens makes no such distinction: although deployed sparingly, slapstick is one of several stylistic methods by which Dickens commits violence against the women of his novels, alongside grotesque caricature and oppressive objectification.

As Kincaid suggests, Quilp's treatment of his wife and her friends asks the reader of *The Old Curiosity Shop* 'to participate in hostile laughter at all women', even those who exhibit 'softness, humility, and gentle subservience' (1971: 83). One enabler of such laughter is the way in which other characters conspicuously fail to notice Quilp's violence towards his wife – Dick Swiveller hears Mrs Quilp's 'suppressed scream' when her husband pinches her, but makes no acknowledgement of the act or the impact of such violence. He 'did not remark on these appearances, and soon forgot them', which provides a cue to the reader to do the same (*OCS* 107). Moreover, in Dickens's harlequinade women are sometimes implicated as would-be participants in the knockabout violence. For Surridge, Mrs Jiniwin and her entourage represent 'the political reality of resistant women' but significantly 'undercuts their resistance as vicious and shrewish, almost as distasteful and in need of reform as Quilp himself' (2005: 159);

by contrast, *Oliver Twist*'s Nancy represents 'Mrs Jiniwin's antitype' (2005: 30) who does not resist Sikes's violence. By inscribing this violence against women as a public performance, Dickens, as Surridge has it, 'dwells almost obsessively on this moment when the 'private' violence of the home enters the public eye' (2005: 18), and as we have seen, this unstable interface between the public and private is a wider and enduring interest for Dickens. However, it further problematises an issue which, while kept private, was containable for Victorian (patriarchal) society, as seen in Dickens's own 'deep ambivalence concerning public intrusion into domestic privacy' (2005: 18). This ambivalence leads Dickens to use slapstick to render comic those who (by contrast to Nancy's devoted silence) make a public spectacle of the violence they suffer and their resistance to it.

This comic treatment of female self-assertion is evident in *Little Dorrit*. Kincaid correctly observes that Affery is 'a real victim of physical cruelty' (1971: 216), but Dickens attempts to obfuscate this through his persistent slapstick tone. By depicting the effects of Flintwinch's violence as exaggerated and impermanent, and by transforming Affery into a Bergsonian automaton, he forces the exchanges between Affery and her violent husband Flintwinch towards the realms of the pantomimic.

Bergson views the stumbling man or the clown who becomes a rigid object when struck or bouncing off other objects as comical due to his 'mechanical inelasticity' and 'rigidity' (1956: 66–7), which make him resemble an automaton: 'The attitudes, gestures and movements of the human body are laughable in exact proportion as that body reminds us of a mere machine' (1956: 79). Affery and Flintwinch move in just such a synchronised, automatic manner, resembling two battling figures in a mechanised clock:

> He kept his eyes upon her, and kept advancing; and she, completely under his influence, kept retiring before him. Thus, she walking backward and he walking forward, they came into their own room. They were no sooner shut in there, than Mr Flintwinch took her by the throat, and shook her till she was black in the face. (*LD* 58)

The pair are regularly characterised in this way, exemplifying Bergson's 'mechanical encrusted on the living'. Flintwinch runs on crooked rails as he prepares to attack his wife, screwing 'himself a curve or two in the direction of the window-seat' and later continuing 'with a menacing grin to screw himself in the direction of his wife' (*LD* 799). Similarly, Affery adopts repetitive actions as a fearful response to her husband's threats: 'In this dilemma, Mistress Affery, with her apron as a hood to keep the rain off, ran crying up and down the solitary paved enclosure several times' (*LD* 365).

Dickens also uses verbal slapstick to disarm and diminish Affery's constant fear of Flintwinch, presenting it as comic repartee with verbal play and punning, in the same way that the shocking impact of working-class domestic violence was defused in accounts of court trials by rendering it in comic terms. Lisa Surridge's *Bleak Houses: Marital Violence in Victorian Fiction* provides more detailed discussion on the wider deployment of this technique. At one point Affery is scared that their house is haunted and so tells her husband that she felt '"a rustle and a sort of trembling touch behind [her]"', to which he responds, '"Affery, my woman [. . .] if you don't get tea pretty quick [. . .] you'll become sensible of a rustle and a touch that'll send you flying to the other end of the kitchen"' (*LD* 203). Flintwinch even makes a dark joke of trying to soothe her nerves, casting his violence and her suffering into a comic frame. To cure her '"distempered antics"', he feels that she '"must have some physic"' and offers to give her '"such a comfortable dose"' when they are alone. However, given that this promise is delivered 'with his fists clenched, and his elbows quivering with impatience to shake her', it is clear what sort of medicine he has in mind (*LD* 657).

By contrast to the pantomime's treatment of women, the elderly man receives no such protection, since during the harlequinade, Grimaldi's principal target for abuse was Pantaloon. In *Harlequin Mother Goose*, Clown 'breaks [a wooden] board in two upon [Pantaloon's] head' (T. Dibdin [1860?]: 16] when he emerges from a basket, while in *Harlequin in His Element*, Clown puts a stinging wasp on the Pantaloon's nose, and then tricks him into sitting on a moving bench which tips him over. Later in a glass factory, Clown 'sweeps [a] stick round, breaks [Pantaloon]'s shins, and knocks him down'. The appropriate response to this assault is signalled by Clown, who 'discovers his mistake, pretends to cry, but laughs aside' (T. Dibdin 1808: 9–10).

Pantaloon is the archetypal old miser and representative of misguided familial authority, and as the nature of these two different vices indicates, the laughter directed at Pantaloon's suffering is both normative and retributive. Mayer characterises Pantaloon as beset by 'egotism and ruthless stupidity' (1969: 43), and, as I explored in Chapter 3, 'The Pantomime of Life' demonstrates that Dickens was aware of Pantaloon's conventional role as a deserved victim of violence. Pantaloon's failures to conform to social norms in relation to his age exculpate both his rough treatment and the almost primal reaction by the audience-mob who surround him. However, the situation also carries a retributive element, by virtue of Pantaloon's attempts to marry his attractive young daughter to an inappropriate suitor, and as part of his role as Clown's master.

The real impact of Pantaloon's suffering is revealed in Andrew Halliday's article 'Pantaloon', in which a retired Pantaloon describes the sufferings caused by his Clown Pelloni. Clown's routine is not merely diverting entertainment but also satisfies the sadism of both Clown himself and his audience:

> He was always very rough at his business. If I missed the slap, Joey would give me a real one, a regular stinger; and the people in the front liked the real thing best. They always laughed more at the real thing, and that encouraged Joey to do the real thing. Once, when he nearly broke my back with the barber's shutter, the gallery went into regular convulsions, and shouted 'Encore'. (1863b: 10)

In the *Memoirs* the supposedly inappropriate behaviour of Billy Coombes, a 'very indifferent actor' who played the Pantaloon to Grimaldi's Clown, makes him a socially sanctioned butt of humour and even violence. The nature of his misdemeanours is kept vague, as we are only told that Coombes had given Grimaldi 'mighty offence upon several occasions, possibly by making his appearance on the stage in a state of intoxication' – in fact, 'Grimaldi forgot the precise cause of affront, but, whatever it was, they deemed it a very great one', implicitly expecting us to trust in Joe's assessment (*MJG* 2: 99).

Dickens incorporates Coombes's 'deserved' punishment in the pantomime act itself, with the full complicity of the spectators: Grimaldi locks him in a chest 'amidst the plaudits of the audience, who thought it was a capital trick' (*MJG* 2: 100), and (maybe) accidentally leaves him there overnight. Even when Coombes emerges from the apparently airtight chest the next morning as a 'truly pitiable object' who was lucky to have survived, Dickens precludes any sympathy by revealing that Coombes had in fact 'got into the chest that morning to turn the tables upon his assailants' (*MJG* 2: 101–2).

Dickens's earliest fictional Pantaloon is Fagin, an avaricious old man who tries to foil the moral and social progress of the hero Oliver. These social infractions enable Dickens to cast Fagin as Pantaloon in a brief scene of slapstick violence when he is caught in a quarrel between two of his accomplices:

> [The] abused Mr Chitling [. . .] rushed across the room, and aimed a blow at the offender, who [. . .] ducked to avoid it; and chose his time so well that it lighted on the chest of the merry old gentleman, and caused him to stagger to the wall, where he stood panting for breath, while Mr Chitling looked on, in intense dismay. (*OT* 169)

The reference to a character's 'timing' is an act of comic misdirection, as Dickens subtly alludes to his own agency in choreographing the scene towards this neat comic finale. Dickens the director cannot resist revealing his hand in events, as he manipulates his characters to provide a final *tableau* for our appreciation, framing attacker and victim.

This scene of comic violence is a gateway to Fagin's much rougher treatment at the end of the novel, when the passive spectators become the active mob and subject Fagin to what Jeremy Tambling calls 'lynch-law': 'no detective is needed when the crowd itself turns detective, as though punishment is being presented here as the due that is owing to an outraged society' (1995: 150). This is a cyclical movement: initially the crowd becomes the mob trying to assault Fagin when he is arrested, 'jumping up, one behind another, and snarling with their teeth and making at him like wild beasts' (*OT* 334), in a manner that recalls the whooping and yelling crowd who stand over the beaten Pantaloon in 'The Pantomime of Life'. They then transform back into a passive but threatening audience for Fagin's final performance at his theatrical trial:

> Before him and behind; above, below, on the right and on the left; he seemed to stand surrounded by a firmament, all bright with gleaming eyes.
>
> He stood there, in all this glare of living light. (*OT* 350)

This continues at his execution scene when the assembled multitude are 'pushing, quarrelling and joking' before 'the black stage' (*OT* 357). Although Fagin's journey from pursuit to trial and final hanging is the conventional melodramatic conclusion for the villainous Pantaloon, Dickens simultaneously acknowledges an equally threatening and destructive impulse within a public audience-mob comfortable with such normative justice from the pantomime.

Dickens returns to the punished Pantaloon much later, in *Our Mutual Friend*. Although Silas Wegg has no daughter to marry off, he interferes in the socially correct love plot of the novel by trying to obstruct the progress of the hero John Rokesmith towards his fortune. Kincaid aligns Wegg with Dickens's earlier pantomimic figures when he comments that Wegg and Venus 'hearken back to much simpler comic types', being 'both completely unselfconscious and quite uncomplex' (1971: 248), and Wegg's amputated leg serves as a suitably slapstick prop. Dickens's preparation of Wegg as a character with elements of the Pantaloon makes his ultimate fate in a 'slosh' scene an entirely expected conclusion. Sloppy is asked to throw him out of the Boffin house:

> but, a scavenger's cart happening to stand unattended at the corner, with its little ladder planted against the wheel, Mr S. found it impossible to resist the temptation of shooting Mr Silas Wegg into the cart's contents. A somewhat difficult feat, achieved with a great dexterity, and with a prodigious splash. (*OMF* 770)

Dickens's carefully placed reference to the fortuitous circumstances of the situation, as the cart is 'happening to stand unattended at the corner', is of course anything but. Moreover, his choice of Sloppy as the agent has also been managed, since throughout the novel Dickens has foregrounded his clownish qualities – his ungainly movement, incessant chuckling and physical appearance ('a very long boy, with a very little head, and an open mouth of disproportionate capacity' [*OMF* 196]). Sloppy thus completes the fulfilment of his conventional role by thwarting Pantaloon and assisting the lovers' progress, and while John Carey censures this scene as 'dutiful, perfunctory business' (1991: 29) Kincaid correctly nuances this scene when he describes it as a ritual of slapstick justice, whereby 'true wisdom [. . .] doesn't reward the cheats but plops them into carts of night-soil' (1971: 250).

## Violence against Children

According to the *Illustrated Sporting and Dramatic News* in 1877, child actors were more suited to the harlequinade's 'brutal buffoonery' than their adult counterparts, because it represented 'essentially the wild frolics of childhood' and 'the utter abandonment of animal spirits only proper to the time of life before care of experience have begun to sober down the temperament of mankind' ([Anon.] 1877a: 365). This is one reason why the child is a frequent conduit for its slapstick violence.

Babies were particularly popular targets: as Wilson relates, Clown would 'kidnap [them] from too-confiding nursemaids' (1946: 38) and then submit them to all manner of cruel pranks and hazardous acrobatics. Contemporary opinion was divided as to the propriety of such routines: for example, Robert Paulet, a foreign visitor to the English pantomime queried, 'Whence can arise the pleasure of seeing children suspended in the air, or tossed about, at the utmost hazard of their lives, to gratify the avarice of unnatural parents?' (Cradock 1828: 66). Similarly, *The Morning Herald* gave a disapproving account of an Adelphi pantomime of 1827, in which 'An effigy of a child was flung towards the pit':

> This incident was loudly applauded. The manner in which the child in the cradle was managed cannot be too reprobated. No one can view the stifling of an infant, even in jest, and the supposed flattening of its body by the pressure of a superior weight, even though that weight should be the ridiculous person of Pantaloon himself, without an unmixed sense of pain. (qtd in Frow 1985: 84)

However, as the audience's reaction suggests, Halliday was not alone in asking forty years later: 'Where is the witticism that can compete with sitting on a baby, and flattening it to the shape of a pancake?' (1863a: 5).

This divided response reflects a more general and ahistorical ambiguity around the place of the child in comedy. For Nelson, the 'nausea of parenthood' and the parents' 'longing not to be responsible for the child in its more repellent aspects' were among 'the many antisocial emotions which comedy allows itself to express'. However comic children can also embody modes that have been closed off to the civilised adult, such as 'liveliness' and 'the natural [and] the instinctual' which make the child a multivalent symbol, representing both the woes of care and a lost state of freedom (1990: 60).

The more frequent appearance of children on the stage in the late eighteenth and early nineteenth century reflected a wider cultural shift in perceptions of the child, which in turn complicated their participation in slapstick routines. As Anne Varty has demonstrated, Romantic conceptions of the child as the guileless natural or the *tabula rasa* superseded previous representations of them as miniature adults and cursed inheritors of original sin, with the stage an important forum for this transition. Varty notes how in an era when 'prejudice against actors and their profession focussed on their doubleness or duplicity', the nineteenth-century 'performing' child was nonetheless situated favourably alongside 'the peasant, the savage, [and] the idiot', as a figure 'in whom the histrionic impulse remains undeveloped' (2008: 12).

Varty also identifies John Ruskin as one of the earliest to situate Dickens's children specifically as a fictional continuation of the Romantic ideals of the child. In 'Fairy Land' (1884) Ruskin notes the prominence of 'child benediction' in Dickens's work, tracing an imaginary London 'pilgrimage' on which one meets 'the Little Nells and boy David Copperfields, and in the heart of it, Kit's baby brother at Astley's, indenting his cheek with an oyster-shell to the admiration of all beholders' (1908: 338).

Much later, Peter Coveney describes the Dickensian child as a principal symbol of innocence and purity in an increasingly sordid and impure machine age, situating Dickens as 'the central figure in the transference of the romantic child into the Victorian novel' (1957: 74). However, while Coveney correctly identifies how Dickens used the pure child as a vehicle for what Coveney calls 'the pivot of his mature art', namely his depiction of 'the struggle of innocence with evil' (1957: 70) he does not account for the child's role in slapstick comedy. For while they were often 'agents in a moral or political thesis' (1957: 65), Dickens's fictional children also functioned as agents of a dark and Regency-inflected humour at odds with many of the author's philanthropic values. In another manifestation of his artistic double vision, he sees the child as both the repository of Victorian sympathy and a small, perfectly malleable receptacle of slapstick violence, whereby they 'may be knocked about and sat upon, or choked with gravy spoons, in the process of feeding, and yet no Coroner be wanted, nor anybody made uncomfortable' (*HW* 4.95: 386). Alongside those famous waifs and sympathetic orphans, the Olivers and Little Nells, come the anonymous and seemingly indestructible miniature clowns that populate his fiction.

Grimaldi's own youth (which Dickens relates in the *Memoirs*) provides the model for Dickens's slapstick child. His father gives him a real and painful beating on stage, but both the father's angry blows and the child's cries are treated as 'a most capital joke' by the audience, welcomed by 'shouts of laughter and peals of applause'. Reviews for that show commented that 'it was perfectly wonderful to see a mere child perform so naturally, and highly creditable to his father's talents as a teacher' and Dickens develops this ambiguity, presenting Grimaldi in a grotesque, liminal state between real, feeling humanity and a performed role. He describes how

> The tears running down his face, which was painted 'an inch thick', came to the 'complexion at last', in parts, and made him look as much like a little clown as like a little human being, to neither of which characters he bore the more distant resemblance. (*MJG* 1: 16)

The performing mask cannot entirely obscure the human feeling beneath because his authentic tears penetrate it and partially reveal the human figure beneath the artifice, and suspend him in an indeterminate position. The reactions to Grimaldi's onstage beating hold two contradictory concepts in tension, as they both demonstrate the desirability and attraction of performing 'naturally', but also acknowledge its performed and taught nature.

The theatrical performance of a fictional narrative must put the pain at a double remove; but in the case of an 1843 production of *Nicholas Nickleby*, the performance was, like young Grimaldi's own plight onstage, closer to felt reality than the audience realised. As Varty describes it, the performing children had been kidnapped and forced onto the stage by the villainous 'Figaro', and once they had been trapped in this stage version of Dotheboys Hall they suffered the same cruelties as Squeers's charges: 'Amidst crying and moaning they were placed on the stage, sitting on benches and kept in order by Figaro's cane – poor children, completely bewildered. When the treacle was administered, most of them cried.'

The audience's reaction is identical to that of the witnesses to Grimaldi's onstage beating; the suffering of the children 'delighted the audience, thinking it was natural (so it was)' (Varty 2008: 21). By privileging the natural and unaffected stage child the audience celebrated enactments of pain that appeared to be natural and unaffected precisely because they were.

A similar dynamic is played out in a more private and domestic scene in the *Memoirs* when, as I described in Chapter 3, Grimaldi's father feigns his own death to assess his two sons' true feelings for him. The stage son Joe uses his training to select an appropriate 'line of conduct', which leads to praise as 'the son who truly and sincerely loved [his father]', whereas his unworldly and authentic brother John provides a natural reaction by openly celebrating his father's demise, and is beaten 'most unmercifully' as a result (*MJG* 1: 28–9). Joe is clearly not the true and sincere child on this occasion, and this episode reminds us that stage children could only ever be manufactured replicas of the 'natural'. However, as Varty comments, 'the license to act out an authentic self that was nevertheless learned, repeatable and various was the special preserve of the child actor' (2008: 12) and so children could suffer real pain under the commonly accepted cultural understanding that all was merely performance. Dickens's beating of a number of his fictional children in a slapstick way, which further distances the violence from reality, represents a novelistic attempt at a similar trick.

As agitation for the improved welfare of children grew, the real pain of child performers became a focus for this debate. Reformists contrasted the suffering child on stage with the protected and comfortable child in the audience: in *Pantomime Waifs; or, A Plea for our City Children*, Ellen Barlee notes that after the end of the show 'few persons [. . .] give a thought to [the] curtain's reverse shadows, or inquire into the well-being of the human machinery which provided their evening's amusement' (1884: xiv). Her phrase 'human machinery' is used to highlight how such children are dehumanised, but in Dickens's work the comic potential of this example of Bergson's living automaton is something to be played with, as the performing child becomes a machine absorbing the blows of the slapstick and then springing up for more punishment.

Stage children were also vulnerable to real machinery as well. As Varty explains, technological advances allowed stage managers to offer more elaborate attractions to spectators, but also threatened the welfare of vulnerable child performers: 'theatrical machinery functioned as a kind of trap, [within which] children were particularly reluctant' (2008: 39). Consequently, Dickens portrays Grimaldi's childhood as a procession through a range of perilous accidents in an echo of Grimaldi's construction of his clown's routine around a series of carefully managed stage traps. For example, when Grimaldi is swung round his father's head 'with the utmost velocity' and the chain snaps, he is 'hurled a considerable distance into the pit'. However, after narrating the facts of this potentially fatal event, Dickens quickly points out that Grimaldi did this 'fortunately without sustaining the slightest injury', and switches the tone to comic effect by adding the detail of the boy's landing 'into the very arms of an old gentleman who was sitting gazing at the stage with intense interest' (*MJG* 1: 19).

In another show, young Grimaldi is dressed in a cat costume, as part of what is known as 'skin work'. Welfare reformers condemned this practice as particularly cruel, with Lord Shaftesbury relating to Parliament in 1872 how children were beaten to fit 'into skins too small for them [. . .] to represent monkeys and devils' ([Anon.] 1872a: c622). Dickens's account initially supports this testimony, as we are told that the 'dress [Grimaldi] wore was so clumsily contrived, that when it was sewn upon him he could not see before him', but then soon shifts towards slapstick. Dickens prefaces the incident with a commentary that glosses the incident as humorous, alluding to the myth of the nine-lived cat as a variation on the indestructible clown: when wearing the cat costume Grimaldi 'met with an accident, his speedy recovery from which would almost induce one to believe that he had so completely identified himself with the character as to have eight additional chances for his life'. This humorous intervention cushions the subsequent impact on the reader when Grimaldi then falls down an open trap-door when 'running about the stage' and suffers severe injury, 'breaking his collar-bone, and inflicting several contusions on his body'. Dickens further compounds the readers' insulation by quickly mentioning Grimaldi's speedy recovery (*MJG* 1: 22).

This humorous presentation of the hazardous existence of stage children contrasts markedly with the presentations of such accidents in stage journals like *The Era*. During an Australian production of *The Slave* in August 1860, a child was thrown across a chasm before his supporting wire had been properly attached and 'the poor little fellow fell on to the stage', causing 'the greatest alarm' in the audience. While Dickens's accounts display little concern for any real hurt caused and continue their narrative unimpeded, this accident pauses both the performance and *The Era*'s description of it. The curtain drops, and the child's offstage recovery becomes the principal drama while the audience wait for news; when his safety is finally assured it is 'warmly welcomed by the house' ([Anon.] 1860a: 12) and the play continues.

Dickens's method in the *Memoirs* of humorously presenting acts of violence against children, accidental or otherwise, continues in two novels of the same period. *Oliver Twist* and *Nicholas Nickleby* are both central in Coveney's presentation of the Dickensian child as 'the symbol of sensitive feeling [within] a society maddened with the pursuit of material progress' (1957: 74), but both often occlude this sensitive feeling for comic effect. While on the one hand Dickens directs 'exaggerated emotions of pathos' (Coveney 1957: 116) towards his principal *loci* of sympathy, Oliver and Smike (both images of his own vulnerable childhood self), on the other there are many anonymous children who merely function as supernumeraries in 'the pantomime of life', with the 'express purpose of being cheated, or knocked down, or both' (*PoL* 504). Moreover, by using highly theatrical and comical figures like Bumble and Squeers as central dispensers of that violence, its pathetic impact is further significantly weakened.

The first section of *Oliver Twist* contains a profusion of such comic business. Just before Oliver is presented to the board 'Mr Bumble gave him a tap on the head, with his cane, to wake him up; and another on the back to make him lively' (*OT* 24), while later at the pauper's funeral, Bumble 'threshed a boy or two, to keep up appearances' (*OT* 49). Bumble becomes synonymous with this cane, his own parochial slapstick, which causes great noise but registers seemingly little physical harm. When Bumble is called by the board to '"step up to Sowerberry's with [his] cane, and see what's best to be done"' after Oliver has beaten Noah, Dickens tells us that Bumble prepares for the visit by 'adjusting the wax-end which was twisted round the bottom of his cane, for the purposes of parochial flagellation' (*OT* 55–6).

Although Bumble is the primary symbol of adult authority, Dickens suggests that the violence towards children is more pervasive and systemic rather than the actions of one individual. The workhouse board ponder possible ways to dispose of Oliver in a similarly grimly ludic spirit, and conclude that sending him to sea may be preferable, where

> the skipper would flog him to death, in a playful mood [. . .] or would knock his brains out with an iron bar, both pastimes being, as is pretty generally known, very favourite and common recreations among gentlemen of that class. (*OT* 36)

Moreover, Gamfield speaks for all employers of child labour when he describes his use of boy sweeps. In response to the serious assertion that young boys are smothered in chimneys, Gamfield gives his own account of his treatment of his young charges that defuses the seriousness through slapstick connotations:

> Boys is wery obstinit, and wery lazy, gen'lmen, and there's nothink like a good hot blaze to make 'em come down vith a run. It's humane too, gen'lmen, acause, even if they've stuck in the chimbley, roastin' their feet makes 'em struggle to hextricate themselves. (*OT* 31)

Surridge has noted how early nineteenth-century reports of working-class marital abuse cases used accented speech in the manner of comic patter to frame their subject matter as humorous, and Dickens's similar appropriation of a working-class idiom here suggests how we might read this scene. The reader is only invited to observe the scene through the humorous proxy of Gamfield and is given no insight into the pain of the boys with roasted feet.

Moreover, Gamfield's treatment acts as a further corollary to his abuse of children. Surridge again notes how violence against animals is an important signifier in Victorian fiction, as writers 'deployed the analogy between wife and animal [. . .] to suggest the connection between wife assault and the legal nonexistence of women' (2005: 87). However, while this is given a serious tone in the relations between Sikes, Bullseye and Nancy, Gamfield's beating of his donkey is given a lighter, comic tone that invites us to read his violence towards young boys in a similar way. Gamfield thinks hard about his financial predicament by 'alternately cudgelling his brains and his donkey', and Dickens dismisses several cruel blows to the animal as mere 'arrangements' before Gamfield approaches the workhouse gate. On observing this performance Bumble 'smiled joyously [. . .] for he saw at once that Mr Gamfield was exactly the sort of master Oliver Twist wanted', indicating a clear correspondence between the actual treatment of the animal and the expected treatment of the boy (*OT* 30). At no point does Dickens ever depict the donkey as crying out in pain nor give us any other indication of his suffering.

Quilp's attitude to childcare is aptly summarised in his assertion that '"I don't eat babies; I don't like 'em"' (*OCS* 166), as he becomes what Kincaid calls 'the deadly enemy of the stock sentiment, of babies and all little, presumably helpless objects of easy tears' (1971: 95). However, Quilp's violence is always mediated through comic spectacle: when he beats the wooden ship's head with an iron bar Dickens notes that 'this might have been a very comical thing to look at from a secure gallery' (*OCS* 463), once again placing the reader into the role of disengaged onlooker, as at the pantomime or *Punch and Judy* show.

As Leach has noted, Quilp closely parallels the 'merry outlaw' Punch in his amused delight in his own sadism, enactment of domestic violence, startling appearance and feigning of death (*OCS* 136). But by reductively characterising Quilp as 'an extreme manifestation of the worser parts of Punch', Leach fails to account for the attraction of Punch's crimes as normative/retributive comedy, and therefore too straightforwardly jumps to the conclusion that 'we do not follow [Quilp's] adventures with the glee we reserve for Punch'. In fact, the positive traits of Punch that Leach ascribes to Dick Swiveller – 'his unquenchable good humour, his frequent self-dramatization, his careless idleness and his refusal to be bound by convention or the law' – equally apply to Quilp.

He represents a more substantial and nuanced incarnation of the Grimaldian clown, who played both hero and (forgivable) villain, and through such figures Dickens resolves what Leach calls 'the contradiction between Punch hero and Punch villain' (1985: 68–9). Sampson Brass astutely recognises his slapstick sensibility when he comments that Quilp would view '"throttling me, and dropping me softly into the river when the tide was at its strongest"' as '"a pleasant joke"' (*OCS* 461). Brass is one of the few figures on whose body Quilp's cruelty is visibly written, for at one point he limps in with 'a scratched face, a green shade over one eye [which covered 'an eye most horribly discoloured'], and a hat grievously crushed' (*OCS* 499). However, the effect of our comprehending such visible harm is doubly diminished: firstly, these injuries are received 'off-stage' between chapters, and secondly, their target is the odious Sampson Brass, rendering such beatings as retributive comedy.

Quilp's propensity for slapstick violence is primarily manifested in his relationship with Tom Scott, who works for him at the wharf and acts as a foil for his pantomimic antics. From Tom's first appearance, their relationship is articulated through the medium of knockabout comedy, as he is aligned with the Bakhtinian 'topsy-turvy' performer of the pantomime. He enters standing on his head and we are told he is 'of an eccentric spirit [with] a natural taste for tumbling'. After he is the right way up, his duel with Quilp begins: 'as soon as his head was in its right position, Mr Quilp, to speak expressively in the absence of a better verb, "punched it" for him'. Tom fights back until Quilp finally gets the upper hand, in a moment when the boy's head seems to take on an autonomous existence: 'dexterously diving in between the elbows and catching the boy's head as it dodged from side to side, [he] gave it three or four good hard knocks' (*OCS* 48). Even with this contest won, Quilp is ready to attack again, 'lying in wait at a little distance from the sash armed with a large piece of wood, which, being rough and jagged and studded in many parts with broken nails, might possibly have hurt him' (*OCS* 49). Here again the comical tone carried in the supposition that such a vicious sounding weapon might only 'possibly' hurt someone provides the 'slap' that diverts us from a realist reading of this potential assault.

In Quilp's scenes with Tom, the hyperbolic nature of the slapstick violence means that it sprays in all directions, with Quilp

> hustling and driving the people about, like an evil spirit; setting Mrs Quilp upon all kinds of arduous and impracticable tasks; carrying great weights up and down with no apparent effort; kicking the boy from the wharf whenever he could get near him; and inflicting with his loads a great many sly bumps and blows upon the shoulders of Mr Brass[.] (*OCS* 111)

For this particular scene, in which Little Nell's house is cleared by Quilp, Dickens eschews a set-piece of pathos and disappointment at the fate of Nell and her grandfather, to present this diverting knock-about skit.

Tom reappears later, once again taunting Quilp with his hand-stands, at which point his master grabs his 'infallible poker' (one of Grimaldi's famous weapons of choice), 'with which, after some dodging and lying in ambush, he paid his young friend one or two such unequivocal compliments that he vanished precipitately, and left him in quiet possession of the field' (*OCS* 507). Framing these blows as 'unequivocal compliments' gives a clear indication of Dickens's desired mood here, as does the adoption of the mock-chivalric 'possession of the field'.

This violent relationship is so integral to Tom's existence that when Quilp is killed, he immediately searches for a replacement sparring partner. He had 'a strong desire to assault the jury' at the inquest into Quilp's death (perhaps refusing to believe his seemingly indestructible master was actually dead) and finds a surrogate Quilp in the form of 'a cautious beadle' who knocks him back to his feet again. The last we hear of Tom is the report that he became a street clown, assuming 'the name of an Italian image lad' and tumbling 'with extraordinary success, and to overflowing audiences' (*OCS* 550).

Sampson Brass acknowledges this confederacy of violence when he comments that 'I believe that boy strews the ground differently every day, on purpose to bruise and maim one; unless his master does it with his own hands, which is more than likely' (*OCS* 461), and Dickens emphasises the unusual and yet compelling nature of their companionship elsewhere. They are a double act in which 'there existed a strange kind of mutual liking between the pair', with Quilp playing the sadist to Tom's masochist: 'Quilp would certainly suffer nobody to contradict him but the boy, and the boy would assuredly not have submitted to be so knocked about by anybody but Quilp, when he had the power to run away at any time he chose' (*OCS* 48). Quilp and Tom thus join Holly Furneaux's 'queer' pairings of other male Dickens characters: this mutually beneficial relationship based on violence offers an unusual example of 'surrogate and adoptive parenting', and while Furneaux's study of 'queer masculinities' focuses on 'particularly tender and nurturing styles of masculinity' (2009: 7), Quilp and Scott offer an alternative model founded on precisely opposite styles, but one no less valid.

In the Dickens pantomime, such rough treatment of children is not a predominantly male characteristic, and a few women also display a careless attitude to the welfare of their charges. The small and immobile nature of well-swaddled babies make them perfect portable props, as Dickens had observed on his travels in Genoa. He visited 'the little country Church of San Martino, a couple of miles from the city' and observed a baptism where a

> curious stiff little instrument, that was passed from one to another, in the course of the ceremony, by the handle – like a short poker – was a child [. . .] I borrowed the child afterwards, for a minute or two (it was lying across the font then), and found it very red in the face but perfectly quiet, and not to be bent on any terms. (*PI* 47)

The nurse, midwife and layer-out Mrs Gamp presents her first acquaintance with Mrs Harris's 'little Tommy' as a comical episode of child suffocation,

> 'with his small red worsted shoe a gurglin in his throat, where he had put it in his play, a chick, wile they was leavin of him on the floor a lookin for it through the ouse and him a chokin sweetly in the parlor'. (*MC* 755)

Once again, the amusing idiom obscures the horrifying detail beneath.

*Nicholas Nickleby* follows a similar pattern of mixed or missing sympathies. In his Preface, Dickens earnestly explains that his intention in writing this novel is to call 'public attention to the system' whereby 'lasting agonies and disfigurements' are 'inflicted upon children by the treatment of the master in these places, involving such offensive and foul details of neglect, cruelty and disease, as no writer of fiction would have the boldness to imagine' (*NN* 3–4).

Thus Bernard Bergonzi describes the novel as 'one huge indictment of the failure of parental responsibility' (1962: 74), and Coveney characterises life at Dotheboys Hall as 'grotesque savagery' (1957: 94). However, the novel also reflects the savagery of the pantomime – Dotheboys Hall is a location that would have fitted into any harlequinade set, and Nelson (amongst others) notes a subtler process at work here; Dickens may set out with the intention to write *Nickleby* as 'pro-child propaganda', but this is 'constantly infiltrated by antifamilial humour, and by the acknowledgement that children are a source of cares as well as blessings' (1990: 64).

Indeed, Dickens declares this himself: after a lengthy description of the suffering pupils, which ends with the rhetorical cry 'What an incipient Hell was breeding there!', he abruptly switches tone: 'And yet this scene, painful as it was, had its grotesque features, which, in a less interested observer than Nicholas, might have provoked a smile' (*NN* 97). As a consequence of casting these children as actors within a pantomime performance, Dickens here positions his readers as those 'less interested observer[s]' and members of the theatre audience who are beyond the apprehension of any physical reality and pain felt by the child performers.

When Mrs Squeers administers the brimstone and treacle using 'a common wooden spoon', we are told in a humorous aside that it 'widened every young gentleman's mouth considerably' (*NN* 97). Such an observation is perfectly acceptable in the jocund world where 'babies may be knocked about and sat upon, or choked with gravy spoons'.

When Squeers later disciplines a crying youngster, the scene is transformed into knockabout comedy when the boy is given clownish powers of elasticity: 'Mr Squeers knocked him off the trunk with a blow on one side of his face, and knocked him on again with a blow on the other' (*NN* 45). As they travel to Dotheboys the coach becomes another site of comic performance:

> The little boys' legs being too short to admit of their feet resting upon anything as they sat, and the little boys' bodies being consequently in imminent hazard of being jerked off the coach, Nicholas had enough to do to hold them on. (*NN* 61)

While Smike largely remains Dickens's repository for sentimental feelings, even the cruelty enacted on him sometimes slips into a comic tone, for example when he is 'pushed by Mrs Squeers and boxed by Mr Squeers' which is a 'course of treatment' aimed at 'brightening his intellects' (*NN* 95). Douglas-Fairhurst feels that in these scenes, Dickens 'dares us to laugh at or ignore child abuse', and in fact 'warns us away from such thoughtless reactions by seeming to expect them so fully' (2011: 113). Yet this expectation is rooted within Dickens's deliberate framing of these scenes within the tropes of the pantomime, which makes the purpose and efficacy of this warning somewhat questionable. If this is Dickens's intention, then the strength of his writing works against him and his most imaginative writing seems to lie in the violence rather than in any social message to be made. Dickens the humanitarian reformer may want to improve social conditions, but in an age of high infant mortality rates, grim laughter remains a dominant response to the rough treatment of children and is a keynote within much of Dickens's black comedy.

Within the theatre, the disregard for children's safety pushed them towards ever greater dangers, as any risks were heavily offset by the opportunities for spectacle (and therefore profit) that they offered to stage managers. As Varty notes, the reformers bitterly rebuked 'the theatre manager [who] treated his juvenile employees as items of theatre property, commodities and props to be disposed of purely with regard to the aesthetic effect they could be made to create and the income this could generate' (2008: 38). Dickens's treatment of his fictional children reflects the same sensibility, as some of his literary progeny become the same 'commodities and props' to be knocked together or thrown around for a particular 'aesthetic effect'.

The Nubbles's visit to Astley's is similarly punctuated with mishaps befalling the children that attract little concern: by the time they have reached the theatre, 'little Jacob was squeezed flat, and the baby had received divers concussions', yet in the space of two paragraphs Jacob is sufficiently recovered to watch the play and applaud at the finale (*OCS* 298). George Cattermole's illustration to this scene, shown in Chapter 3 of this study, underscores the perils attendant on the children. The two dangle precariously over the balcony with the rest of the audience banked in steep rows bearing down upon them. The riotous diversity of the crowd presents a variety of potential dangers: drunks, pickpockets and a man on the right-hand side of the frame who menacingly wields a stick above the baby's head. These threats are either unobserved or treated with smiles and laughter rather than horror or surprise.

At the dinner afterwards, the baby seems constantly at risk of inflicting pain on himself, for if he is not 'trying to force a large orange into his mouth', he is 'making indentations in his soft visage with an oyster-shell' (*OCS* 301). As we saw, Ruskin fondly read this scene as simple infant innocence, but the baby's receptiveness to whatever violent impressions Dickens can mark upon him can also be seen as emblematic of the author's slapstick treatment of children. The small children in *Dombey and Son* are similarly pliable, in contrast to the earnest hardness of Dombey and his son Paul.

Mrs Chick's eldest boy gets a 'blister on his nose' when 'the little creature, in his mother's absence, smelt a warm flat iron' (*DS* 26), while Mrs Mac Stinger's son Alexander is often described as 'black in the face, with holding his breath', which his mother resolves using 'a cool paving-stone' – 'usually found to act as a powerful restorative in such cases' (*DS* 361).

When a parent does attempt to display parental concern, Dickens chooses to frame it in a comic manner: while travelling with the single gentleman, Kit's mother imagines all manner of exaggerated mishaps that may have befallen her children in her absence. She suffers

> maternal apprehensions that perhaps by this time little Jacob, or the baby, or both, had fallen into the fire, or tumbled down stairs, or had been squeezed behind doors, or had scalded their windpipes in endeavouring to allay their thirst at the open spouts of tea-kettles. (*OCS* 355)

Such vivid depictions of potential accidents highlight the exaggerated nature of her maternal worries in a way that draws us away from any felt sense of real peril for the children.

## Conclusion

Returning to poor Kit in the jailhouse, it apparently seems that the turnkey's reading matter has not completely inoculated him against sympathy. In response to his irritated inquiry, Mrs Nubbles replies that she has something for Kit to eat, which she would like to see him have:

> The turnkey looked as if he thought the request a strange one and rather out of the common way, but nevertheless he laid down his paper, and coming round where Kit's mother stood, took the basket from her, and after inspecting its contents, handed it to Kit, and went back to his place. (*OCS* 459)

And so it is with Dickens. For while the occasion of violence provides him with a rewarding source of comedy (for both author and reader alike) it is only by framing it within a theatrical and pantomimic sensibility that it can be developed to full comic fruition. Like the turnkey, Dickens is also able to 'lay down his paper' and treat violence with serious emotion elsewhere; his own mental and physical reaction to his readings of Sikes's murder of Nancy is perhaps the most tangible (and tragic) evidence of this, but one thinks also of Jo the crossing-sweeper, whose institutional mistreatment occasions little comedy beyond bitter laughter at the sanctimony of Chadband.

However, much of the spark and flourish of Dickens's writing is lost with the laughter: here in the prison, the jailer's 'serious' mode of conduct is a flat, functional one as he deals with the matter of Kit's food in a mechanical mode in five brief subclauses without further comment. A full exploration of Dickens's own 'serious' mode is the subject of a different study beyond the scope of this study, but its undeniable emotional impact on 'my lords and gentlemen', 'Right Reverends and Wrong Reverends of every order' and 'men and women, born with Heavenly compassion in your hearts' (*BH* 572) is another measure of Dickens's versatility, and of the delicate tension at stake in his writing whenever his pantomimic sensibility intrudes.

Chapter 8

# The Clothed Clown

## Introduction

In this final chapter I will explore how Grimaldi and Dickens use the clothing of their clownish characters to explore the transformative power of garments. A pair of biographical episodes neatly illustrates the use of clothing as a discourse in the sartorial transactions of both men.

As we saw earlier Grimaldi once had to run to the theatre in full costume and makeup, but after being recognised by an excited mob he was detained until he had performed a brief impromptu performance. His 'onstage' costume incriminated him as the clown, leaving him entirely at the mercy of the interpretation of his audience and forced to act according to their narrow expectations of what a clown should do, whereas public appearances in his 'offstage' clothes rarely provoked comment.

The second episode concerns an entirely unbidden performance by a young Dickens. His daughter 'Mamie' relates how one evening the Hogarths were sitting quietly in their drawing room:

> when suddenly a young sailor jumped through one of the open windows into the apartment, whistled and danced a hornpipe, and before they could recover from their amazement jumped out again. A few minutes later my father walked in at the door as sedately as though quite innocent of the prank and shook hands with everyone; but the sight of their amazed faces proving too much for his attempted sobriety, his hearty laugh was the signal for the rest of the party to join his merriment. (Dickens [1897]: 30–1)

Unlike Grimaldi, Dickens here performed contrary to audience expectations, as the sailor's costume served multiple functions – as an outlet for his innate theatricality, as a release valve for his seemingly limitless energy and as a momentary refuge from the stifling expectations of the great Victorian novelist. Dickens thus takes control of the image that he projects to the world, and in a calculated two-fold performance manages his audience's reaction in a way that defuses a potentially awkward encounter with his future in-laws. This careful control is something that he would sustain in his fiction, as he replicated this sartorial investment in his own characters by adapting the fixed costume of the older style folk clown. Moreover, he also harnessed the metamorphic power of the clown's wider sartorial repertoire, to play with and interrogate the social encoding of clothes, whereby the wearer was often granted a power that went no deeper than the fabric.

When contextualising Dickens's sartorial choices alongside the clown's transformative possibilities, Thomas Carlyle's *Sartor Resartus* is an important bridging text, because it both looks back to the clothes-based antics of the carnivalesque clown and looks forward to Dickens's imaginative presentations of clothing. Carlyle's 'Satirical Extravaganza on Things in General' (*LTC* 6: 396), was serialised in *Fraser's Magazine* from 1833 to 1834, and comparisons with Dickens's early sketch 'Meditations in Monmouth-Street' suggest that Dickens was aware of it soon after.[1]

Carlyle once observed that 'I have under all my gloom a genuine feeling of the ludicrous; and could have been the merriest of men, *had I not* been the sickest and saddest' (*LTC* 6: 449), a statement that informs the tone of parts of *Sartor*, belying conceptions of Carlyle as the epitome of Victorian earnestness. *Sartor*'s ludic sensibility is registered in several ways, perhaps most directly through the paratextual Editor's commentary, which highlights the pantomimic grotesque within Teufelsdröckh's 'original' work. As the text resists categorisation and takes on ever more exaggerated proportions, the Editor notes the Professor's 'more and more discernible humouristico-satirical tendency' (*SR* 150). The Editor variously describes the work as an 'enormous, amorphous Plumpudding, more like a Scottish Haggis, which Herr Teufelsdröckh [has] kneaded for his fellow mortals' (*SR* 214), and, in a gustatory analogue for the harlequinade, as an all-inclusive Grimaldian feast:

> some mad banquet, wherein all courses had been confounded, and fish and flesh, soup and solid, oyster-sauce, lettuces, Rhine-wine and French mustard, were hurled into one huge tureen or trough, and the hungry Public invited to help itself. (*SR* 26)

Carlyle's verbal inventiveness also closely parallels Grimaldi's physical inventiveness and pantomimic extemporising. Defending his linguistic improvisation in *Sartor*, Carlyle argues that 'if one has thoughts not hitherto uttered in English Books, I see nothing for it but that you must use words not found there, must *make* words' (*LTC* 135) and in coining such evocative neologisms as 'humano-anecdotal' (*SR* 58) and 'diabolico-angelical' (*SR* 174), he verbally mimics Grimaldi's sartorial tricks which reconfigure and reanimate incongruous, inanimate materials.

Moreover, *Sartor* includes several comic-grotesque images which foreground clothing. In the 'Miscellaneous-Historical' chapter Teufelsdröckh explains how medieval nobles wore little bells in their girdle 'so that when a man walks it is with continual jingling', and likens male dress to grand architectural structures such as 'peaks and Gothic-arch intersections'. Such phallic images recall Grimaldi's bodily protuberances, as does the growth of the hyperbole as men compete with women in the outlandishness of their costumes and don such ridiculous garments as 'doublets of fustian, under which lie multiple ruffs of cloth, pasted together with batter [. . .] which create protuberance enough' (*SR* 37–8).

But *Sartor* does not present clothing as something merely frivolous or inconsequential beyond its comic potentialities, it is also a controlling metaphor within Carlyle's political and spiritual discourse. As I shall argue in this chapter, Grimaldi and Dickens extend this further to insert clothing within theatrical discourse (Grimaldi's use of clothing in his non-verbal bodily performance), social discourse (Dickens's own sartorial strategies) and literary discourse (the treatment of clothing in Dickens's work).

Roland Barthes regards clothing as an 'articulate language through which it is possible to analyse a culture as system and process, institution and individual act' (qtd in Calefato 2004: 7), which holds a peculiarly liminal status. Alexandra Warwick and Dani Cavallero further suggest how clothes perform two potentially oppositional functions simultaneously; clothing both '*frames* the body and insulates private fantasies from the Other' but also 'connects the individual self to the collective Other and fashions those fantasies on the model of a public spectacle' (1998: xvi). Both Grimaldi and Dickens play with this ambiguity by using the clothing of their characters to interrogate this often uneasy duality between the individual and society.

External elements were central to the signifying system of eighteenth- and early nineteenth-century theatre, and genres such as melodrama placed a primacy on facial expression, gesture and clothing as the index to a character. Deborah Vlock's study of early Victorian reading and theatre-going practices supports this: while the voice would later become the key signifier of semiotic value within theatre, 'the stage was from the beginning a forum for the semiotic display of bodies, and certainly Victorian dramaturgy played on collective social assumptions about bodily signs' (1998: 82).

Thus in theatre, rather than concealing the character, clothing is a mechanism for its revelation, and for Juliet John 'Dickens keeps [the] underside [of his characters] clearly and flagrantly on display' (2001: 3). Rather than adopting a simple binary surface/depth model of appearance (in which the surface conceals the 'true' character beneath) here the surface *is* the character and is 'read' to gain access to the internal, rather than being a barrier. Clothes, then, are phrases within the body-text and an essential part of the non-verbal presentation of character, and the liberty provided by 'dressing-up' gave actors the licence to both explore these signifiers in a material way and negotiate a range of contested boundaries, such as gender, class and nationality.

In the rest of this chapter I want to examine three key boundaries that Grimaldian and Dickensian clowns negotiate. Firstly, clothing is regularly deployed as an expression of individual liberty in defiance of the oppressive controlling mechanisms of the conservative society within which the clown operates. Secondly, and in relation to this, clowns demonstrate how clothes can be used to dehumanise the human body, through the imposition of a proscriptive sartorial code whose meaning and definition is controlled by others, but conversely rehumanise the body through an appropriation, manipulation and subversion of this sartorial code in a manner unintended by its original imposers. Finally, as a representative case study, I will closely examine the presentation of the clothing of two related cultural archetypes of interest to both Dickens and Grimaldi, namely the clothes-fixated dandy and his relation, the swell.

## Clothing as a Symbol of Individual Liberty

In what *Sartor*'s Editor calls his 'interminable disquisitions of a mythological, metaphorical, cabalistico-sartorial and quite antediluvian cast' (*SR* 29), Teufelsdröckh describes how society 'is founded upon Cloth' (*SR* 48). He asserts that clothes are a primary means of differentiating and determining the power relations between individuals, regarding 'the solemnities and paraphernalia of civilized

Life' as 'nothing but so many Cloth-rags'. He cites the example of two men, 'one dressed in fine Red, the other in coarse threadbare Blue' (*SR* 47), who become, through the symbolic power of clothing, a judge sentencing a prisoner, and to Teufelsdröckh such symbolism provides our 'individuality, distinctions [and] social polity' (*SR* 32). This is reflected in a variety of artefacts, including a crown ('an implement [. . .] in size and commercial value, little differing from a horse-shoe' [*SR* 168]) and a sceptre ('a piece of gilt wood' [*SR* 170]). By drawing attention to the material nature of garments, Carlyle conversely demonstrates the extent to which their power relations are determined by their accepted place in the semiotic code rather than by any inherent qualities. Clothing is thus an empty signifier and so resembles language itself; indeed, Teufelsdröckh calls language 'the Garment of Thought' (*SR* 57).

This treatment of clothing by Grimaldi and Dickens as both material garment and immaterial symbol, signifier and signified, exemplifies what Valentine Cunningham describes as the interplay between the word and the world, or 'the wor(l)d' (1994: 11). Clothing sits on the border between Cunningham's 'textual stuff' and 'worldly stuff' (1994: 80) and Grimaldi and Dickens use it to show how meaning resides in what Cunningham calls 'the busy overlap, interaction [and] clash' between 'aesthetic, textual stuff' and 'the historico-worldly Other beyond the text' (1994: 61).

By highlighting the insubstantiality of clothing as a symbol, Carlyle joins a chorus of anxiety that had begun in the previous century, as cultural commentators decried the schism between signifier and signified that had been precipitated by the commercialisation of clothing during the consumer revolution. This divergence contributed to the erosion of existing power structures based on more uniform and predictable patterns of dress. Within these incumbent structures, clothing was instrumental in what Jennifer Craik calls 'a technique of acculturation' which 'denotes and embodies conventions of conduct that contribute to the etiquette and manners of social encounters' (1994: 10). Here, clothing's symbolic power was co-opted to impose social order – as Warwick and Cavallero describe, dress 'renders [the body] analysable, either forcibly through required clothing, or voluntarily through self-selected garments; it becomes manipulable through the effects of being dressed' (1998: 75). Calefato also recognises this appropriation of the symbolic and argues that clothes can 'cage' the body and reduce it to 'the forced task of representing a [particular] social role, position or hierarchy'. In this way, specific costumes such as uniforms 'can be a controlling device for the body, sanctioning a closed system of correspondences between external appearance and social order' (2004: 2). As Catherine Spooner notes, it is therefore unsurprising that one of the principal state mechanisms for the 'discipline and surveillance' of the 'Foucauldian [docile] body' was 'the management and observation of the surface' (2004: 12), in which clothes played an important role.

According to Warwick and Cavallero, when clothing operates on this symbolic level it is 'symptomatic of our introjections of sartorial and vestimentary codes and conventions', and is embodied in regular, static and repeated uniforms. By contrast, on the imaginary level 'dress represents a projection of the ideal egos which we seek to embody and with which we wish to identify', and is unique, ever-evolving and based on personal rather than social codes (1998: xvi). Barthes calls the symbolic level 'Costume' and the imaginary level 'Dress', and any single sartorial act plays out the tension between these two divergent positions to produce what Maria K. Bachman calls 'a desiring and a disciplinary subject' (2005: 172).

Conversely, the clown inherently operates against this as a representative of anarchic anti-establishment values, and disrupts or subverts such controlling mechanisms through his own strategies of clothing. In fact, both Dickens and Grimaldi, as well as their clown characters, carefully manipulate the 'symbolic' level into becoming the 'imaginary' level in many of their sartorial transactions. As celebrity artists, both men were regularly subject to attempts to fix their identity through appearance, being expected to dress and act according to the social conventions of their class and profession. This chapter opened with a chilling example of the sartorial prison-house built around Grimaldi, and Dickens's choice of garments was regularly scrutinised and prescribed. A number of those who met him expressed dismay at the confounding of their expectations as Dickens used dress to resist their preconceived categorisation. Thomas Adolphus Trollope recounted how:

> We were at first disappointed, and disposed to imagine there must be some mistake! No! That is not the man who wrote 'Pickwick'! What we saw was a dandified, pretty-boy-looking sort of figure [. . .] with a slight flavour of the whipper-snapper genus of humanity. (2010: 110)

Other disenchanted fans found that 'His dress was foppish; in fact, he was overdressed' in waistcoats that were 'somewhat on the flash order' and 'vivid tints [that] were very conspicuous' (Payne 1927: 9, 49, 60).

A closer comparison of prevailing fashions and Dickens's *couture* shows how he was deliberately at odds with his times. Clair Hughes has plotted the divergent movement of male and female fashion from the 1840s onwards, summarising the trend as 'macho musculature and sombre austerity' that 'offset and formed a background to an exaggerated and colourful femininity'. Earlier in the century, male and female garments had corresponded, but a shift towards female 'docility and secluded domesticity' after Victoria's accession was emblematised in a significant sartorial rift. While women's clothes ballooned outwards and took on a broader range of colours, male fashions became 'increasingly angular, severely vertical and monochrome', with heavier garments and darker colours (2006: 61–2). As John Harvey asserts, 'colour died in menswear in the nineteenth century' and the 'stark formula of black men and bright women' became 'another of that century's sharpened severities' (1995: 195–6).

While Ellen Moers reads Dickens's resistance as partly juvenile indulgence ('a näive, almost childlike pleasure in dressing up') and partly a more calculated attempt to 'further ambition with the drama of dress' (1960: 222), Dickens was clearly challenging the symbolic determinism of clothing and defining a unique identity for himself. A primary model for such behaviour was offered by Grimaldi, and while reworking the *Memoirs* Dickens learned about Grimaldi's struggles to preserve the imaginary while all those around him privileged the symbolic. Episodes in Dickens's narrative (most notably the 'appearing in public' anecdote) demonstrate that throughout his stage life many audiences read only the surface of Grimaldi's appearance according to the culturally accepted role of the clown, and failed to see any other dimension of his identity – such as a feeling or suffering human – underneath. Even without his slap and motley, his attempts to set aside his clownish persona were obstructed and his identity continued to be controlled by 'unofficial' audiences away from the playhouse: as Dickens tells us, Byron tricked him into that grimly comic routine with food at a dinner party and he was invited to houses to sing or entertain others rather than demonstrate any other aspect of himself.

However, one strategy which Grimaldi used to attempt to assert control over his public identity was to refashion the clown's traditional costume and make it unique and personal to him. After the retirement of his mentor Dubois in 1801, Grimaldi managed every aspect of his Clown persona, including his innovative appearance, the choreographing of his knockabout routines, and the design of his complex stage contraptions. His collaborator Charles Dibdin describes how Dubois and other clowns 'seldom wore anything but old-fashioned, outre, liveries' and only ever dressed themselves as 'a rustic booby, with red hair' with their faces painted 'merely in imitation of florid nature', but Grimaldi made his clown dress 'more extravagant' (1956: 47).

Verbal accounts often highlight how Grimaldi transformed existing models. Wilson's head-to-toe catalogue signals how each layer was an idiosyncratic variation of contemporary social codes:

> In burlesquing [the conventional style] Grimaldi turned up the wig at the back, wore a large ruffle instead of a lace collar and pulled the breeches above the knees so as to make them baggy and provide them room for pockets big enough to hold the legs of mutton, geese and other stolen goods. He exaggerated the 'clocks' on the stockings and the rosettes on the shoes and covered the costume with bright-coloured spots and patches. (1949: 47)

Grimaldi's subtle sartorial variations showed Dickens a potential means of resisting reductive categorisation based on appearance – even if such resistance was only temporary – a method he subsequently followed in his characters. Rather than adopting the sober and well-cut clothes of the respectable gentleman, they parody or burlesque the prevailing sartorial codes to resist conformity and express their individuality. To Barthes, this meant playing with the markers of difference between dress and costume, such as

> how untidy a garment is, what it lacks, how it fits and how it is worn (crooked buttons, sleeves too long etc), improvised clothing, colour (except in special circumstances, like mourning), and the characteristic gestures of the wearer. (Calefato 2004: 8)

Dickens was attuned to the importance of such distinctions and repeatedly integrated them into his characterisation. The use of colour, the lack of fit, the move towards shapelessness and the presence of various protuberances all break down the monolithic, hermetically sealed and textureless male figure.

A number of Dickens's clowns dress in a manner that projects them into discourse as knowing 'artificial' fools, who consciously critique the activities and habits of those around them. When the Misses Pecksniff visit Todgers's for Sunday tea, Bailey displays his resistance to standard sartorial codes by burlesquing Sunday best and 'courting' attire: he appears in 'a complete suit of cast-off clothes several sizes too large for him' and 'a clean shirt of such extraordinary magnitude, that one of the gentlemen (remarkable for his ready wit) called him "collars" on the spot' (*MC* 146). In the same novel, Tom Pinch is 'drest in a snuff-coloured suit, of an uncouth make at the best, which, being shrunken with long wear, was twisted and tortured into all kinds of odd shapes' (*MC* 28). Although it may initially appear that Tom has been forced into this shape by his oppressive employer Pecksniff (impressing a costume upon a docile body) it progressively becomes a signifier of Tom's resolute idiosyncrasy and his subtle challenge to the Pecksniff household.

The tumbling and grimacing Bob Sawyer also uses his clownish attire to significant effect when he becomes embroiled in a political discussion with the hack reporter Mr Pott at the Saracen's Head. Pott propounds the virtues of his preferred candidate, Samuel Slumkey of the Blue Party, while disparaging his opponent Horatio Fizkin of the despised Buff Party whenever he can. Pott interrogates Bob and Ben in his usual self-aggrandising and pompous style, asking '"[A]re both [of you] imbued with those blue principles, which so long as I live, I have pledged myself to the peoples of these kingdoms to support and maintain?"' Bob hesitates, stating '"I don't exactly know about that . . . I am – "' – prompting Pott's worst fears: '"Not buff, Mr Pickwick . . . your friend is not buff, Sir?"' – but then resorts to a sartorial reference to provide a disarmingly straightforward answer: '"No, no, . . . I'm a kind of plaid at present; a compound of all sorts of colours."' Pott negatively concludes that Bob is '"a waverer"', but here Bob's uncomplicated attitude to life and refusal to limit his thinking to any single ideology has exposed the narrowness of Pott's conceptions and punctured his lofty (and flawed) pretensions (*PP* 679).

Newman Noggs's clothing also functions at the imaginary level, and wholly reflects Barthes's sense of dress as a form of individual rebellion. Like Tom Pinch, Noggs wears 'a suit of clothes (if the term be allowable when they suited him not at all) much the worse for wear, very much too small, and placed upon such a short allowance of buttons that it was marvellous how he contrived to keep them on' (*NN* 24). This description signals that this dress rejects the accepted bounds of Noggs's perceived position, and the final clause introduces the magical possibilities of his appearance, which disregards regular rules of tailoring and operates according to the sartorial laws of the pantomime. Another detail which underlines Noggs's non-conformity is his deliberate utilisation of clothing in ways contrary to its intended use. At one point Noggs removes a house key from his hat, 'in which, by-the-bye, in consequence of the dilapidated state of his pockets, he deposited everything' (*NN* 136). Noggs's hat here serves as a Grimaldian pocket, that fantastically bottomless hold-all that Gerald Frow notes was a 'receptacle of all sorts of edibles and occasionally of kettles of boiling water and even of lighted candles' (1985: 74).

Montague Tigg is a final example of a character whose 'shabby-genteel' wardrobe reflects his personality. His clothes constantly reveal their deviation from the norm: 'his fingers were a long way out of his gloves', 'the soles of his feet were at an inconvenient distance from the upper leather of his boots' and his nether garments were 'violent in its colours once' but are 'sobered now with age and dinginess'. Moreover, these later items operate outside of their wearer's control, as they 'were so stretched and strained in a tough conflict between his braces and his straps, that they appeared every moment in danger of flying asunder at the knees'. To complete the effect, Tigg transforms a piece of costume – a coat 'in colour blue and a military cut' 'buttoned and frogged, up to his chin' – into dress by virtue of its inclusion within this heterogeneous ensemble (*MC* 53). Tigg's choice of garment and method of wearing it also warn the observer of his predisposition towards rule-breaking in a wider sense, but also leaven this more profound point by bringing in an element of comic absurdity through his speculative courting of the Chuzzlewit daughters, itself a comic commentary on their father's pretensions to gentility. However, as I shall explore in the next section, just as there are two Tiggss in the novel, so there are two Tigg wardrobes, and Montague Tigg's subsequent transformation into Tigg Montague, aided by a change of costume, offers a cautionary alternative perspective on the ability of garments to indicate character.

## Dressing to Transform

Tigg's fraudulent social performance demonstrates how the transformative opportunities provided by costume represented a threat that was symptomatic of a wider discomfort at the erosion of traditional class distinctions. This had become a matter for more general debate throughout the eighteenth and nineteenth centuries: previously clothing had been a reliable indicator of its wearer's social standing, as tailors only made clothes for those who could afford them and sumptuary laws ensured that the best garments were only available to a confined elite – Richard Steele confidently asserted at the start of the eighteenth century 'each by some particular in their dress shows to what class they belong' (qtd in McKendrick et al. 1982: 55). However, as manufacturers began to produce more garments, and served an ever-growing group of middle-class consumers who could now afford them, clothing was no longer a dependable index of class and became a site of increasing social competition.

Some contemporary commentators expressed concern at this disturbance within the social strata. A letter to *The London Magazine* lamented that 'the lower orders of the people (if there are any, for distinctions are now confounded) are equally immerged in their fashionable vices' ([Anon.] 1772: 321) and three years later another noted that 'whenever a thing becomes the mode it is universally and absurdly adopted from the garret to the kitchen, when it is only intended for some very few Belles in the first floor' ([Anon.] 1775: 495). This phenomenon did not pass quickly for, in 1817, William Davis noted that 'a fondness for Dress may be said to be the folly of the age, and it is to be lamented that it has nearly destroyed those becoming marks whereby the several classes of society were formerly distinguished' (1817: 23).

As residents of London, described by McKendrick as 'the radiant centre of the fashion world and conspicuous consumption' (1982: 41), Grimaldi and Dickens were ideally placed to participate within these developments, which were made manifest and circulated through a variety of channels, not least drama and literature. McKendrick comments that 'Rarely, if ever, has the fashionable imitation of so much of the rest of society been so frequently mocked, so accurately recorded and so pointedly revealed in so many different art forms' (1982: 57) than during this period.

Dickens himself was all too aware of the unstable and double-edged status of clothing, and how misinterpretations could be double-edged. Ackroyd relates how Dickens arrived for his first day as a young apprentice at Ellis and Blackmore 'in what was undoubtedly a brand-new uniform – a blue jacket and a military-looking cap which had a strap under the chin'. Here, Dickens was already trying to transform himself from a lowly 'writing clerk' into a more masculine and heroic figure through costume, and to add another personal flourish he carried his cap 'rather jauntily on one side of his head'. However, this transformation fails to impress his audience, as he returns from his first errand on Chancery Lane 'bearing a black eye'. Ackroyd continues:

> Dickens explained to a fellow clerk that 'a big blackguard fellow knocked my cap off as I was crossing over Chancery Lane [. . .] He said 'Halloa, sojer' which I could not stand, so I at once struck him and he then hit me in the eye.' (1991: 123–4)

Dickens regularly inscribed such scenes of misinterpretation in his work, and their prevalence in his early writing bespeaks the social neuroses of a young man finding his place in the world. I earlier described one such misreading from the *Memoirs*; when Grimaldi was a young boy, his father had dressed him as a 'gentleman', yet the public reaction echoes Dickens's own unfortunate reception on Chancery Lane and reconfigures him as something ridiculous – a 'monkey', a 'bear dressed for a dance' or a 'cat going out for a party' (*MJG* 1: 24).

In the parallel episode in *Oliver Twist*, the young protagonist suffers an identical fate: dressed in a new suit of clothes to signal his change of status, Oliver is accosted on an errand and is designated as a 'young wretch' and 'little brute' by the crowd. Later in Fagin's den, Charley Bates's mockery focuses on Oliver's clothes: '"Look at his togs, Fagin!" said Charley, putting the light so close to his new jacket as nearly to set him on fire. "Look at his togs! – superfine cloth, and the heavy-swell cut!"' (*OT* 111). Charley's reference to the 'heavy-swell', a type of vulgarised dandy, further nuances this attack on Oliver as a sartorial one.

Yet despite such anxieties Grimaldi and Dickens were alert to the satirical possibilities of the sartorial and used clothes as a prop to radically challenge the fabric of authority, particularly in its most parochial form. In *Harlequin in His Element*, Grimaldi suggests that anyone can become a parish watchman merely by donning the appropriate clothing: after getting the constable drunk, Grimaldi puts on his greatcoat and hat, takes up his other accoutrements of authority – his lantern and rattle – and parades the stage in such a convincing performance that Harlequin requests a wake-up call for the following morning.

Dickens similarly critiques such authority figures by demonstrating how they carry no intrinsic or 'natural' authority and instead derive it solely from their costume and props. The beadle Mr Grummer in *Pickwick* is described as 'an elderly individual in top-boots' whose role only becomes clear to Pickwick when he produces 'from the breast-pocket of his coat, a short truncheon surmounted with a brazen crown, with which he beckoned to Mr Pickwick with a grave and ghost-like air' (*PP* 322), in an evocation of *Hamlet*'s opening scene that further highlights the inherent theatricality and insubstantiality of Grummer.

Mr Bumble constantly draws attention to his clothing to assert his perceived authority and reassure himself of it. When he goes to collect Oliver from Mrs Mann, he sits down in the parlour and

> officiously deposited his cocked hat and cane on the table before him. Mr Bumble wiped from his forehead the perspiration which his walk had engendered; glanced complacently at the cocked hat; and smiled. Yes, he smiled. Beadles are but men; and Mr Bumble smiled. (*OT* 22)

This complacent glance at his hat emphasises Bumble's symbolic investment of power into his clothes, especially as it is accompanied by the assertion that Bumble is 'but' a man. Indeed, the unworldly Oliver accidentally identifies where the real authority lies, for when asked to bow to Bumble, he makes a bow 'which was divided between the beadle on the chair, and the cocked-hat on the table' (*OT* 23).

When Bumble becomes master of the workhouse Dickens highlights how his previous authority was reliant on his costume: Bumble's new outfit 'announced that a great change had taken place in the position of his affairs', whereby his 'mighty cocked-hat was replaced by a modest round one' (*OT* 239). He then includes a passage which replicates Carlyle's discussion of the men in red and blue:

> There are some promotions in life, which, independent of the more substantial rewards they offer, acquire peculiar value and dignity from the coats and waistcoats connected with them [. . .] Strip the bishop of his apron, or the beadle of his hat and lace; what are they? Men. Mere men. Dignity, and even holiness, too, sometimes, are more questions of coat and waistcoat than some people imagine.

Thus another 'beadle had come into power; and on him the cocked-hat, gold-laced coat, and staff, had all three descended' (*OT* 239–40). Whereas Grimaldi's clown punctured authority by dressing in its robes, Dickens here strips off the robes to reveal the clown beneath. Ultimately Bumble's incompetence and weakness reveal how wholly unsuitable for any position of authority he is, further underscoring the hollowness of his symbolic costume.

Dickens presents a similar 'dressing-down' in *Little Dorrit*, at the moment when Pancks reveals the superficially benevolent Casby to be an avaricious villain squeezing his tenants for their last penny. Pancks's explosive verbal exposure of Casby as 'a driver in disguise, a screwer by deputy, a wringer, and squeezer, and shaver by substitute [. . .] a philanthropic sneak [and] a shabby deceiver!' (*LD* 833) significantly concludes with a ritual of defrocking, as Pancks 'snipped off short, the sacred locks that flowed upon [Casby's] shoulders' and 'caught the broad-brimmed hat out of the astounded Patriarch's hand, cut it down into a mere stewpan, and fixed it on the Patriarch's head' (*LD* 836). Dickens indicates throughout the novel how some of the reverence and awe around Casby is founded on the symbolic power of his hair, which is worn long and grey 'like floss silk or spun glass, which looked so very benevolent because it was never cut' (*LD* 160) and his clothes, which 'looked patriarchal' (*LD* 163). After these apparatuses are removed his power is gone, and all that is left of Casby is a 'bare-polled, goggle-eyed, big-headed, lumbering personage [. . .] not in the least impressive [and] not in the least venerable' (*LD* 836).

The Grimaldian clown also presented a positive model of sartorial transformation through his endless harlequinade inventions. Pantomime's constantly metamorphic world meant that the clown was not merely confined to the distinctive livery that Grimaldi had devised for him, and that clothing assisted in his transformation into other personas – the society dandy, swaggering soldier or drunken watchman – who provided a release from his conventional appearance as Clown.

Grimaldi's pantomimes circulated fashions through their inclusion of their contemporary material objects and their commentary on current tastes: as Mayer observes, 'Commerce constitutes one of the firmest foundations of the nineteenth-century London harlequinade' (1969: 206), and clothing was one of its principal commercial commodities. Juliet John's view of pantomimic selfhood as 'not circumscribed but protean' (2001: 12) is epitomised by Clown's propensity to put on and cast off a variety of garments emblematic of different identities. Clown's centrality in the surreal, improvisational harlequinade meant that he could explore a variety of genders, nationalities, occupations and social positions within a single performance. Clown's dressing-up, combining calculated satire with a more playful and inventive element, is thus doubly potent – not only is authority undermined through his sartorial impersonation but also through the implication that anyone could do the same.

A principal topic for Grimaldi's brand of 'costumewit' was the Napoleonic wars. For example, in *Harlequin and the Swans* he dons 'a rattling, shiny uniform of saucepan lids and dish-covers' in an act of idiosyncratic self-projection (Frow 1985: 78) and then assembles an 'awkward squad' of conscripts made from household items. This trick originated in *Harlequin and the Red Dwarf* (Covent Garden, 1812), and was, according to *The Times*, prompted by 'A Hussar officer, in all the extravagant and foolish finery of the corps' crossing the stage, after which 'Clown [was] determined to be a hero and a Hussar in his own person'. To convert the soldier's costume into dress, he first created a pair of boots from 'two black varnished coal-scuttles', heeled with 'two real horseshoes' and spurred with candlesticks. To complete his outfit, he

> equipped his legs in an [*sic*] uniform almost as clattering, unwieldy, and absurd, as the most irresistible of our whiskered *propugnatores*. A white bear-skin formed his pelisse, a muff his cap, and a black tippet finished his toilet, by giving him a beard, whiskers and pendant mustaches [*sic*]. ([Anon.] 1813: 3)

This elaborate turn was soon popularised in prints such as William Heath's.[2]

In a clear reference to the real Hussar's costume, *The Times* also noted that the audience laughed 'in the spirit of general contempt of these miserable imitations of foreign foppery' and the 'merited ridicule' of this satire became even more 'pointed' and 'intelligent' due to 'the presence of a row of genuine Hussar Officers in the stage box, covered de *cap à pied*, with chains and catskins' ([Anon.] 1813: 3). Grimaldi's comical performance on stage is thus made doubly piquant by an adjacent public performance by the Hussars themselves. Moreover, in combining the traditionally masculine blacksmith's wares of coal-scuttles and horseshoes with the feminine tippet and muff, Grimaldi reflects how, in Clair Hughes's words, 'traditional masculine aggression' can become 'ritualized, sentimentalized and confused with colourful dressing up' (2006: 52).

Such heterogeneous ensembles are another embodiment of Bakhtin's grotesque '"carnival and culinary" anatomy' that I introduced in Chapter 6, whereby everyday domestic objects appear in the carnival procession as oversized foodstuffs (such as giant sausages and buns), which are attended by a convoy of guards who wield kitchen utensils as weapons. Usage and meaning are inverted as objects are 'turned inside out [and] utilized in the wrong way, contrary to their common use' (1968: 411), and in his Hussar routine Grimaldi uses objects 'in the wrong way' by inverting a collection of miscellaneous and quotidian objects into a soldier's costume.

Dickens's adaptation and realisation of Grimaldi's methods also clearly owes a debt to Carlyle's ideas. The conjuring of new life and character from a collection of inanimate items is a theme of both *Sartor* and Dickens's early sketch, 'Meditations in Monmouth-Street'. Teufelsdröckh treats empty, or 'cast', clothes with a holy reverence:

> With awe-struck heart I walk through that Monmouth Street, with its empty Suits, as through a Sanhedrim of stainless Ghosts. Silent are they, but expressive in their silence: the past witnesses and instruments of Woe and Joy, of Passions, Virtues, Crimes, and all the fathomless tumult of Good and Evil in 'the Prison men call Life'. (*SR* 178)

Empty clothes are thus simultaneously imaginary and symbolic, reflecting the past of the individual life but now representing something more universal in their own 'afterlife'. Similarly for Dickens, the clothes displayed in Monmouth Street (that 'burial-place of the fashions' and the 'extensive groves of the illustrious dead' [*SkB* 98]) represent the life-texts of their owners, to be read by the musing sketch-writer on the street corner. One set of clothes displayed together prompts the comment that 'There was the man's whole life written as legibly on those clothes, as if we had his autobiography engrossed on parchment before us' (*SkB* 99). Dickens thus performs an act of Grimaldian necromancy by merely observing a set of clothes and fitting them 'upon some being of our own conjuring up, and endeavouring, from the shape and fashion of the garment itself, to bring its former owner before our mind's eye' (*SkB* 98). The rest of the sketch narrates the lives, interests, circumstances and even eventual fate of long-departed people, all surmised from the clothes that they may have worn.

Cruikshank's print supports these themes: the proximity between the human figures and empty clothes on display makes it hard to differentiate between them, a problem exacerbated by the wreaths of smoke enveloping one of the 'filled' sets of clothes and several 'empty' sets. Moreover, the insubstantiality of the clothing of the children in the foreground contrasts with the more detailed 'skeleton suit' hanging empty in the top left-hand corner (Fig. 8.1).

Dickens regularly animates collections of empty clothes and other objects in this way to create complex configurations of meaning. Fagin meditates in prison just as 'Boz' had meditated on Monmouth Street, but this time imagining the reverse journey from life to death: 'With what a rattling noise they went down; and how suddenly they

**Figure 8.1** George Cruikshank, 'Monmouth Street', 'Meditations in Monmouth-Street'. Reproduced by courtesy of Charles Dickens Museum, London.

changed, from strong and vigorous men to dangling heaps of clothes' (*OT* 352–3). Dickens reworks this image with Dennis the hangman prior to his own hanging in *Barnaby Rudge*, when overcome with his fear of the scaffold he 'sank down a mere heap of clothes between the two attendants' (*BR* 694), and again later when describing the hanging of George Manning and his wife, 'a limp, loose suit of clothes as if the man had gone out of them; the woman's, a fine shape, so elaborately corseted and artfully dressed, that it was quite unchanged in its trim appearance as it slowly swung from side to side' (*HW* 6.136: 146). Dickens's characters remain associated with their clothes after they have died or temporarily vacated them, giving them an independent existence like the enchanted garments of Monmouth Street.

Mrs Gamp is a figure who would have certainly frequented Monmouth Street, and one that we are encouraged to 'read' through her clothes. We are told that 'She wore a very rusty black gown, rather the worse for snuff, and a shawl and bonnet to correspond'; she wore these particular clothes since they 'at once expressed a decent amount of veneration for the deceased, and invited the next of kin to present her with a fresher suit of weeds' (*MC* 303). In a city populated by hypocrites and actors of all kinds, Mrs Gamp assumes respectability and professionalism in her ministrations as a private nurse and performs 'swoons of different sorts' (*MC* 740) depending on the circumstances. Her clothing choice is deliberately calculated for her own personal gain, as she recognises the symbolic power of clothing (particularly mourning costumes) and yet also manages to impose the imaginary upon them (through details like the snuff stains). The imaginary act of the previous wearer inhabiting their empty clothes here is another call-back to both 'Monmouth Street' and the Covent Garden pantomime.

The description of the clothing that Mrs Gamp wears for 'night-watching' her sick patient is another clownish improvisation. Her yellow nightcap is 'of prodigious size' and 'in shape resembling a cabbage' and is worn in place of another piece of artificial semi-animate headwear, 'a row of bald old curls that could scarcely be called false, they were so very innocent of anything approaching to deception'. She completes this ensemble with one of Grimaldi's favourite prop garments that enables both a transformation and an act of reanimation:

> Finally, she produced a watchman's coat, which she tied round her neck by the sleeves, so that she became two people; and looked, behind, as if she were in the act of being embraced by one of the old patrol. (*MC* 394)

Following the science-confounding laws of the harlequinade, Dickens's imagination enables Mrs Gamp to become two people at once, revert to just herself again, and finally perform a comic *pas de deux* with a watchman's ghost. In an interface between the material and the symbolic (which Cunningham calls the 'curiously mixed existence' [1994: 82) of dress), her coat and the imagined embrace associate her with the derided institution of the watch and so offer an ironic commentary on her own incompetence in 'watching' the sick.

In a further echo of Grimaldi's tricks of construction Dickens often draws on what John Carey calls 'the enchantment' and 'rich humanity of improvised junk' (1991: 49) and directs the dehumanising effect of this slippage between the inanimate and animate towards a satirical purpose. In *Hard Times*, the unfeeling figures of Bounderby and Gradgrind are constructed through metaphors and similes which indicate that they are less than entirely organic compositions. Gradgrind's hair is 'a plantation of firs to keep the wind from the shining surface' of his head, which was 'like the crust of a plum pie' (*HT* 5). Dickens answers the question 'who *was* Mr Bounderby?' by describing how the pompous industrialist was a 'man made out of a coarse material, which seemed to have been stretched to make so much of him' who had 'a pervading appearance on him of being inflated like a balloon, and ready to start' (*HT* 15). This idea of Bounderby as a balloon develops through the narrative as his bombast continues to inflate him to yet greater dimensions, like Grimaldi at the Aldgate pump. On the verge of another of his outbursts he 'swelled to such an extent' (*HT* 181), and when 'Mrs Pegler' reveals herself to be his mother he 'had every moment swelled larger and larger' (*HT* 196). Dickens opts for another hair-related simile when, during another angry spell, Bounderby's hair becomes 'like a hayfield wherein his windy anger was boisterous' (*HT* 181).

Schlicke notes that these allusions to pantomime transformation denote the pervasive power of fancy and the imagination, and the uncontainable nature of the circus spirit. They also certainly suggest another Bakhtinian grotesque body: both Gradgrind and Bounderby, despite their conscious attempts to represent limitation and control, are corporeally so malleable and fluid that their appearance transforms to represent their predominant emotion or mental state, in defiance of their own prescriptions of socially acceptable behaviour. At one point these transformative powers seem to have possessed Bounderby's hat, for on discovering that the bank has been robbed he discusses the matter with Harthouse and 'with his hat in his hand, gave a beat upon the crown at every little division of his sentences, as if were a tambourine' before he finally puts it on his head 'like an oriental dancer' (*HT* 140–1). Dickens has transformed Bounderby into a sideshow entertainer, without Bounderby himself being aware of it, and while he tries to oppose everything that the circus stands for ('art and fiction and the whole tradition of story and metaphor' [1994: 134] as Cunningham puts it), he briefly becomes 'a gargantuan mess of fictions' (1994: 138) himself.

While many of these characters are unconsciously transformed by their creator, others deliberately and self-consciously utilise the transformative possibilities of clothing and exploit the possibilities of misinterpretation for personal gain. When Montague Tigg later reappears as Tigg Montague (in a chapter entitled 'Showing that Old Friends may not only Appear with New Faces, but in False Colours'), he dresses very differently, and Dickens adjusts his tone accordingly. Now

> his clothes, symmetrically made, were of the newest fashion and the costliest kind. Flowers of gold and blue, and green and blushing red, were on his waistcoat; precious chains and jewels sparkled on his breast; his fingers, clogged with brilliant rings, were as unwieldy as summer flies but newly rescued from a honey-pot. (*MC* 407)

Dickens makes it clear that we already know this man; even if he had 'changed his name, and changed his outward surface', it was still 'the same Satanic, gallant, military Tigg', and although 'the brass was burnished, lacquered, newly stamped' it 'was the same true Tigg metal notwithstanding' (*MC* 408). This somewhat over-wrought intervention betrays Dickens's anxious desire that the reader clearly recognises Tigg as the same person as before, despite his outward transformation. This is understandable, given the powerful and dangerously persuasive nature of his change: when Tigg first appeared, he could barely scrape together 'the ridiculously small amount of eighteenpence', but he can now separate wealthy businessmen from their substantial fortunes (*MC* 60). Indeed, given this transformative power of cloth, it is perhaps no coincidence that a branch of the Anglo-Bengalee Disinterested Loan and Life Insurance Company operates 'in a first floor over a tailor's' (*MC* 410). Dickens expresses and explores this anxiety more thoroughly through the figure of Pip in *Great Expectations*, who, like Dickens himself, tries to transform himself and those around him through dress, and I shall return to him later.

Tigg Montague's 'young gentleman in livery' Bailey similarly adopts a uniform appropriate to his elevation from boarding-house boot-boy to footman. However, his clownish impulses cannot be restrained, and he performs a comic routine for his friend Poll Sweedlepipe to demonstrate the inherently hollow and ridiculous nature of his costume, going 'round and round in circles, for the better exhibition of his figure' (*MC* 399). Branwen Bailey Pratt describes how Bailey operates 'beyond both occupational categories and expected norms of behaviour' and here he turns his costume into dress through the way he wears it (1975: 186). Like the clown promenading the stage he puts 'his hands into the pockets of his white cord breeches, swaggering along at [his friend's] side' and engages his awestruck audience in some boastful repartee:

> 'D'ye know a pair of top-boots when you see 'em, Polly? – look here!'
> 'Beau-ti-ful!' cried Mr Sweedlepipe.
> 'D'ye know a slap-up sort of button, when you see it?' said the youth. 'Don't look at mine, if you ain't a judge, because these lions' heads was made for men of taste: not snobs.'
> 'Beau-ti-ful!' cried the barber again. 'A grass-green frock-coat, too, bound with gold! and a cockade in your hat.'
> '*I* should hope so,' replied the youth. 'Blow the cockade, though; for, except that it don't turn round, it's like the wentilator that used to be in the kitchen winder at Todgers's.' (*MC* 399–400)

These clothes elevate Bailey in Poll's estimation and through a pantomimic transformation Bailey switches between the imaginary and symbolic modes of appearance. We are told that Paul 'was so perfectly confounded by [Bailey's] precocious self-possession, and his patronising manner, as well as by his boots, cockade, and livery, that a mist swam before his eyes', and he saw not the old boot-boy Bailey from Todgers, but 'a highly-condensed embodiment of all the sporting grooms in London' (*MC* 401). This description brings us close to Grimaldi's representations of sporting dandies (as seen in pantomimes such as *Harlequin and Padmanaba, or The Golden Fish* (Covent Garden, 1811)), which Bailey reinforces with some comic gymnastics: while talking to Poll, he performs 'a straddling action of the white cords, a bend of the knees, and a striking-forth of the top-boots' (*MC* 400). He repeats this in front of Jonas Chuzzlewit when he comes to visit Montague, performing his 'favourite action of the knees and boots' (*MC* 427).

Here Bailey's actions offer an oblique commentary on the actions of his master, who has been entirely transformed by his own clothing and gestures from the scrounging chancer into a respected man of business. Our laughter with Bailey as he implicitly points out the folly of his supposed betters is resolutely Bergsonian and corrective, and a direct antecedent of the actions of another young clown apprentice, Trabb's boy in *Great Expectations*, to whom I will return later.

## The Dandy as Clown

These two notions of dress as performance and of deploying clothing in a manner which both liberates one from restrictive social mores and then critiques them from a distance culminate in the cultural figure of the dandy, a character who was a common concern for

Grimaldi, Carlyle and then Dickens. Although *Sartor* has often been read as thoroughly opposed to dandyism, its often ambiguous tone reflects a more nuanced and ambivalent attitude prevalent at the time.[3] Clair Hughes notes that 'while frivolity of dress was clearly "wrong"', Victorian men found 'something attractive, even nostalgic' in the way that the dandy 'made a success (however despicable and trivial) of *absolute selfishness*' (2006: 51), while Sima Godfrey describes 'the essential paradox of the Dandy' as 'a man who is at once ridiculous and yet dictates fashion' (1982: 24). Although the dandy's grotesqueness could be lampooned, his perceived carelessness about the dictates of society made him an attractive site for imaginative release, and both Grimaldi and Dickens play with the possibilities of this ambiguity. The dandy-clown thus becomes a third subcategory alongside the two Dickensian dandy types identified by Ellen Moers – the earlier theatrical dandy-villains (such as Mulberry Hawk and Sir John Chester) and the later, more developed and ambiguous 'grey men' (1960: 16) (including Eugene Wrayburn and Henry Gowan).

Grimaldi's tricks of construction, which invest the material everyday with symbolic value, find a correlation with the dandy's fetishism of his clothing. Moody has identified how Grimaldi's Clown 'subverted the boundaries separating nature and culture, destroying spectators' assumptions about the distinction between that which is alive, and that which has been manufactured' (2000: 224), which parallels Benjamin's view of fashion as a celebration of fetishism, which, to quote Calefato, 'transforms the human body [. . .] into the sum of its parts, each of which is considered a cult object in itself [. . .] it is [also] the form in which merchandise, the inorganic object, reveals an unexpected fascination' (2004: 112).

The 'protean' nature of the dandy and the importance he places on what Regenia Gagnier calls 'presentation as a spectacle' (1986: 68), aligns him with the pantomime clown, and unsurprisingly Grimaldi's repertoire included a dandy figure, akin to the 'swell'. Spooner recognises that 'dandyism emerged through a variety of social configurations', from genuine aristocratic figures to the gaudier 'Swells' or 'Gents', those lower-class but aspiring middle-class clerks and shop assistants 'who briefly counted Dickens among their number' (2004: 91). Richard Altick calls the swell 'the dandy's leisured middle-class imitator' (1991: 244) who sought to emulate the style of the dandy, but merely 'vulgarized it with loud colours and fancy, eccentric cuts' (1991: 287).

Grimaldi went further than topical laughs and developed the swell's status as the grotesque extreme of dandy style and sensibility which, as Moody points out, could encompass both 'excessive physical consumption' and 'grotesque bodily contortion' (2000: 224). One principal manifestation of this was Grimaldi's character of Dandy Lover, described by Mayer as 'the foolish, vain, and insipid young man personifying the deservedly spurred suitor' (1969: 169), and who appeared in pantomimes such as *Harlequin and Cinderella* (Covent Garden, 1820) and *Harlequin and Friar Bacon*.

Eigner describes John Chivery as 'the sad Clown of *Little Dorrit*' (1989: 30), who renounces his love for Amy to clear the path for the more acceptable choice of Arthur Clennam, but he also has close affinities with Dandy Lover, and for Dickens he embodies the comic sartorial business of earnest young men from the lower classes who attempt to elevate their status through dress. Dickens describes John's Sunday attire for visiting his would-be father-in-law in terms that echo the Grimaldian dandy-swell figure:

> He was neatly attired in a plum-colored coat, with as large a collar of black velvet as his figure could carry; a silken waistcoat, bedecked with golden sprigs; a chaste neck-kerchief much in vogue at that day, representing a preserve of lilac pheasants on a buff ground; pantaloons so highly decorated with side-stripes, that each leg was a three-stringed lute; and a hat of state, very high and hard [. . .] the prudent Mrs Chivery perceived that in addition to these adornments her John carried a pair of white kid gloves, and a cane like a little finger-post, surmounted by an ivory hand marshalling him the way that he should go[.] (*LD* 232)

In Dickens's fulsome description we are presented with a dazzling array of sartorial details encompassing colours, textiles, designs and accessories. The inclusion of cigars in a later ensemble when he is seen 'in his best clothes, with his tall hat under his arm, his ivory-handled cane genteelly embarrassing his deportment, and a bundle of cigars in his hand' (*LD* 659), immediately implicate him in the 'swell' class.

Grimaldi's Clown burlesques dandy style in other ways. In *Furibond, or Harlequin Negro* (Drury Lane, 1807), he visits a tailor in a 'fashionable green coat, with a large Belcher handkerchief hanging out of each breast pocket'. He quickly adopts dandy attitudes and dismisses the tailor's demands for payment in the 'tone of a Bond Street Lounger' suggesting that '"Oh, my dear fellow, never trouble yourself"' (Mayer 1969: 176–7). Dickens emulates such behaviour in 'The Pantomime of Life', in his portrayal of the clown 'taking lodgings which he has not the slightest intention of paying for, or obtaining goods under false pretences' (as discussed in Chapter 3).

In *Harlequin and the Red Dwarf* Grimaldi's Clown plays an auctioneer selling off a variety of dandy clothing: 'And here's a famous lot of Man Millinery – a pair of Stays for a Beau – a Frill to wear without a shirt for a Buck, pair of ruffles for a Blood, and a cravat for a Bang-up.' To further exaggerate the comedy of this routine, Mayer describes how, rather than using real articles of clothing, Grimaldi used 'either ridiculously enlarged versions of dandy apparel, or everyday objects that [he] combined to burlesque dandy haberdashery' for the amused contemplation of the audience (1969: 177).

In 1815, Grimaldi's song 'All the World's in Paris' from *Harlequin Whittington, Lord Mayor of London* drew attention to the ridiculousness of dandy dress and aligned it with the inflated pretensions of its wearers: 'Lawk! Who's that, with monstrous hat, / Her parasol who handles? / 'Tis Miss Flame, the Borough dame, / Who deals in tallow-candles.'[4] In Cruikshank's depiction of the scene, Grimaldi wears an oversized hat and a coat with enlarged fur cuffs and collars.[5] Artists such as Cruikshank and Richard Dighton caricatured the dandy through what Moers calls their 'persistent sense of the relation between anatomy and dress' (1960: 61–2), channelling the same sense of the bodily grotesque as Grimaldi and supporting his teasing of the dandy figure.

In *Lacing a Dandy*, Dighton depicts a figure that looks barely human and who is as malleable and subject to bodily extremes as Grimaldi's Clown.[6] This dandy is grossly disproportioned, with a minuscule head surmounted on a ridiculously high collar and hidden between two large clumps of *bouffant* hair, carrying limbs and a torso that alternate between the stick-thin and the inflated. Cunningham notes how farce is linked thematically and etymologically with *farce*, an Old French derivation of the Latin '*farcire*' (to stuff) (1994: 220), and here Dighton depicts the farcical stuffing of the dandy body into a misshapen and ill-conceived costume.

Cruikshank's annual series 'Monstrosities, or London Dandies' drew similar attention to the grotesque and exaggerated fashions that transformed their wearers into alien figures. In these prints, the broad kaleidoscope of colours and unusual shapes of the figures – such as puffed sausage legs, angular spindles, swollen chests, absurdly high collars and tiny hats and shoes – make their wearers seem to be other than human.

These themes of comically grotesque dandyism are parallelled both visually and verbally in the figure of Mr Toots in *Dombey and Son.*

**Figure 8.2** Hablot K. Browne ('Phiz'), 'Mr Toots becomes Particular – Diogenes also', *Dombey and Son*. Reproduced by courtesy of Charles Dickens Museum, London.

Phiz captures him in full Dandy Lover mode as he tries to kiss Susan Nipper (Fig. 8.2).

The stiff angular shapes of his pantaloons and long jacket echo the clean straight lines of a shop window mannequin, and a sense of the inanimate is enhanced through the surrounding furniture – the table, the umbrella stand and the bannister – which emphasises long verticals. The angle of his cane leaning against the table and its proximity to the hat can be compared with Toots's torso and legs in a manner which further reduces him to a mere collection of clothes. His remarkable thinness (caused by the tailoring he has undergone) is thrown into relief by the broader figure of Susan Nipper and the wild shapelessness of Diogenes the dog, while his spindly legs and the fluffy curls of hair bunched either side of his head also echo the grotesquer elements of Dighton's print.

The clownish Toots serves as a complement to the sober businessman Dombey, who projects a different kind of dandyism. Benjamin notes that dandyism was created by 'the English who were leaders in world trade' (1985: 96) as a means for business leaders to mask the unpredictable nature of trading and fluctuating stock markets, and so preserve commercial confidence. Figures like Dombey and Merdle therefore put on their own performances of inscrutability, and suppress any anxieties and strain while in public, but the comical dandy reflects the chaotic, free energy lurking just beneath the surface of the contained, controlled facade of the businessman.

Thus in *Dombey and Son*, Toots's 'blaze of jewellery and buttons' (*DS* 221) is contrasted with the more conventional colours and clothes of Mr Dombey, and even when Dombey breaks away from his usual black, he remains within the rules of propriety: as Schaffer notes, 'blues and purples' were 'acceptable colours for men's outfits on especially celebratory occasions', making the 'blue coat and lilac waistcoat' that 'the ultra-respectable Mr Dombey' dons for his wedding to Edith socially permissible (2000: 46).

Moreover, unlike Dombey's predictable and understated wardrobe, Mr Toots indulges in a variety of comic sartorial business, as he goes through various private agonies to keep up with fluctuations in contemporary fashion:

> Mr Toots appeared to be involved in a good deal of uncertainty whether, on the whole, it was judicious to button the bottom button of his waistcoat, and whether, on a calm revision of all the circumstances, it was best to wear his wristbands turned up or turned down. Observing that Mr Feeder's were turned up, Mr Toots turned his up; but the wristbands of the next arrival being turned down, Mr Toots turned his down. The differences in point of waistcoat-buttoning, not only at the bottom, but at the top too, became so numerous and complicated as the arrivals thickened, that Mr Toots was continually fingering that article of dress, as if he were performing on some instrument; and appeared to find the incessant execution it demanded, quite bewildering. (*DS* 221)

As Grimaldi's routine in *Harlequin Negro* suggests, the tailor was an important protagonist in such sartorial dramas, and took on greater significance as clothing became an important commodity within the consumer revolution. *The London Tradesman* wryly noted that 'to some [the tailor] not only makes their Dress, but [. . .] may be said to make themselves' and consequently there are 'Numbers of Beings in and about this Metropolis who have no other identical Existence than what the Taylor [*sic*], Milliner, and Perriwig-Maker bestow upon them' (Campbell 1747: 191).

In *Sartor* the tailor carries a theological significance, characterised as 'not only a Man, but something of a Creator or Divinity', who transforms ordinary men into greater beings:

> Man is by the Tailor new-created into a Nobleman, and clothed not only with Wool but with Dignity and a Mystic Dominion, – is not the fair fabric of Society itself, with all its royal mantles and pontifical stoles, whereby, from nakedness and dismemberment, we are organised into Polities, into Nations, and a whole co-operating Mankind, the creation, as has here been often irrefragably evinced, of the Tailor alone? (*SR* 212)

Dickens recognised the value of his own tailor, calling him 'my artist' in a letter to Macready; signing himself as 'The Unwaistcoated One', he asked to borrow a waistcoat for a wedding – specifically, the one 'wherein certain broad stripes of purple disported themselves by a combination of extraordinary circumstances'. By wearing it, Dickens planned to 'ha, ha, ha, ha! – eclipse the bridegroom!' (*LCD* 4: 406–7), a jesting comment that recognises the power of clothing within social ritual.

Toots similarly relies on the ubiquitous tailors of Burgess and Company, and in an echo of Dickens's letter 'attires himself as if he were at least the Bridegroom' for Dombey's wedding (*DS* 478). Throughout the novel Dickens wields the tailor's power and constantly reminds us of Toots's reliance on his tailors for not only his dress, but his very mode of existence. His engagement with Burgess and Co. begins very early: soon after meeting young Paul Dombey at Blimber's school, Toots turns the conversation to sartorial origins:

> 'Who's your tailor?' inquired Toots, after looking at him for some moments.
>
> 'It's a woman that has made my clothes as yet,' said Paul. 'My sister's dress-maker.'
>
> 'My tailor's Burgess and Co.,' said Toots. 'Fash'nable. But very dear.' (*DS* 175–6)

Toots's comment is humorously precocious in contrast to Paul's more homely response, but these 'very dear' tailors become a principal vehicle for this shy young man to articulate his thoughts. He consciously uses tailoring as a metaphor when he explains to Captain Cuttle his frustration at not being able to adequately express himself, as clothing becomes the language of thought: '"You know," said Mr Toots, "it's exactly as if Burgess and Co. wished to oblige a customer with a most extraordinary pair of trousers, and *could not* cut out what they had in their minds."' (*DS* 849).

We are reminded of Toots's attire on nearly every occasion that he appears, and clothes also dominate his thoughts on emotional matters – Toots views himself through his clothes, Dickens shows him to us through his clothes, and other characters see him through his clothes. When Florence accompanies him on a walk to Blimber's, Toots's infatuated awkwardness is realised in reference to his attire: 'though he is splendidly dressed, he feels misfits, and sees wrinkles, on the masterpieces of Burgess and Co., and wishes he had put on that brightest pair of boots' (*DS* 628). Toots further acknowledges his 'wasting away' at a time of emotional distress (caused by his love for Florence) by stating that '"Burgess and Co. have altered my measure, I'm in that state of thinness"' (*DS* 730). As part of this love sickness, Toots lets his appearance become 'wild and savage', admits that he is in such a '"rash state"' that '"I haven't had my clothes brushed"' (*DS* 761) and even warns his boxing companion The Game Chicken against polishing his boots. At the resolution of this love-episode, when Toots steps aside for Walter, he not only pledges to be Florence's friend but also '"to make the best of myself, and to – to have my boots as brightly polished, as – as circumstances will admit of"' (*DS* 846). Finally, he describes his sadness at Paul's premature death in terms of clothes; '"Poor Dombey! I'm sure I never thought that Burgess & Co. – fashionable tailors (but very dear), that we used to talk about – would make this suit of clothes for such a purpose"' (*DS* 279).

Clothing is also an agent of being and of change in *Great Expectations*. Pip, whose attention to his clothes and those of others resembles Toots's, is confronted by two different attitudes to sartorial metamorphosis: resistance, represented by Joe Gargery, and burlesque, represented by Trabb's boy.

Although Mary Shelley's *Frankenstein* would not appear until 1818 Grimaldi had obliquely pre-empted her narrative of reanimation by giving life and new purpose to similar collections of miscellaneous parts. As mentioned in Chapter 2, *The Times* noted how Grimaldi 'was a sort of Shakspeare [*sic*] in his way, – he exhausted natural monsters, and then "imagined new". *Frankenstein* was nothing to him' ([Anon.] 1828b: 3) and like Frankenstein's monster, Grimaldi's inventions repeatedly rose up and battled against their creator. These complementary notions of the tailor as man's creator and Grimaldi as Dr Frankenstein combine in Dickens's presentation of Pip's relationships with Joe and Magwitch, who resist the potential annihilation of the self threatened by Pip's attempts to transform them into docile, 'respectable' bodies.

As Pip observes, Joe is most comfortable in the 'costume' of his trade: 'In his working clothes, Joe was a well-knit characteristic-looking blacksmith; in his holiday clothes, he was more like a scarecrow in good circumstances, than anything else' (*GE* 23). He wears his smarter attire in a way that unconsciously draws out his simple clownishness rather than the assumed formality that the pompous Pip desires. On one appearance in his 'court-suit', Joe 'pulled up his shirt-collar so very high behind, that it made the hair on the crown of his head stand up like a tuft of feathers' (*GE* 80), in the manner of Dighton's parodic prints.

At Pip's chambers, Joe indirectly resists Pip's attempts to render him docile by interacting comically with his thoroughly alien clothing. Pip knows that Joe has arrived even before he sees him, as he recognises 'his clumsy manner of coming upstairs' sounded by 'his state-boots' which were 'always too big for him' (*GE* 169). This ill-fitting and excessively-sized clothing stands in opposition to the neatly tailored clothes mistakenly prized by Pip. This entrance is the precursor to Joe's lengthy comic business with his hat: he spends a considerable amount of time looking for a suitable place to put it ('as if it were only on some very few rare substances in nature that it could find a resting-place') until finally settling on an inappropriate spot on the corner of the chimney piece 'from which it ever afterwards fell off at intervals' (*GE* 171). This falling hat consumes his entire attention, and he devotes to it 'a quickness of eye and hand, very like that exacted by wicket-keeping'. Despite his disappointment, Pip describes this performance in the manner of a fascinated pantomime spectator:

> He made the most extraordinary play with it, and showed the greatest skill; now, rushing at it and catching it as neatly as it dropped; now merely stopping it midway, beating it up, and humouring it in various parts of the room and against a good deal of the pattern of the paper on the wall, before he felt safe to close with it; finally splashing it into the slop-basin, where I took the liberty of laying hands upon it. (*GE* 172)

As he leaves, Joe reiterates verbally what he had eloquently expressed in his physical performance, explaining how he feels '"wrong in these clothes"' (*GE* 173) and we see the salutary effects of this performance in Pip's retrospective comments. In retrospect he acknowledges that Joe retained his 'simple dignity' despite 'the fashion of his dress' (*GE* 174) which he had worn to accord with Pip's elevated circumstances.

In a further development of the Frankenstein motif, Pip's other attempts to transform those around him through dress have more serious consequences. For example, a 'boy in boots' is quickly 'created' according to Pip's design for a gentleman's errand-boy, but he soon quashes Pip's grander plans for him, becoming a 'monster' whom Pip 'had to find [. . .] a little to do and a great deal to eat; and with both of those horrible requirements he haunted [his] existence' (*GE* 169). In calling him a 'monster' created out of 'refuse', Pip foregrounds the unnatural state of this idle, all-devouring descendent of Sam Weller and Bailey, who parodies both the consumer revolution and the dandy ideal.

This haunting of the creator by his monster foreshadows Pip's relationship with Magwitch. Magwitch's attempts to forge his own existence, and his resistance to Pip's efforts to recreate him, lead Pip towards the same analogy: 'The imaginary student pursued by the misshapen creature he had impiously made were not more wretched than I, pursued by the creature who had made me' (*GE* 253–4). Like Joe Gargery's 'court-suit', Pip's disguise for Magwitch fails to transform its wearer and he seems doomed to be discovered even before he has set out on his flight from London: 'The more I dressed him and the better I dressed him, the more he looked like the slouching fugitive on the marshes' (*GE* 252).

A second attitude to Pip's social-sartorial engineering is presented by Trabb the tailor's boy, who enacts an exaggerated style of metamorphosis to burlesque and shows the folly of Pip's own attempts at transformation. He is positioned as a clown when Pip comments that he 'had too much vivacity to spare' and 'it was in his constitution to want variety and excitement at anybody's expense' (*GE* 321), which is borne out in his sartorial imitation of Pip and a masterstroke of improvisation:

> This time he was entirely changed. He wore the blue bag in the manner of my great-coat, and was strutting along the pavement towards me on the opposite side of the street [. . .] Words cannot state the amount of aggravation and injury wreaked upon me by Trabb's boy, when, passing

> abreast of me, he pulled up his shirt-collar, twined his side-hair, stuck an arm akimbo, and smirked extravagantly by, wriggling his elbows and body, and drawling to his attendants, 'Don't know yah, don't know yah, pon my soul don't know yah!' (*GE* 188)

Trabb's boy mimics Pip's new suit of clothes with whatever he has to hand, in this case the costume and accessories of his trade. According to his clown's prerogative, he also offers an oblique commentary on Pip's own shortcomings in a manner which entirely disconcerts Pip, putting him into a state of 'inexpressible terror, amazement, and indignation' and leaving him 'utterly confounded' (*GE* 188).

This burlesque of Pip's obsession with the transformative powers of dress and his reliance on unstable signifiers to denote social standing should be read alongside the scenes of Joe Gargery's awkwardness. Joe's most comfortable dress is entirely at variance with Pip's social norms of gentility, which are shown to be based on performance, and Trabb's boy accentuates this theatricality of the dandy yet further, with a grotesquely exaggerated (and amusing) performance.

## Finishing Touches

As I have outlined here, both Grimaldi and Dickens recognised the value of clothing as a versatile and polyvalent material symbol. Grimaldi's Clown pushed the concept of the theatrical costume change much further than his pantomimic predecessors, both developing a new clown dress from the conventional costume and devising new garments from whatever everyday objects he had available to him. In this way, he was able to use his clothing to mark out his own autonomous clowning space outside convention, transcend boundaries of class and station, and playfully lampoon the pretensions of his time.

These ideas spoke directly to Dickens, who adopted this use of clothing in both his own sartorial choices, and to a greater extent, those of his characters. Carlyle had anticipated this pantomimic use of clothing in prose, but it was in the work of Dickens, the theatrical novelist, that it received its fullest expression. Like Grimaldi, Dickens recognised the multi-faceted power of clothing and tried to harness it at appropriate moments during his fiction. In his rebellious clowns clothing becomes not just a convenient shorthand for their non-conformity and refusal to bow to social expectations, but a fully-realised element of it. Elsewhere, Dickens explores its transformative powers and ability to puncture the hollow pretensions of both authority figures and dandyesque social climbers, whose power and self-worth seem to exist entirely in their garments.

## Notes

1. See Oddy and Schwarzbach 1978.
2. William Heath, 'Grimaldi's Bold Dragoon in the Popular Pantomime of Red Dwarf' (1812), Victoria and Albert Museum.
3. For accounts of its anti-dandyism, see Laver 1968, p. 85, and Moers 1960, p. 170 and p. 178.
4. W. Ware, *London now is out of town, a comic song, sung by Mr Grimaldi, in the pantomime of Harlequin Whittington, or Lord Mayor of London composed by W. H. Ware* (London: Power, 1811).
5. George Cruikshank, 'J. Grimaldi, Sung in Character – "All the World's in Paris"' (1815), Museum of London.
6. Richard Dighton, 'Lacing a Dandy' (1819), Museum of London.

# *Bibliography*

Ackroyd, Peter. *Dickens*. London: Minerva, 1991.

Altick, Richard D. *Lives and Letters: A History of Literary Biography in England and America*. New York: Alfred A. Knopf, 1966.

– . *The Presence of the Present: Topics of the Day in the Victorian Novel*. Columbus: Ohio State University Press, 1991.

Amigoni, David. 'Introduction: Victorian Life Writing: Genres, Print, Constituencies'. In *Life Writing and Victorian Culture*. Ed. David Amigoni. Aldershot: Ashgate, 2006, pp. 1–20.

Andrews, Malcolm. *Dickens and the Grown-Up Child*. Basingstoke and London: Macmillan, 1994.

Andrin, Muriel. 'Back to the "Slap": Slapstick's Hyperbolic Gesture and the Rhetoric of Violence'. In *Slapstick Comedy*. Ed. Tom Paulus and Rob King. New York and London: Routledge, 2010, pp. 226–35.

[Anon.] 'To the Editor of the London Magazine'. *London Magazine or Gentleman's Monthly Intelligencer*. July 1772, pp. 321–2.

– . 'Harlequin, No. XXVI'. *London Magazine or Gentleman's Monthly Intelligencer*. October 1775, pp. 495–6.

– . 'Memoranda Dramatica, &c.'. *The Monthly Mirror: Reflecting Men and Manners with Strictures on their Epitome, the Stage*. London: Wright, 1807. Vol. 1, pp. 428–37.

– . 'Covent-Garden Theatre'. *The Times*. 5 January 1813, p. 3.

– . *The New Pantomime of Harlequin and Fortunio; or Shing-Moo and Thun-Ton, with a Sketch of the Story, etc.* London: Glendinning, 1815a.

– . 'The New Pantomimes'. *The Champion*. 31 December 1815b, p. 421.

– . 'Literary and Scientific Intelligence'. *The Edinburgh Magazine and Literary Miscellany*. August 1818, pp. 167–71.

– . 'Covent-Garden'. *European Magazine and London Review*. January 1821, pp. 67–70.

– . 'Covent-Garden'. *The Times*. 27 December 1823, p. 3.

– . 'Covent-Garden Theatre'. *The Times*. 27 December 1824, p. 3.

– . 'Memoir of Joseph Grimaldi'. *Oxberry's Dramatic Biography and Histrionic Anecdotes*. Ed. Catherine and William Oxberry. Vol. 2. London: Virtue, 1825a, pp. 109–22.

– . 'Covent-Garden Theatre'. *The Times*. 28 December 1825b, p. 3.

–. 'Punch'. *The Pocket Magazine Robin's Series*. February 1827, pp. 90–6.

–. 'Review of Collier's Punch and Judy'. *The London Literary Gazette*. 9 February 1828a, pp. 82–4.

–. 'Drury-Lane'. *The Times*. 27 December 1828b, p. 3.

–. 'Adelphi Theatre'. *The Times*. 27 December 1832, p. 3.

–. 'Review of Second Series of *Sketches by Boz*'. *The Spectator*. 24 December 1836, pp. 16–17.

–. 'Some Recollections of Grimaldi'. *The New Monthly Magazine and Humorist*. Ed. Theodore Hook. Vol. 2. London: Colburn, 1837. pp. 375–84.

–. 'Review of *Memoirs of Joseph Grimaldi*'. *The Athenaeum*. 17 February 1838a, pp. 114–17.

–. 'Life of Grimaldi'. *The Literary Gazette; and Journal of Belles Lettres, Arts, Sciences. &c*. 17 February 1838b, pp. 97–9.

–. 'Life of Grimaldi – 2nd notice'. *The Literary Gazette*. 24 February 1838c, pp. 118–19.

–. '*Memoirs of Joseph Grimaldi* – 2nd Notice'. *The Athenaeum*. 3 March 1838d, pp. 164–5.

–. 'Review of *Memoirs of the Late Joseph Grimaldi, the Clown*'. *The Idler, and Breakfast-Table Companion*. 3 March 1838e, pp. 66–7.

–. '*Memoirs of Grimaldi, the Clown* – 2nd Notice'. *The Idler, and Breakfast-Table Companion*. 10 March 1838f, pp. 74–5.

–. 'New Books – Memoirs of Joseph Grimaldi, edited by Boz'. *The Mirror of Literature, Amusement and Instruction*. 17 March 1838g, pp. 169–71.

–. 'Review of *Memoirs of Joseph Grimaldi, the Clown*'. *The Monthly Magazine, or British Register*. April 1838h, pp. 434–5.

–. 'Review of *Memoirs of Joseph Grimaldi*'. *The Knickerbocker, or New-York Monthly Magazine*. May 1838i, pp. 463–5.

–. 'Review of *Memoirs of Joseph Grimaldi*'. *The Gentleman's Magazine*. 2.6 (June 1838j), pp. 416–19.

–. 'The Christmas Pantomimes'. *The Times*. 27 December 1842, p. 5.

–. 'Mr. Dickens and his New Work'. *The Mirror of Literature*. 27 December 1845, p. 402.

–. 'Theatricals in Australia', *The Era*. 12 August 1860a, p. 12.

–. 'Theatre Royal – The Pantomime'. *Manchester Times*. 22 December 1860b, p. 5.

–. 'Pantomimes', *All the Year Round* 17.408 (16 February 1867a), pp. 189–92.

–. 'Boxing Night at the Theatres'. *The Era*. 29 December 1867b, p. 10.

–. 'Acrobats Bill – Second Reading'. *Hansard*. 4 July 1872a. Vol 212, cc618–23.

–. 'Covent Garden Theatre'. *The Morning Post*. 30 August 1872b, p. 6.

–. 'Our Captious Critic', *Illustrated Sporting and Dramatic News*. 6 January 1877a, p. 365.

–. 'The Pantomime: Blue Beard'. *Nottingham and Midland Counties Daily Express*. 27 December 1877b, p. 4.

Assael, Brenda. *The Circus and Victorian Society*. Charlottesville and London: University of Virginia Press, 2005.

Axton, William F. *Circle of Fire: Dickens' Vision and Style and the Popular Victorian Theater*. Lexington: University of Kentucky Press, 1966.

Bachman, Maria K. 'Bulwer-Lytton's *Pelham*: The Disciplinary Dandy and the Art of Government'. *Texas Studies in Literature and Language* 47.2 (Summer 2005), pp. 167–87.

Baer, Marc. *Theatre and Disorder in Late Georgian London*. Oxford: Clarendon Press, 1992.

Bagehot, Walter. 'Charles Dickens'. *National Review* 7.14 (October 1858), pp. 458–86.

Bakhtin, Mikhail. *Rabelais and His World*. Trans. Helene Iswolsky. Cambridge, MA: Massachusetts Institute of Technology, 1968.

Barlee, Ellen. *Pantomime Waifs; or, A Plea for our City Children*. London: Partridge, 1884.

Baudelaire, Charles. 'Of the Essence of Laughter, and Generally of the Comic in the Plastic Arts'. In *Selected Writings on Art and Literature*. Trans. and Int. P. E. Charvet. London: Penguin, 2006, pp. 140–61.

Beizer, Janet. *Thinking through the Mothers: Reimagining Women's Biographies*. New York: Cornell University Press, 2008.

Bell, Robert H. *Shakespeare's Great Stage of Fools*. New York: Palgrave Macmillan, 2011.

Benjamin, Walter. *Charles Baudelaire: A Lyric Poet in the Era of High Capitalism*. Trans. Harry Zohn. London: Verso, 1985.

Berger, Peter L. *Redeeming Laughter: The Comic Dimension of Human Experience*. New York and Berlin: Walter de Gruyter, 1997.

Bergson, Henri. 'Laughter'. In *Comedy*. Ed. Wylie Sypher. Baltimore: The Johns Hopkins University Press, 1956, pp. 59–190.

Bergonzi, Bernard. 'Nicholas Nickleby'. In *Dickens and the Twentieth Century*. Ed. John Gross and Gabriel Pearson. Toronto: University of Toronto Press, 1962, pp. 65–76.

Bevis, Matthew. 'Dickens by the Clock'. In *Dickens's Style*. Ed. Daniel Tyler. Cambridge: Cambridge University Press, 2013, pp. 46–72.

Booth, Michael. *Victorian Spectacular Theatre 1850–1910*. Boston, MA and London, Henley: Routledge and Kegan Paul, 1981.

Boswell, James. *Life of Johnson*. Ed. George Birkbeck Hill and L. F. Powell. 6 vols. Oxford: Oxford University Press, 1934.

Bradshaw, Penny. 'The Politics of the Platter: Charlotte Smith and the "Science of Eating"'. In *Cultures of Taste/Theories of Appetite: Eating Romanticism*. Ed. Timothy Morton. New York and Basingstoke: Palgrave Macmillan, 2004, pp. 59–76.

Bratton, Jacky. 'Pantomime and the Experienced Young Fellow'. In *Victorian Pantomime*. Ed. Jim Davis. Basingstoke: Palgrave Macmillan, 2010, pp. 87–99.

Bryant, Arthur. *The Age of Elegance 1812–1822*. London: Collins, 1950.

Burke, Peter. *Popular Culture in Early Modern Europe*. Aldershot: Scolar Press, 1994.

Butwin, Joseph. 'The Paradox of the Clown in Dickens'. *Dickens Studies Annual* 5 (1976), pp. 116–32.

Calefato, Patrizia. *The Clothed Body*. Oxford: Berg, 2004.

Campbell, Robert. *The London Tradesman*. London: Gardner, 1747.

Carey, John. *The Violent Effigy: A Study of Dickens's Imagination*. London: Faber, 1991.

Carlyle, Thomas. 'Biography'. *Fraser's Magazine for Town and Country* 27 (April 1832), pp. 253–60.

–. *On Heroes, Hero-Worship, and the Heroic in History*. London: James Fraser, 1841.

–. *Past and Present*. London: Chapman and Hall, 1843.

Chambers, Robert (ed.). *The Book of Days*. 2 vols. Edinburgh: W. and R. Chambers, 1881.

Chesterton, G. K. *Charles Dickens: A Critical Study*. New York: Cornell University Library, 1909.

–. *Appreciations and Criticism of the Works of Charles Dickens*. London: Dent, 1911.

Chittick, Kathryn. *Dickens in the 1830s*. Cambridge: Cambridge University Press, 1990.

['Christopher North']. 'Lectures on the Fine Arts. No. 1. On George Cruikshank'. *Blackwood's Edinburgh Magazine* (July 1823), pp. 18–26.

Clayborough, Arthur. *The Grotesque in English Literature*. Oxford: Clarendon Press, 1965.

Collins, Philip. *Dickens: The Critical Heritage*. London: Routledge and Kegan Paul, 1971.

Connor, Steven. 'Introduction'. In *Charles Dickens*. Ed. Steven Connor. London: Longman, 1996, pp. 1–33.

Cook, Dutton. *A Book of the Play*. 2 vols. London: Sampson Low, 1876.

Coolidge, Archibald. *Charles Dickens as Serial Novelist*. Iowa: Iowa State University Press, 1967.

Coveney, Peter. *Poor Monkey: The Child in Literature*. London: Rockcliff, 1957.

Cradock, Joseph. *Literary and Miscellaneous Memoirs*. London: Nichols, 1828.

Craik, Jennifer. *The Face of Fashion: Cultural Studies in Fashion*. London: Routledge, 1994.

Creed, G. 'Pantomimes'. *The Drama; or Theatrical Pocket Magazine*. London: T. and J. Elvey, 1822. Vol. 1, pp. 125–30.

Cunningham, Valentine. *In the Reading Gaol: Postmodernity, Texts, and History*. Oxford: Blackwell, 1994.

Davis, Jim (ed.). *Victorian Pantomime*. Basingstoke: Palgrave Macmillan, 2010.

–. and Victor Emeljanow. *Reflecting the Audience: London Theatregoing, 1840–1880*. Hatfield: University of Hertfordshire Press, 2001.

Davis, William. *Friendly Advice to Industrious and Frugal Persons*. London: Bensley, 1817.

Dibdin, Charles. *Songs and other vocal compositions in the pantomime called . . . Jan Ben Jan, or, Harlequin and the forty virgins. Performing at the Aquatic Theatre, Sadler's Wells*. London: Glendinning, 1807.

– . [The Astrologer.] *Songs, Duets, Trios, Glees, Chorusses, &c., with a description of the scenery and an outline of the plot, in the new comic pantomime, called the Astrologer: or Harlequin and Moore's Almanack, etc.* London: Glendinning, 1810a.

– . *Songs, Duets, Trios, Chorusses, &c. &c. with a description of the scenery in the new comic pantomime, called Bang Up! or, Harlequin Prime, etc.* London: Glendinning, 1810b.

– . *[London.] Songs, and other Vocal Compositions, in the pantomime called London; or, Harlequin & Time, etc.* London: Glendinning, 1814.

– . *Professional and Literary Memoirs of Charles Dibdin the Younger*. Ed. George Speaight. London: Society for Theatre Research, 1956.

Dibdin, Thomas. *Harlequin in his Element; or, Fire, water, earth, & air; a favourite pantomime, etc.* London: Appleyards, 1808.

– . *Harlequin and Mother Goose; or, the Golden Egg! A comic pantomime*. London: Thomas Hailes Lacy, [1860?].

Dickens, Charles. 'Theatrical Examiner'. *The Examiner*. 21 October 1843, p. 660.

– . 'A Preliminary Word'. *Household Words* 1.1 (30 March 1850), pp. 1–2.

– . 'The Amusements of the People [i]'. *Household Words* 1.1 (30 March 1850), pp. 13–15.

– . 'The Amusements of the People [ii]'. *Household Words* 1.3 (13 April 1850), pp. 57–60.

– . and W. H. Wills, 'A Curious Dance Round A Curious Tree', *Household Words* 4.95 (17 January 1852), pp. 385–9.

– . and G. A. Sala. 'First Fruits'. *Household Words* 5.112 (15 May 1852), pp. 189–92.

– . 'Lying Awake'. *Household Words* 6.136 (30 October 1852), pp. 145–8.

– . 'Where We Stopped Growing'. *Household Words* 6.145 (1 January 1853), pp. 361–3.

– . 'Gone Astray'. *Household Words* 7.177 (13 August 1853), pp. 553–7.

– . 'Out of the Season'. *Household Words* 13.327 (28 June 1856), pp. 553–6.

– . 'The Uncommercial Traveller [iii]' ['Two Views of a Cheap Theatre']. *All the Year Round* 2.44 (25 February 1860), pp. 416–21.

– . 'The Uncommercial Traveller [xi]' ['Dullborough Town']. *All the Year Round* 3.62 (30 June 1860), pp. 274–8.

– . and Henry Spicer. 'Paradise Revisited'. *All the Year Round* 15.352 (20 January 1866), pp. 30–4.

– . *The Uncollected Writings of Charles Dickens: Household Words 1850–1859*. Ed. Harry Stone. 2 vols. London: Allen Lane, 1969.

Dickens, 'Mamie' (Mary). *My Father As I Recall Him*. Westminster: The Roxburghe Press, [1897].

Disher, Maurice Willson. *Clowns and Pantomimes*. London: Constable, 1925.

Dollimore, Jonathan and Alan Sinfield (eds). *Political Shakespeare: New Essays in Cultural Materialism*. Manchester: Manchester University Press, 1985.

Douglas-Fairhurst, Robert. *Becoming Dickens: The Invention of a Novelist*. London and Cambridge, MA: The Belknap Press of Harvard University Press, 2011.

Eagleton, Terry. 'First Class Fellow Traveller'. [Review of Sean French, *Patrick Hamilton: A Life*]. *London Review of Books*. 2 December 1993, p. 12.

Eakin, Paul John. *How Our Lives Become Stories: Making Selves*. New York: Cornell University Press, 1999.

Eigner, Edwin M. *The Dickens Pantomime*. Berkeley and Los Angeles: University of California Press, 1989.

Erasmus, Desiderius. *In Praise of Folly*. Trans. John Wilson. New York: Dover, 2003.

Feaver, William. *George Cruikshank Exhibition Catalogue*. Arts Council of Great Britain, 1974.

Findlater, Richard (ed.). *Memoirs of Joseph Grimaldi*. London: Macgibbon and Kee, 1968.

– . *Joe Grimaldi: His Life and Theatre*. Cambridge: Cambridge University Press, 1978.

Fitzgerald, Percy. 'Harlequin Fairy Morgana!'. *All the Year Round* 12.278 (20 August 1864), pp. 40–8.

[Fleetwood, Charles]. 'Drury-Lane'. *General Advertiser*, 22 November 1744, p. 1.

Forster, John. *The Life of Charles Dickens*. Ed. A. J. Hoppé. 2 vols. London: Dent, 1966.

Frost, Thomas. *The Old Showmen and the Old London Fairs*. London: Tinsley, 1874.

Frow, Gerald. *Oh Yes It Is!: A History of Pantomime*. London: BBC, 1985.

Furneaux, Holly. *Queer Dickens: Erotics, Families, Masculinities*. Oxford: Oxford University Press, 2009.

Gagnier, Reginia. *Idylls of the Marketplace*. Stanford: Stanford University Press, 1986.

Godfrey, Sima. 'The Dandy as Ironic Figure'. *SubStance* 11.36 (1982), pp. 21–33.

Gunning, Tom. 'Mechanisms of Laughter: The Devices of Slapstick'. In *Slapstick Comedy*. Ed. Tom Paulus and Rob King. New York and London: Routledge, 2010, pp. 137–51.

Halliday, Andrew. *Comical Fellows or The History and Mysteries of the Pantomime*. London: J. H. Thomason, 1863a.

– . 'Pantaloon'. *All the Year Round*. 8.177 (13 September 1863b), pp. 10–13.

– . 'My Pantomime [ii]'. *All the Year Round*, 10.238 (14 November 1863c), pp. 272–6.

– . 'Poetry and Pantomime'. *All the Year Round* 13.310 (1 April 1865), pp. 229–33.

Harvey, John. *Men in Black*. London: Reaktion, 1995.
Hill, Jonathan E. 'Cruikshank, Ainsworth, and Tableau Illustration'. *Victorian Studies* 23.4 (Summer 1980), pp. 429–50.
Hill, T. W. 'The Oyster: A Close-Up'. *The Dickensian* 36 (Spring 1940), pp. 139–46.
Hobbes, Thomas. *The Elements of Law Natural and Politic*. Ed. J. C. A. Gaskin. Oxford and New York: Oxford University Press, 1994.
Hollington, Michael. *Dickens and the Grotesque*. London and Sydney: Croon Helm, 1984.
Hood, Thomas. 'A Serio-Comic Reminiscence'. In *Hood's Own, or Laughter from Year to Year*. London: Edward Moxon, 1868, pp. 113–15.
– . *The Complete Poetical Works of Thomas Hood*. Ed. Walter Gerald. London and New York: Henry Frowde, 1906.
Hornback, Robert. *The English Clown Tradition from the Middle Ages to Shakespeare*. Woodbridge and Rochester, NY: Brewer, 2009.
Houston, Gail Turley. *Consuming Fictions: Gender, Class and Hunger in Dickens's Novels*. Carbondale and Edwardsville: Southern Illinois University Press, 1994.
Hughes, Clair. *Dressed in Fiction*. Oxford and New York: Berg, 2006.
[Hunt, Leigh]. 'Theatrical Examiner'. *The Examiner*. 26 January 1817, pp. 8–9.
– . 'The Drama'. *The London Magazine*. Vol 1. London: Baldwin, Cradock and Joy, 1820. pp. 569–78.
James, Louis. 'Cruikshank and Early Victorian Caricature'. *History Workshop* 6 (Autumn 1978), pp. 107–20.
John, Juliet. *Dickens's Villains: Melodrama, Character, Popular Culture*. Oxford: Oxford University Press, 2001.
Johnson, Samuel. *The Rambler* 60 (13 October 1750), pp. 30–6.
– . '[Observations on] The Second Part of *Henry IV*'. In *The Yale Edition of the Works of Samuel Johnson, Vol 7: Johnson on Shakespeare*. Ed. Arthur Sherbo. New Haven, CT: Yale University Press, 1968, pp. 490–524.
Jones, Michael Wynn. *George Cruikshank: His Life and London*. London: Macmillan, 1978.
Kayser, Wolfgang. *Praisers of Folly: Erasmus, Rabelais, Shakespeare*. London: Victor Gollancz, 1964.
Kincaid, James R. *Dickens and the Rhetoric of Laughter*. Oxford: Clarendon Press, 1971.
Kolakowski, Leszek. 'The Priest and the Jester'. In *Toward a Marxist Humanism: Essays on the Left Today*. Trans. Jane Zielonko Peel. New York: Grove Press, 1968, pp. 9–37.
Lackington, James. *Memoirs of the First Forty-Five Years of the Life of James Lackington*. London: Lackington, 1792.
Laver, James. *Dandies*. London: Weidenfeld and Nicolson, 1968.
Leach, Robert. *The Punch and Judy Show: History, Tradition and Meaning*. London: Batsford Academic and Educational, 1985.

Ledger, Sally. *Dickens and the Popular Radical Imagination*. Cambridge: Cambridge University Press, 2007.

Loftus, Donna. 'The Self in Society: Middle-Class Men and Autobiography'. In *Life Writing and Victorian Culture*. Ed. David Amigoni. Aldershot: Ashgate, 2006, pp. 67–86.

Lynch, James J. *Pit, Box and Gallery: Stage and Society in Johnson's London*. Berkeley and Los Angeles: University of California Press, 1953.

Macklin, Charles. *Memoirs of the Life of Charles Macklin Esq*. Ed. James Kirkman. 2 vols. London: Lackington, Allen and Company, 1799.

Marcus, Laura. *Auto/biographical Discourses: Criticism, Theory, Practice*. Manchester and New York: Manchester University Press, 1994.

Marcus, Steven. *Dickens: From Pickwick to Dombey*. London: Chatto and Windus, 1965.

Mayer, David. *Harlequin in His Element: The English Pantomime, 1806–1836*. Cambridge, MA: Harvard University Press, 1969.

– . 'Documents of Performance: George Cruikshank, "The First Appearance of William Shakespeare on the Stage of the Globe with Part of his Dramatic Company in 1564"'. *Nineteenth Century Theatre and Film* 30.1 (Summer 2003), pp. 53–64.

Mayhew, Henry. *London Labour and the London Poor*. 4 vols. New York: Dover Publications, 1968.

McKendrick, Neil, John Brewer and J. H. Plumb. *The Birth of a Consumer Society: The Commercialization of Eighteenth-Century England*. London: Europa Publications, 1982.

Meisel, Martin. *Realizations: Narrative, Pictorial, and Theatrical Arts in Nineteenth-Century England*. Princeton: Princeton University Press, 1983.

Miles, Henry Downes. *The Life of Joseph Grimaldi with Anecdotes of his Contemporaries*. London: Charles Harris, 1838.

Miller, J. Hillis, 'The Fiction of Realism: *Sketches by Boz*, *Oliver Twist* and Cruikshank's Illustrations'. In J. Hillis Miller and David Borowitz. *Charles Dickens and George Cruikshank: Papers Read at a Clark Library Seminar on May 9 1970*. Los Angeles: William Andrew Clark Memorial Library, University of California, 1971, pp. 1–69.

Moers, Ellen. *The Dandy: Brummell to Beerbohm*. Lincoln and London: University of Nebraska Press, 1960.

Moody, Jane. *Illegitimate Theatre in London, 1770–1840*. Cambridge: Cambridge University Press, 2000.

Moore, Mark. *The Memoirs and Adventures of Mark Moore*. London: Myers, 1795.

Moore, Tara. 'National Identity and Victorian Christmas Foods'. In *Consuming Culture in the Long Nineteenth Century: Narratives of Consumption 1700–1900*. Ed. Tamara S. Wagner and Narin Hassan. Lanham, MD: Lexington Books, 2007, pp. 141–54.

Morton, Timothy (ed.). *Cultures of Taste/Theories of Appetite: Eating Romanticism*. New York and Basingstoke: Palgrave Macmillan, 2004.

– . 'Introduction: "Consumption as Performance: The Emergence of the Consumer in the Romantic Period". In *Cultures of Taste/Theories of Appetite: Eating Romanticism*. Ed. Timothy Morton. New York and Basingstoke: Palgrave Macmillan, 2004, pp. 1–17.

– . 'Preface'. In *Cultures of Taste/Theories of Appetite: Eating Romanticism*. Ed. Timothy Morton. New York and Basingstoke: Palgrave Macmillan, 2004, pp. xv–xxi.

Munden, Thomas Shepherd. *The Memoirs of Joseph Shepherd Munden, Comedian*. London: Bentley, 1846.

Murphy, Arthur. *The Life of David Garrick*. Dublin: Smith, 1801.

Murray, D. L. *Candles and Crinolines*. London: Jonathan Cape, 1930.

Nelson, T. A. *Comedy: An Introduction to Comedy in Literature, Drama, and Cinema*. Oxford: Oxford University Press, 1990.

Newman, S. J. *Dickens at Play*. London and Basingstoke: Macmillan, 1981.

North, Julian. *The Domestication of Genius: Biography and the Romantic Poet*. Oxford: Oxford University Press, 2009.

O'Brien, John. *Harlequin Britain: Pantomime and Entertainment, 1690–1760*. Baltimore and London: The Johns Hopkins University Press, 2004.

Oddy, William and F. S. Schwarzbach. 'Dickens and Carlyle Again: A Note on an Early Influence'. *The Dickensian* 53 (Summer 1978), pp. 149–54.

Ollier, Edmund. 'Ghostly Pantomimes', *Household Words*, 8.196 (24 December 1853), pp. 397–400.

Patten, Robert. 'Conventions of Georgian Caricature'. *Art Journal* 43.4 (Winter 1983), pp. 331–8.

– . *George Cruikshank's Life, Times, and Art*. 2 vols. Cambridge: The Lutterworth Press, 1992, 1996.

Payne, Edward F. *Dickens Days in Boston*. Boston, MA and New York: Houghton Mifflin, 1927.

Planché, James Robertson. *The Reflections and Recollections of J. R. Planché*. 2 vols. London: Tinsley Brothers, 1872.

Poole, Adrian. *Shakespeare and the Victorians*. London: Arden Shakespeare, 2004.

Pratt, Branwen Bailey. 'Dickens and Freedom: Young Bailey in *Martin Chuzzlewit*'. *Nineteenth-Century Fiction* 30.2 (September 1975), pp. 185–99.

Rede, Leman Thomas. *The Guide to the Stage*. New York: Samuel French, 1868.

Richards, Jeffrey. *The Golden Age of Pantomime*. London and New York: I. B. Tauris, 2015.

Rhodes, Neil. *Elizabethan Grotesque*. London: Routledge, 1980.

Robson, William. *The Old Play-Goer*. London: Longman, 1846.

Ruskin, John. *The Stones of Venice*. New Universal Library edition. 3 vols. London: Routledge, 1907.

–. 'Fairy Land'. In *The Works of John Ruskin, Vol 33: The Art of England*. Ed. E. T. Cook and Alexander Wedderburn. London: George Allen, 1908, pp. 327–49.

Sala, George Augustus. 'Getting Up a Pantomime'. *Household Words* 4.91 (20 December 1851), pp. 289–96.

Schaffer, Talia. 'Fashioning Aestheticism by Aestheticizing Fashion: Wilde, Beerbohm, and the Male Aesthetes' Sartorial Codes'. *Victorian Literature and Culture* 28.1 (2000), pp. 39–54.

Schlicke, Paul. *Dickens and Popular Entertainment*. London: Unwin, 1985.

Shakespeare, William. *A Midsummer Night's Dream*. Ed. Peter Holland. Oxford: Oxford University Press, 2008a.

–. *Hamlet*. Ed. G. R. Hibbard. Oxford: Oxford University Press, 2008b.

Sidney, Philip. *The Defense of Poesy*. Ed. Albert Cook. Boston, MA: Ginn and Company, 1890.

Slater, Michael. *Charles Dickens*. New Haven, CT and London: Yale University Press, 2009.

[Smith, Horatio]. 'Mr Grimaldi'. *The Drama; or Theatrical Pocket Magazine*. Vol. 2. London: T. and J. Elvey, 1822, pp. 53–60.

Spooner, Catherine. *Fashioning Gothic Bodies*. Manchester and New York: Manchester University Press, 2004.

Stauffer, Donald A. *The Art of Biography in Eighteenth Century England*. Princeton: Princeton University Press, 1941.

Stein, Richard L. 'The Case for Cruikshank'. *The Threepenny Review* 2 (Summer 1980), pp. 27–9.

Stott, Andrew McConnell. *Comedy*. New York and London: Routledge, 2005.

–. *The Pantomime Life of Joseph Grimaldi*. Edinburgh: Canongate, 2009.

Stott, Rebecca. *Oyster*. London: Reaktion Books, 2004.

Sullivan, Jill A. *The Politics of the Pantomime: Regional Identity in the Theatre 1860–1900*. Hatfield: University of Herts Press and The Society for Theatre Research, 2011.

Surridge, Lisa. *Bleak Houses: Marital Violence in Victorian Fiction*. Athens: Ohio University Press, 2005.

Sypher, Wylie. 'The Meanings of Comedy'. In *Comedy*. Ed. Wylie Sypher. Baltimore: The Johns Hopkins University Press, 1956, pp. 191–255.

Tambling, Jeremy. *Dickens, Violence and the Modern State*. Basingstoke: Macmillan, 1995.

Taylor, Millie. *British Pantomime Performance*. Bristol: Intellect Books, 2007.

Thackeray, William Makepeace. *An Essay on the Genius of George Cruikshank*. London: Hooper, 1840.

–. *The Four Georges*. London: Murray, 1869.

Thoms, William J. 'A Chapter on Clowns, and such like Comicalities'. *Bentley's Miscellany*. Vol. 3. London: Richard Bentley, 1838, pp. 617–24.

Thomson, Philip. *The Grotesque*. London: Methuen, 1972.

Trollope, Thomas Augustus. *What I Remember*. Cambridge: Cambridge University Press, 2010.

Tromp, Marlene. *The Private Rod: Marital Violence, Sensation, and the Law in Victorian Britain*. Charlottesville and London: University Press of Virginia, 2000.

Tyler, Daniel (ed.). *Dickens's Style*. Cambridge: Cambridge University Press, 2013.

Varty, Anne. *Children and Theatre in Victorian Britain*. Basingstoke: Palgrave Macmillan, 2008.

Videbaek, Bente. *The Stage Clown in Shakespeare's Theatre*. Westport, CT: Greenwood Press, 1996.

Vlock, Deborah. *Dickens, Novel Reading and the Victorian Popular Theatre*. Cambridge: Cambridge University Press, 1998.

Wallace, Jennifer. 'Keats's Frailty: The Body and Biography'. In *Romantic Biography*. Ed. Arthur Bradley and Alan Rawes. Aldershot and Burlington: Ashgate, 2003, pp. 139–51.

Warwick, Alexandra and Dani Cavallero. *Fashioning the Frame: Boundaries, Dress and the Body*. Oxford: Berg, 1998.

Wiles, David. *Shakespeare's Clown: Actor and Text in the Elizabethan Playhouse*. Cambridge: Cambridge University Press, 1987.

Wilkinson, Tate. *Memoirs of His Own Life*. 4 vols. York: Wilson, Spence, and Mawman, 1790.

Wilson, A. E. *Christmas Pantomime: The Story of an English Institution*. London: Allen and Unwin, 1934.

–. *Pantomime Pageant*. London: Stanley Paul, 1946.

–. *The Story of Pantomime*. London: Home and Van Thal, 1949.

Woolf, Virginia. 'The Art of Biography'. In *The Death of the Moth*. London: Hogarth Press, 1981, pp. 119–26.

Youngquist, Paul. 'Romantic Dietetics! Or, Eating Your Way to a New You!'. In

*Cultures of Taste/Theories of Appetite: Eating Romanticism*. Ed. Timothy Morton. New York and Basingstoke: Palgrave Macmillan, 2004, pp. 237–55.

# *Index*

CPSIA information can be obtained
at www.ICGtesting.com
Printed in the USA
JSHW052224061120
9310JS00001B/3

9 781474 463928